Yugoslavia in Crisis

Yugoslavia in Crisis

HAROLD LYDALL

CLARENDON PRESS · OXFORD
1989

Oxford University Press, Walton Street, Oxford OX2 6DP
Oxford New York Toronto
Delhi Bombay Calcutta Madras Karachi
Petaling Jaya Singapore Hong Kong Tokyo
Nairobi Dar es Salaam Cape Town
Melbourne Auckland
and associated companies in
Berlin Ibadan

Oxford is a trade mark of Oxford University Press

Published in the United States
by Oxford University Press, New York

British Library Cataloguing in Publication Data
Lydall, Harold, 1916–
Yugoslavia in crisis.
1. Yugoslavia. Economic conditions
I. Title
330.9497'024
ISBN 0–19–828695–3

Library of Congress Cataloging in Publication Data
Lydall, Harold.
Yugoslavia in crisis / Harold Lydall.
Bibliography: p.   Includes index.
1. Yugoslavia—Economic conditions.
2. Yugoslavia—Politics and government—1945–   .
3. Management—Yugoslavia—Employee participation.   I. Title.
HC407.L95 1989   338.9.497—dc19   88–7633
ISBN 0–19–828695–3

Set by Hope Services, Abingdon
Printed in Great Britain
at the University Printing House, Oxford
by David Stanford
Printer to the University

The Serbocroatian Language

Yugoslavia is a country of many languages. In a population of nearly 23 million there are five major languages which are spoken by at least one million people. These are Serbian, Croatian, Slovenian, Albanian, and Macedonian. In addition, in the province of Vojvodina, Hungarian is spoken by about half a million people; and in Yugoslavia as a whole there are many thousands of people who speak Turkish, Romany, Slovakian, Romanian, Bulgarian, Czech, Ruthenian, Italian, Wallachian, and Ukrainian.

About two-thirds of the whole population speak Serbocroatian as their mother tongue. Serbocroatian is the name for two very similar languages, nearly as similar as British and American English. But Serbian is written in the Cyrillic script (rather like Russian), while Croatian is written in a Latinized script. This latter script, which is used for Serbocroatian words in this book, contains some letters additional to the Latin alphabet; and some of the letters are pronounced differently from their pronunciation in English. The main differences are as follows:

The Croatian letter *c* is pronounced *ts*.

The Croatian letters *č* and *ć* are pronounced *tch*.

The Croatian diphthong *dž* is pronounced as *j* in *jam*.

The Croatian letter *j* is pronounced as *y* in *yet*.

The Croatian letter *š* is pronounced *sh*.

The Croatian letter *ž* is pronounced as *s* in *leisure*.

Preface

When I was working on my previous book on Yugoslavia (Lydall 1984), I came to realize that the Yugoslav system of 'socialist self-management' suffered from a number of serious defects. A large part of that book was, in fact, devoted to an attempt to elucidate the nature of those defects. But up to 1979, which was the terminal year for most of the annual statistics then available to me (in 1982 and 1983), the Yugoslav economy had done rather well. What I did not then know, or did not fully grasp, was that, precisely from 1979, the Yugoslav economy had entered a prolonged period of stagnation and decline. As I write these words, the rate of decline is, at least in some respects, accelerating, although the new anti-inflationary programme of the government (agreed with the IMF) offers the hope of a partial recovery.

It is now clear that for the past nine years Yugoslavia has been in a state of economic crisis. This is accepted by everyone in Yugoslavia: in the Party, in the government, and among the population generally. The number of Yugoslav books with titles containing the word 'crisis' is already large, and growing. It is no wonder. For the greatest claim of socialist (or communist) regimes—especially in poorer countries—is that they are able to raise the standard of living of their subjects. A socialist regime that produces only a declining standard of living is, therefore, in danger of losing its legitimacy.

The Yugoslav story has become a tragedy. So many high hopes were raised by the idea of 'self-management', not only in Yugoslavia but also among sympathizers in the West. Even now, there are Western socialists who hope to rescue their ideology by renouncing 'state' socialism in favour of some vaguer concept of social ownership, which would include 'self-management'. Not surprisingly, there are still many Yugoslavs of the older generation who continue to insist that 'self-management' is, in theory, an ideal system, and that the only trouble is that it has not been operated as it should be. The wiser, and hence the more

disillusioned, have come to realize that it is a system designed, in
Professor Županov's words, 'for angels and not for men'.
Unfortunately, the creators of Utopias too easily end by putting
humanity in an intolerable material and mental straitjacket.

An analysis of the underlying causes of the present crisis of the
Yugoslav system, such as is attempted in this book, can yield
important lessons for all who are interested in the future of
socialism. But the people who have most to lose from a failure to
learn those lessons, and the most to gain from a correct analysis
of the situation, are the people of Yugoslavia itself. By their
heroic resistance to foreign occupation in the Second World War,
and by their defiance of Stalin's attempt to absorb them
thereafter, they have earned the right to a better life. In my
judgement, if only their present shackles could be removed, they
would rapidly create a thriving and prosperous society.

In the preparation of this work, I have received assistance from
many quarters. First and foremost, I must acknowledge the
indispensable help of the Leverhulme Trust, which gave me an
Emeritus Fellowship grant to cover the expenses of the study.
But that alone would have been insufficient without the aid of a
number of Yugoslav scholars, who were kind enough to send me
copies of their articles or books, or to explain puzzling aspects of
their country's institutions, laws, or behaviour. Behind them,
also, stands a much larger number of Yugoslav economists,
sociologists, political scientists, journalists, politicians, and
directors of enterprises, who have published valuable articles,
books, and interviews. The reader will find quotations from
many of these sources in this book. There is little that is written
here that has not been said or written by one or more Yugoslavs
themselves. I stand on their shoulders; and I am deeply indebted
to them.

More specifically, I should like to express my gratitude to
Professor Aleksander Bajt, of Ljubljana University, for reading a
first draft of Chapter 4; and to Professor Wlodzimiercz Brus, of
Wolfson College, Oxford, for reading the whole text. I have made
a number of changes in the light of their comments, but they
cannot be held responsible for the final version. I am also grateful
to Professor Laura Tyson, of the University of California at

Berkeley, for drawing my attention to a previously unpublished paper by Professor Jože Mencinger.

Thanks are also due to the Oxford University Institute of Economics and Statistics for the use of its library and other facilities, and to the Bodleian Library and St Antony's College, Oxford, for access to their Yugoslav materials.

Finally, I owe a great debt, as usual, to my wife for many kinds of assistance with this project.

Oxford University Institute of Economics and Statistics   H. F. L.
August 1988

Contents

List of Tables   xi

 1.   Introduction   1
 2.   The Yugoslav Economic and Political System   11
 3.   The Main Symptoms of Crisis   24
 4.   The Decline of the Economy and the
      Government Response   40
 5.   Underlying Causes of the Crisis   72
 6.   Enterprise Self-management   102
 7.   Enterprise Income and its Distribution   126
 8.   Taxation and Money   144
 9.   Foreign Trade   172
10.   Regional Problems   186
11.   Politics   213
12.   General Conclusions   235
Appendix   Adjusted Estimates of Social Product   245
References   249
Index   251

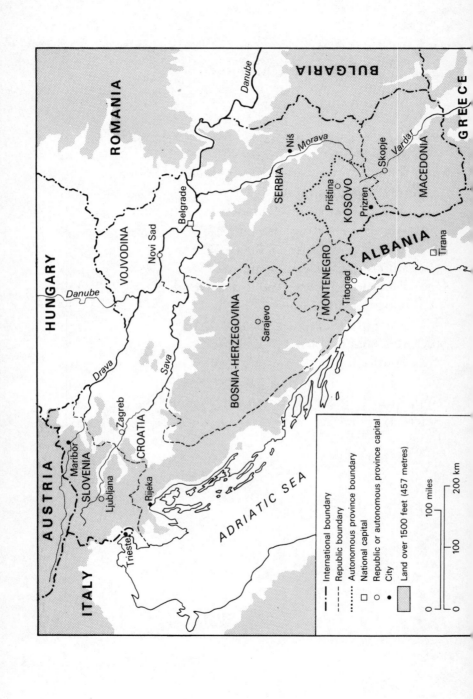

List of Tables

4.1 Growth and Decline of the Yugoslav Economy   41

4.2 Changes in Major Components of Demand, 1979–1985   45

4.3 Changes in Gross Fixed Investment   47

4.4 Volume of Imports of Goods by Category, 1975 and 1979–1985   48

4.5 Major Components of Current Balance of Payments as Percentages of Social Product, and End-of-year Foreign Debt, 1975–1985   49

4.6 Changes in Prices of Imports, Exports, and Industrial Products, Volume of Exports, and the Real Exchange Rate, 1975–1985   56

4.7 Cycles of Changes in Consumer Prices (Cost-of-living Index), 1980–1986   58

4.8 Percentage Changes in Real Earnings and Related Variables, 1979–1985   61

4.9 Changes in Nominal Money Supply, Social Product and Prices, Index of Real Money Supply, and Velocity of Circulation, 1977–1985   66

7.1 Net Saving of Social Sector Enterprises, before and after Stock Appreciation Adjustment, 1977–1985   129

7.2 Net Saving, Changes in Assets, Liabilities, and Net Worth, and the Ratio of Net Debt to Net Physical Assets, Productive Social Sector, 1977–1985   132

8.1 Revenues of Governments and other Agencies as Per-centage of Adjusted Social Product, 1979–1987   145

8.2 Consolidated Public Sector Revenue and Expenditure as Percentage of Adjusted Social Product, 1979–1987   147

8.3 Nominal and Real Interest Rates, 1975–1985   161

8.4 Changes in Cost of Living and Money Supply, 1977–1987   163

9.1 Values and Volumes of Commodity Trade, 1977–1987   174

9.2   Structure of Balance of Payments, Selected Years,
      1973–1985   175
9.3   Commodity Trade by Area, 1979, 1984, and 1987   177
9.4   Commodity Composition of Foreign Trade, Average
      of 1980–1984 Values   178
10.1 Regional Differences in Productivity and Income,
      1986   188
10.2 Other Indicators of Regional Differences   190
10.3 Net Enterprise Saving per Worker and Net Personal
      Income per Worker, 1987   192
11.1 Trends in Public Opinion, 1983–1987   223
A1.   Estimates of Stock Appreciation Adjustment and
      Adjusted Social Product, 1975–1985   246

I

Introduction

Among the communist countries of eastern Europe, Yugoslavia is the only one that has ever acquired a wide popularity among liberal-minded people in the West. This was, in the first place, a response to the success of the Yugoslav partisans during the Second World War, the only resistance movement in occupied Europe to hold a continuous base of operations with its own organs of government. The heroism of the partisans won the admiration of Churchill and of many British officers sent to work with them. In the extremity of war, the fact that Tito and his colleagues were fervent Stalinists, dedicated to the introduction of a Soviet-style dictatorship in Yugoslavia, was partially ignored, and Tito was welcomed into the alliance for the liberation of Europe and for the implementation of the principles of the Atlantic Charter. Towards the end of the war Marshal Tito, in a splendid uniform, began to emerge on to the world stage.

When the war ended in Europe, the Yugoslav Communist Party took control of Yugoslavia, suppressed all other parties, monopolized the media, banned free expression of opinion, and established the 'dictatorship of the proletariat'. Yugoslavia became Stalin's most dedicated satellite, supporting Soviet international policy on almost every point and, in domestic affairs, following the Stalinist path of nationalization, collectivization, and suppression of individual freedom.

But in 1948 a very surprising event occurred: Yugoslavia was denounced by the Cominform as a traitor to socialism, and expelled. Stalin tried at first to incite a pro-Soviet revolt in Yugoslavia, and when that failed he imposed a total blockade on Yugoslavia's trade with the Cominform countries. The effect of the blockade on the Yugoslav economy was disastrous, but the situation was made even worse by a serious drought and by a wanton decision to try to force collectivization on the peasants. Within the next two years, however, the Yugoslav communists came to recognize that they had been finally excluded from the Soviet camp, that they now had to search for a new policy, and that they would need to build bridges with the West. Collectivization was abandoned, and in 1950 Tito announced the slogan of 'The factories to the workers'. Yugoslavia started on its long path towards 'socialist self-management'.

During the next three decades Yugoslavia attracted much interest from socialists, and even from some liberals, and it acquired considerable prestige as a pioneer of a new kind of socialist society. Central planning was abandoned, the previously nationalized industries were progressively transferred to the control of elected workers' councils, and enterprises began to operate in the market. But it was never a free market, even for goods and services, and there was no market for labour or capital. Despite official party denunciations of 'statism' (the diagnosed sin of the Soviet Union), and the change of the Party's name to League of Communists, which was intended to signify some relaxation of its monopoly position, the Party continued to run the country as its private fief. The delegates elected to workers' councils were carefully vetted and kept under party control (directly or through the trade unions), while party-controlled governments at all levels continued to exert dominant influence on enterprise decisions, either directly or through the banks. Nevertheless, there was some increase in freedom. Workers in enterprises were given more information; they were allowed to ask questions; they had some say in the election of workers' councils; and they could even criticize, and in the final analysis demand the removal of, their managers.

During the 1960s, the movement towards greater market freedom was slightly accelerated, especially in the period of the Economic Reform. Unemployment began to rise, and workers were allowed to emigrate to West Germany and other Western countries in search of work. At its peak, about one million Yugoslavs were working abroad. Some took their wives and children with them, but almost all returned from time to time to visit Yugoslavia. They brought with them news of life in the West, and much-needed foreign currency to supplement Yugoslavia's weak balance of payments. The need for foreign currency also prompted the development of a considerable tourist industry, especially along the beautiful Adriatic coast, and this opened the doors to a large annual influx of Western tourists. Most Yugoslavs were allowed to travel freely to other countries, and in recent years the number of recorded exits of Yugoslavs, mainly to neighbouring countries on short shopping expeditions, has been larger than the total population.

As a consequence of these changes in policy, Yugoslavia has become a country of deep internal contradictions. It has broken with most aspects of Stalinism; it has abandoned central planning and compulsory collectivization; it has created a market economy (although subject to considerable state interference); it has opened its frontiers, both to foreigners and, more important, to its own citizens; and it has given its workers some nominal rights of 'self-management'. Yet Yugoslavia is still a one-party communist state; there are no free elections; there is no free press and no right of free assembly or organization; books and papers are censored; dissidents are imprisoned and banned from their normal employment; there is anti-religious propaganda, and defamatory attacks on the Church, especially the Catholic Church, are common; the trade unions are servile and their leaders are almost completely out of touch with the workers; the Party has a monopoly of all key positions in government, the trade unions, the press, and education; there is deep official hostility towards any kind of private enterprise; and there has been a great effort to indoctrinate children (and to some extent the whole population) with Marxism.

Despite these contradictions, for most of the period from 1950 to 1979 Yugoslavia not only survived but prospered. Real national product rose rapidly; millions of ex-peasants were given jobs in the social sector; industrial production expanded rapidly, and exports of manufactured products came to dominate the export trade; social services were extended and improved; supplies of consumer goods increased; and Yugoslavia's prestige in the outside world, especially as one of the leaders of the 'non-aligned' countries, became considerable. These advances were made possible by a number of factors. First, there was a genuinely popular post-liberation enthusiasm, which was harnessed and directed by the all-pervasive Party. Second, there was the stimulating effect of the introduction of a market economy.

Third, although the workers had been granted the right to 'self-management', for a long time wages (or 'personal incomes') were kept low, and enterprises were forced to save heavily. Fourth, Yugoslavia received large foreign loans, mainly from the United States in the 1950s, later from the World Bank, and in the 1970s from commercial banks relending OPEC money. Finally, Yugoslavia had Tito, both as a figurehead and as a strong leader capable of knocking heads together and enforcing decisions.

Unfortunately, by the early 1980s all these advantages had disappeared. Revolutionary enthusiasm had been replaced by massive work-shirking and cynicism. The market system had been weakened by persistent and increasing government intervention, and by the 'social compact' system established under the 1974 Constitution. The shares of enterprise income paid out in the form of taxes, contributions, and personal incomes had increased and the share of savings had fallen. After the second oil shock of 1979 and the start of the world recession, foreign lending dried up, and in any case Yugoslavia could no longer afford to accept the burden of more debt. And in 1980 Tito died. So all the props were removed, and the Yugoslav economy was suddenly brought face-to-face with the underlying reality. Since 1980, Yugoslavia has been in a continuous state of economic crisis; and the crisis has spread into the social, political, 'national' (or ethnic), and intellectual spheres. There is no agreement, even in the Party, on what to do about it, and all forecasts of the future are gloomy.

The main symptoms of the crisis are as follows. First and most fundamentally, in the economic sphere real social product (adjusted for stock appreciation) has fallen, by nearly 6 per cent from 1979 to 1985 and even further since then. Despite this decline in output, under strong political pressure, social sector enterprises have been forced to take on extra workers, with the consequence that labour productivity in the social sector fell in the same period by about 20 per cent, and the real personal incomes of social sector workers by about 25 per cent. The standard of education, health, and housing services has also fallen. Universities are unable to replace essential equipment or to buy foreign journals; hospitals and patients are short of drugs; and, despite a heavy backlog of demand, completions of new social sector flats have fallen. Real earnings of teachers in schools and universities have been reduced even more than in most other occupations. The rate of inflation has accelerated, and at the end of 1987 reached over 150 per cent per annum. Despite a vast amount of overmanning, both in industry and in government and semi-government employment, there are more than a million persons registered as seeking work, four-fifths of whom are young people.

Throughout the social sector, work discipline is at a low level. There are large numbers of work-shirkers, who arrive late, leave early, slack on the job, take excessive sick leave, and try to get early retirement on grounds of ill-health. Investment and imports have been severely squeezed, and many firms are unable to meet demands of their customers for want of raw materials, components, and spare parts for their machinery. Exports have grown a little, but the quality of many Yugoslav products is not internationally competitive, and export prices have often been cut to uneconomic levels. The population in general has borne the cost of this export weakness through a low rate for the dinar, export subsidies, and compensatory price rises on goods sold on the domestic market. The burden of servicing the foreign debt accumulated in the 1970s is very heavy, and in practice most repayments of principal have been postponed, either by re-scheduling or by raising new loans. The foreign debt hangs like a Sword of Damocles over the country.

While successive Yugoslav governments in the 1980s showed some courage in trying to master the economic crisis, especially by cutting back investment and imports, they completely failed to control inflation, the growth and acceleration of which has corroded the whole fabric of society. There have been temporary price freezes, longer-term price controls on some products, and on two occasions—in the first quarter of 1983 and in the first quarter of 1987—complete incomes freezes in the social sector. But the effects of all these measures on the rate of inflation have been scarcely perceptible. The business accounts of enterprises have been severely distorted by inflation, with inventory gains appearing as income and depreciation allowances falling in real terms. Believing, for these reasons, that their incomes were larger than they really were, enterprises have paid out higher personal incomes, taxes, and contributions, and their real savings have fallen. New accounting rules, prescribed in a 1987 law, are designed to eliminate these distortions; but, if the law is applied rigorously, it will precipitate widespread bankruptcies.

When they come to this point, previous governments have always run away. Loss-making enterprises have been bailed out with bank credits or by the forcible transfer of funds from more profitable firms. Although occasional, rather feeble, efforts have been made to limit the expansion of the money supply, the government has never voluntarily renounced the drug of new money, which is seen as the ultimate remedy for all social ills. In May 1988 the government signed an agreement with the IMF under which, in return for new foreign loans and the rescheduling of maturing foreign debt, the government undertook to keep a tight control over the expansion of bank credits, with the aim of bringing the rate of inflation down by the end of the year to 95 per cent. This is the first serious attempt to use monetary policy to slow down inflation. Although it is unlikely that the immediate inflation target will be met, a firm continuation of a tight monetary policy will eventually bring inflation under control. The transitional economic and social problems will undoubtedly be serious, but if the government and the Party have the courage to face them, the Yugoslav economy will eventually be in a much healthier condition.

The economic crisis has also produced symptoms of a social crisis. Many households have suffered growing impoverishment, especially those with only one earner. The more fortunate households are those with relatives working abroad, or with one or more members working on a family farm or in some form of 'moonlighting'. Households who own villas or flats on the coast can also make good incomes out of renting to tourists, often collecting the rent in foreign exchange. Since all citizens are allowed to hold foreign exchange accounts (in a wide range of currencies), and since these retain their foreign value, this form of savings is hedged against inflation. In recent years the interest rates on term deposits in dinars have been raised to 80 per cent of more, which has given some protection to the holders of such deposits. But the real rate of interest, even on such deposits, has continued to be negative, and on holdings of cash or sight deposits, heavily so. Economic and social conditions have especially deteriorated in the southern parts of Yugoslavia (southern Serbia, Kosovo, Macedonia, and Montenegro), which were already the most backward regions. Personal income per worker in the social sector in Macedonia is now only half the corresponding level in Slovenia (although the cost of living is lower), and per capita income in the southern republics and the province of Kosovo is further reduced by the greater proportion of small peasant households and by the larger average size of families. There has been a general increase in crime, but especially of 'economic crime'—robberies and frauds at the expense of socialized enterprises. There is a growing number of strikes; there are increasing signs of tension between various 'national' (or ethnic) groups, especially between Serbs and Albanians in Kosovo; and there are widespread cynicism and disillusion among young people, most openly expressed in Slovenia.

The political and intellectual symptoms of the crisis are mostly not exhibited publicly. But more and more members of the federal parliament (the Skupština) openly express loss of confidence in the government, and some have even called for its resignation. A start has been made on the laborious and time-consuming process of amending the Federal Constitution, and some people have been urging the desirability of introducing direct elections. But, since the main impetus for changing the Constitution comes from Serbia, which wants thereby to establish its direct rule over Kosovo, and since direct elections are considered by the dominant section of the Party to be dangerous to its maintenance of power, this proposal is unlikely to be accepted, except perhaps for some offices of trivial importance.

Almost all reputable intellectuals are deeply disillusioned with the present system. Although most of them do not write openly about its fundamental defects—one-party rule, the absence of real democratic rights, the impotence of the people to influence government policy, and the heavy burden of dogma—they keep emphasizing the need for freer market relations, true self-management, more democracy within the existing system, and more responsible behaviour by political leaders. But these are all officially approved ideas and, no matter how often they are repeated, their restatement has no significant effect so long as the core of the system remains intact.

As a result of the economic decline of the 1980s, the people of

Yugoslavia have experienced an increasing sense of crisis. They have been told that in these years neighbouring countries like Greece and Turkey—even Turkey!—have done better than socialist Yugoslavia. Hundreds of thousands of Yugoslavs now travel to Istanbul to find goods that are unobtainable in their own shops. Yugoslavia is remorselessly slipping back in the world league, especially in Europe, where it is now the 'sick man'. Because Yugoslavia's world prestige has fallen, the pilgrims who used to come to study the miracles of self-management have disappeared. Apart from tourists sunning themselves on Adriatic beaches, the main pilgrimage today is to Medjugorje, a small village in Herzegovina where a group of local people claims to have seen the Madonna.

How did things come to this pass? Why were all the high hopes of 'self-management' disappointed? It is now clear that many of the successes of the latter part of the 1970s were illusory. During that period Yugoslavia was living on borrowed time—and money. The system was fundamentally defective, especially after the introduction of the Constitution of 1974 and the Law on Associated Labour of 1976. These led to a fragmentation of enterprises, an undermining of managerial efficiency, a weakening of work discipline, and the strangulation of the economy in a mass of 'social compacts' and 'self-management agreements'. Government and semi-government institutions expanded at the expense of productive enterprises, and when the world economic recession arrived Yugoslav industry was incapable of responding with vigorous counter-measures, but instead used up its energies in trying to cope with a stifling tangle of red tape. As time passed, more and more strands of tape were added. By the second half of the 1980s some people were even advocating the complete scrapping of the Law on Associated Labour, and the abandonment of 'social planning' and the whole 'social compact' system.

The purpose of this book is to bring to light the fundamental causes of the failure of the Yugoslav socialist self-management system. Its analysis and conclusions will be relevant not only to Yugoslavia but also to other communist countries that are experimenting with the introduction of markets and, in some cases, moving in the direction of self-management. They will also be relevant to current discussions about the future of socialism, and of socialist parties, in non-communist countries.

Before we start our detailed analysis, it may be helpful for readers to be given a brief summary of the unique Yugoslav economic and political system, and of the special terminology that accompanies it. Chapter 2 is, therefore, devoted to this task. Chapter 3 reviews the general trends of the Yugoslav economy in the 1980s and the macroeconomic symptoms of the economic crisis. While the official figures reveal the disastrous decline in economic performance, they give a picture that is in some respects rosier than the true one. The decline in the standard of living has been so great that it is difficult to think of any other country that would not have responded with major political changes, or even revolution. This chapter also describes some of the social and political effects of the economic crisis.

Chapter 4 is concerned with the proximate causes of the economic crisis, and with government efforts to deal with it. The crisis was brought on by the oil shocks of the 1970s, the sharp rise in foreign indebtedness, and the world recession of the early 1980s. But it was exacerbated by the inadequacy and inconsistency of government policies.

In Chapter 5 we turn to a consideration of the underlying and long-term causes of the crisis. 'Self-management' can take various forms; but all of them have a certain defect, namely, that there is a lack of clarity about the ownership of capital. This leads to a waste of capital, and a low mobility of both capital and labour. It has often been suggested that a self-management system enjoys a great advantage over capitalism through the sense of solidarity engendered by the co-operative form of organization. But this sense of solidarity does not seem to be very durable, especially in large organizations. These problems would exist even in a *laissez-faire* competitive system of industrial co-operatives; but they are greatly increased in Yugoslav conditions, where the system is one of *socialist* self-management. For socialism is, by definition, a system in which the state is all-powerful and is actively involved in the economy, not only at a macroeconomic level but also in the detailed regulation of individual enterprises. The situation in Yugoslavia is even further complicated by the high degree of federalization of the country. The ways in which government (and party) intervention in the economy has been maintained, and even increased, under Yugoslav conditions of 'federalized socialist self-management' will be described in detail. We shall then be able to address the central question of Chapter 5, namely, how such a system responds to an economic crisis, and why the results have been so unsatisfactory.

The following six chapters are devoted to a consideration of the effects of this system on behaviour in a number of important areas. Chapter 6 examines the actual operation of the self-management system in Yugoslav enterprises, and assesses the extent to which it yields the advantages claimed for it. One of the crucial areas of enterprise decision-making over which the government wishes to establish firm control is the distribution of income; and the methods by which the government is trying to achieve this objective are discussed in Chapter 7. Chapter 8 is concerned with taxation and the monetary system; it considers, in particular, why the fiscal and monetary systems of Yugoslavia have been so ineffective in restraining inflation. The organization and regulation of foreign trade are the subjects discussed in Chapter 9; and problems of regional development, together with the sources of 'national' (or ethnic) conflicts, are considered in Chapter 10. In the final analysis, the future of Yugoslavia, as of all countries, depends on the nature of its political system, and this is discussed in Chapter 11. In conclusion, Chapter 12 summarizes the reasons for the failure of socialist self-management in Yugoslavia and discusses the lessons to be learned from this experience.

2

The Yugoslav Economic and Political System

The economic and political system of Yugoslavia has no parallel in any other country. After evolving gradually over the first thirty years after the war, it was radically changed by the Constitution of 1974. This Constitution was further elaborated, and applied to the economic side of life, by the Law on Associated Labour of 1976. The installation of a communist government in 1945 had already led to the replacement of Western concepts of economics by Marxist concepts, with corresponding changes in terminology. From that time onwards, old words, like 'productive' and 'democracy', were given new meanings, and old terms were replaced by new ones. (For example, 'saving' became 'accumulation'.) Similarly, a firm with no net investment was described as being in a state of 'simple reproduction', while one that had positive net investment was engaged in 'expanded reproduction'. But these terms are familiar in all communist countries. The Yugoslav Constitution added a completely new language, previously unknown, and so far not adopted in any other country.

Not only is the Yugoslav system very complex, but its actual behaviour differs widely from its theoretical behaviour. There is not space in this chapter to give a full account of the system or of the difference between its theory and its practice; these can be found in my previous book (Lydall 1984). Nevertheless, readers may find it useful to have a brief outline of the system, with an explanation of the main economic and political terms in general use in present-day Yugoslavia. The actual behaviour of the system in recent years will be the subject of discussion in subsequent chapters.

1. The Economy

Major sectors

The Yugoslav economy is divided in two independent dimensions. First, there is a distinction between the social sector and the individual, or private, sector; second, there is a distinction between 'productive' and 'non-productive' activities. The social sector consists of all enterprises that were originally nationalized and later transferred to self-management, together with new self-management enterprises established subsequently. These are regarded as being owned by 'society', a term that is not defined, but whose practical meaning will become clearer in subsequent chapters. The social sector also includes government institutions, the social services, and the 'socio-political organizations' (the Party, the trade unions, the Socialist Alliance, and the youth and veterans' organizations). The private sector consists mainly of small peasants and small urban businesses, such as artisan workshops, small retail businesses, restaurants, and road transport operators.

The distinction between 'productive' and 'non-productive' activities, or between 'the economy' and 'the non-economy', is widely believed to be based on one made by Marx; but it is in fact based on a different distinction made by Adam Smith. However, since it was taken over from Soviet practice, it is now sacrosanct. 'Productive' activities include all enterprises producing goods, and some related services, such as transport and trade, as well as catering, hotels, and public utilities. 'Non-productive' activities include government administration, the armed forces and police, social services, the work of the socio-political organizations, banking and insurance, and personal services. According to an approximate estimate, made for the year 1980 (Lydall 1984, 93), out of a total occupied work-force of 9.5 million (but apparently excluding the army and the police), 5.8 million were employed in the social sector (of which 4.8 million were in productive and nearly 1 million in non-productive activities), while 3.7 million were employed or self-employed in the private sector (3.5 million in productive and 0.2 million in non-productive activities).

The Yugoslav social product, or 'gross material product', is equal to the sum of gross value added in all productive enterprises, whether in the social or the private sectors. Compared with the Western definition of gross domestic product, this excludes value added in those service industries that are not regarded as 'productive'. In 1980 these industries employed approximately 12 per cent of the work-force, but the inclusion of their wages and salaries in the value of social product would have increased the latter by only about half as much. Estimates of the rate of growth of gross material product differ from corresponding estimates of the rate of growth of gross domestic product to the extent that the proportion of the work-force engaged in non-productive activities is changing, or that income per worker in the non-productive sector changes in comparison with value added per worker in the productive sector.

Enterprise organization

Under the 1974 Constitution and the subsequent Law on Associated Labour, all Yugoslav enterprises were completely reorganized. So far as possible, enterprises, which were now called 'work organizations of associated labour', were divided into smaller units, such as departments of a factory or even parts of a railway system. These were called 'basic organizations of associated labour'. Each basic organization is supposed to be financially and commercially independent, although it is linked with other basic organizations in the same work organization by a system of 'self-management agreements'. (Self-management agreements can also be made between organizations of associated labour which are not members of the same work organization.) In some cases, work organizations are grouped into 'complex organizations of associated labour', i.e. into larger combines. Some of these complex organizations now consist of dozens of basic organizations arranged in a structure of work organizations. In the larger work organizations there is usually a 'work community' of white-collar workers doing clerical, administrative, and technical work. This is also 'self-managed', but it has fewer rights and duties than a basic organization of 'productive' workers. Organizations of associated labour and work communities are also formed in the non-productive social sector; but their financial powers and responsibilities are limited in comparison with those of organizations in the productive social sector. For example, since they are 'non-productive', they are not allowed to 'accumulate'.

The workers in every organization of associated labour employing more than thirty workers elect a workers' council and various other committees, including a disciplinary committee. They also elect 'delegates' to form part of the stratum of 'delegations' which lies at the base of one section of the political pyramid, and numerous other 'delegates' to all sorts of other organizations, including the 'self-management communities of interest' (see below). The workers' council is the principal organ through which the self-management rights of the workers are supposed to be exercised. But important questions are submitted to mass meetings ('assemblies'), and in some cases to a referendum. Among its other tasks, the workers' council appoints the director, but only from a short list of candidates submitted by the nomination committee, on which the Party is strongly represented, partly through representatives of the local commune and partly through the local trade union organization. In principle, the division of responsibilities between the workers' council and the director is clear. The workers' council takes all major business decisions, while the director carries out those decisions and organizes the work of the enterprise. In practice, however, the decisions of the workers' council are heavily influenced by the recommendations made by the director and his senior staff.

Banks, which occupy a crucial position in the economy, are supposed to be under the control of their 'founders', which are usually local productive organizations of associated labour. Banks are not allowed to make profits; but often make losses. They are, in practice, very much under the control of governments—communal, republican or provincial, and federal—and of the Party.

Social services

Social services, such as education and health services, and also pension funds and some other activities, are financed by proportional 'contributions' levied on the income of organizations of associated labour and on the personal incomes of their employees.

Although the level of such contributions is supposed to be agreed voluntarily, in practice they are almost entirely compulsory. The provision of these services is in the hands of 'self-management communities of interest', which are supposed to be controlled by delegates from the contributing organizations, the workers employed in the service, and the commune or republic (or province). In practice, control is mainly in the hands of the officials of these organizations, although their employees have some partial self-management rights.

Allocation of enterprise income

The purpose of productive organizations of associated labour is defined as being to maximize their 'net income', which is (or was until 1987) approximately equivalent to gross value added minus allocations for depreciation, taxes, contributions, and interest on loans. At the end of each year, when the accounts are made up, the workers' council recommends to the assembly a division of net income between 'collective consumption' (mainly expenditure on housing, transport of workers to and from work, and meals at work), 'personal incomes' payable to the work-force (the term 'wages' is not used), reserves, and saving ('accumulation'). The reserve allocation is mainly a compulsory contribution towards reserve funds, which can be used to cover current losses of other organizations in the same commune or republic (or province), or future losses made by the organization itself. The allocation to personal incomes is 'gross', the amount eventually received by the workers being reduced by personal contributions towards self-management communities of interest and membership dues paid to the Party, the trade unions, and other socio-political organizations. Gross personal income minus contributions is called 'net personal income'.

Each month, on the recommendation of the management, the workers' council agrees on advance payments of personal incomes to the workers. At the end of the year (more precisely, in March of the following year) these advances may need to be corrected in the light of the final accounts for the year. But there is strong resistance to any downward revision, and it is the allocation to accumulation that acts as a residual. An organization that has paid out more in advances of personal incomes and on expenditure for collective consumption than it can cover by its final net income is considered to be making a loss. Such organizations are obliged to find someone (usually its bank, sometimes another organization) to cover the loss by giving additional credit. In principle, if it fails to cover the loss in this way, it can be declared bankrupt and taken under direct management by the local commune. In practice, however, this has very rarely happened. As a result, the banks are burdened with many bad debts, as losses are transferred from enterprises to their banks. Even if enterprise losses are 'covered' in this way, enterprises are not supposed to go on accumulating losses, and they may be obliged to reduce the level of personal incomes paid to their workers. Net personal incomes are not permitted to fall below a 'guaranteed' level, which is a fixed proportion of the previous year's average for the republic or province in which the organization is located. The value of this 'guarantee' is clearly much diminished under conditions of rapid inflation.

Taxation

Taxes are levied at three levels of government: the federation, the republic or province, and the commune. The bulk of tax revenue comes from turnover taxes, which are levied by all three categories of government. Other sources include customs duties, taxes on the net income of productive organizations, and some minor taxes, such as those levied on very high personal incomes and on personal property (mainly private houses). Peasants and other private businesses are also taxed on their assessed incomes and in other ways, sometimes at absurdly high rates which encourage evasion.

Social planning

As soon as the Yugoslav communists decided to move towards a system of decentralized enterprise decision-making through self-management, they realized that this implied the acceptance of a market economy. But they never abandoned their devotion to socialism. Since socialism implies planning, some method would need to be found for reconciling the market with planning. The solution, which was eventually found in the 1970s, was to create a system of *voluntary* planning, called 'social planning'. Five-year plans, and sometimes plans for longer periods, are supposed to be made 'from the bottom up' through the agreement of all the organizations concerned. These organizations include all enterprises (and their component organizations), all governments (including 'local communities', which cover sub-areas of communes), and all other institutions, such as self-management communities of interest, which employ labour and produce goods or services. After prolonged discussions, a plan is drawn up for each republic or province, and some attempt is made to make these plans consistent with a federal plan, which is framed from the top downwards. When the plans are agreed, the next stage is to formulate them in a series of 'social compacts', which are signed by governments and sometimes also by trade unions, and by 'economic chambers', which represent industries or groups of industries. Enterprises and basic organizations and other bodies also make 'self-management agreements' with one another about particular aspects of the plan, such as the amount of new capacity for each product to be installed during the plan period, or in the form of normal commercial agreements about the supply of materials or components.

The whole process of social planning is somewhat of a mystery, and there is no evidence that it has had any beneficial effect on economic performance. One of its weaknesses is that, since social compacts are, in principle, voluntary (although there is often a great deal of political pressure to ensure that they are signed), they are unenforceable. Since the system began, many thousands of social compacts have been signed, and nobody now knows how many of them are still supposed to be in operation. Except in rare instances, and then only when the government steps in to enforce them, they are simply ignored. Social planning absorbs a great deal of valuable time, especially the time of managements, which might otherwise be used in improving efficiency. The main beneficiaries have probably been economists, lawyers, and bureaucrats, who have obtained large numbers of well-paid jobs from the system.

2. Politics

The political system of Yugoslavia is also very complex. The country is a federation of six republics (Slovenia, Croatia, Serbia,

Bosnia and Herzegovina, Montenegro, and Macedonia) and two autonomous provinces (Vojvodina and Kosovo). Nominally, Vojvodina and Kosovo form part of Serbia; but for almost all purposes they are treated as if they were semi-republics. Statistics usually show them separately from 'Serbia without the provinces', which is sometimes called 'Serbia in the narrow sense'. (Their constitutional position in relation to Serbia is currently a fierce political issue.) Within each republic or province there are large numbers of 'communes', or local governments, amounting to about 500 in the country as a whole. Governments at all levels are called 'socio-political communities'.

Delegates and assemblies

Every commune, republic, and province has an assembly and an executive council. The assemblies consist of three chambers, representing, respectively, associated labour, citizens in general, and the socio-political organizations. Thus, many people are represented in three or more ways. (A worker in the social sector will be represented through his organization of associated labour, through his 'local community', and possibly through several different socio-political organizations.) The members of the first two chambers are elected by 'delegates', who have themselves been elected by workers in organizations of associated labour or by citizens in local communities. For each of these 'elections' there is a single list of candidates, drawn up by the trade unions and the Socialist Alliance, respectively. Members of the socio-political chamber are appointed by the socio-political organizations, without even the semblance of an election. Members of republican and provincial chambers are usually elected from among the members of the basic 'delegations' by the members of the corresponding chambers in the communes.

At the federal level there is also an assembly (the Skupština, or parliament). This consists of two chambers, each of which is elected by the assemblies of the republics and provinces. The Federal Chamber consists of thirty delegates from each republic and twenty delegates from each province, chosen from among the delegates elected at the lowest level of the electoral pyramid, but excluding persons who are already members of republican or provincial assemblies. The Chamber of Republics and Provinces consists of twelve delegates from each republic and eight delegates from each province, elected by the republican or provincial assemblies *from among their own members*. This chamber is of great importance, because it has jurisdiction over all economic questions. Voting in this chamber is by republican or provincial delegation, each voting in a block on the instructions of its own assembly. Except in special circumstances, no measure can be passed by this chamber without the unanimous approval of all delegations. This is the famous republican and provincial 'veto'.

Socio-political organizations

There are five 'socio-political organizations': the League of Communists of Yugoslavia (formerly the Communist Party of Yugoslavia and still popularly, and correctly, called 'the Party'), the Socialist Alliance of the Working People of Yugoslavia, the Trade Union Federation, the Veterans' Federation, and the League of Socialist Youth. The Party is the usual communist 'vanguard' organization, although it now has about 2 million members. It is supposed to provide intellectual, political, moral, and organizational leadership for virtually everything that happens in Yugoslavia, especially in the spheres of economics and politics. It is officially Marxist, but it follows a different path in some respects from communist parties in other countries. Although the Party is dedicated to the task of creating an ideal socialist, or communist, society, where there will be abundance for everyone, its main practical function under existing conditions is to hold on to power, and hence to provide important jobs for its members. Because Yugoslavia is more decentralized than other communist countries, local officials in the communes and in the republics and provinces have much more power than elsewhere. So there is a larger number of influential jobs to be distributed. No one can reach the top in politics, the civil service, the army, the police, the trade unions, the media, education, or banking without being a member of the Party; and very few directors of large enterprises are non-party members.

The Socialist Alliance has a membership which embraces virtually the whole adult population, but it is run as a satellite organization of the Party. It has the important responsibility of nominating persons for election as delegates from local com-

munities in the first stage of the electoral process. The Socialist
Alliance is the nominal owner of the principal Yugoslav daily
paper, *Borba*, which carried on its front page the slogan 'Workers
of all lands unite!' But the Socialist Alliance is a hollow shell, and
its local branch meetings are attended by a few pensioners and
housewives.

Although membership of a trade union is officially voluntary,
most workers in the social sector are members and have their
membership dues subtracted from their pay. Trade union
officials are, probably without exception, party members, who
ensure that the trade unions faithfully support party policies, not
only in industry but in general. It has never been quite clear
what the functions of a trade union should be in a 'self-managed'
enterprise, in which there is no obvious division between
employer and employees. As a result, trade union officials have
found it difficult to occupy their time, and they have tried to
create work for themselves by organizing holidays and the
purchase of commodities in short supply on behalf of their
members.

Local trade union officials keep a watchful eye on the
operation of self-management within each enterprise, and they
are officially responsible for nominating—which in fact means
selecting—the members of the workers' councils. They are also
represented on the committee for nominating suitable candidates
for the post of director of each organization of associated labour.
Trade unions at various levels sign 'social compacts', especially
those relating to industry, and in this way they 'commit' their
members to obey such compacts. But this has little effect on their
members' behaviour.

Strikes are not officially recognized in Yugoslavia (when they
occur, they are euphemistically called 'work stoppages'), and
until recently they were comparatively rare. But in 1987, as a
result of a government-imposed incomes freeze, there were two
waves of strikes, some of which lasted for several weeks. In the
past, trade union officials have regarded it as their primary duty
to suppress strikes; but, with the recent emergence of mass
protests, officials are beginning to change their attitude, and
have been known to give them half-hearted support.

The Veterans' Federation is a tight organization of veterans of
the Second World War, dominated by ex-partisans. The

organization takes a hard line about national policies, and its pronouncements give the impression that it considers that present-day Yugoslavia has degenerated in comparison with the glorious days of the liberation struggle and the revolution. The organization is also very diligent in looking after its members' interests, especially in relation to pensions and health benefits.

The League of Socialist Youth is a nursery for future party members, and its officials often move on to important jobs in the Party, the trade unions, or the Socialist Alliance. It tries in various ways to arouse the enthusiasm of young people for socialism, but it does not have much success at a time when there are more than 1 million registered job-seekers, of whom 80 per cent are under the age of twenty-five.

The Party uses the other four socio-political organizations as a platform for expressing its own views, as a source of statements and resolutions supporting party policy, and as instruments for implementing that policy. Except on rare occasions, and then only briefly, these organizations never show the slightest sign of independent thought or action. They contribute practically nothing to the much-vaunted idea of Yugoslavia as a superior kind of democratic society, in which there is a 'pluralism of self-management interests'.

Rotation

Since Tito's death, there is no Yugoslav who commands the confidence of the people in all republics and provinces; and recently some Serbs have even begun to question whether the 'Croat' Tito was impartial in his attitude towards Serbia. Foreseeing this type of difficulty, Tito proposed before his death that top positions in the federal government should be regularly rotated, with careful balancing of the representation of each republic and province. This rule now applies to the Federal Executive Council, or government, and to the Presidency of the Federation, which is a collective body carrying out some of the duties that would be carried out in other countries by a single president. The Presidency elects one of its members to serve as president of the Republic for a year, with regular rotation among the representatives of the republics and provinces.

There is much rotation also in the governments of the

republics and provinces, and even in the socio-political organizations, at both federal and republican levels. Leading party
members move around from jobs in government, the Party, or its
satellite organizations in the republics and provinces to a similar
range of jobs at the federal level. From time to time they may be
appointed as ambassadors, editors of leading newspapers, or
to other key positions. When their term of office in one job finishes,
the 'Cadres Department' takes care to find them another job
elsewhere. Unless they show any sign of 'deviating', they are
guaranteed jobs for life, with many fringe benefits, including
eventually a comfortable pension. They never, at any time, have
to submit to the ordeal of popular election.

Ideology

Like all communist parties, the Yugoslav Party subscribes to the
ideology of Marxism–Leninism, the central tenets of which are
the 'dictatorship of the proletariat', and the role of the Party as a
'vanguard', whose function it is to carry out that dictatorship.
The broad purpose of the dictatorship is to eliminate capitalism
and establish socialism; and in a largely peasant country, such as
Yugoslavia was in 1945, this means not only socializing existing
industry but also expanding industrial employment as rapidly as
possible. Most communist countries have tried to follow the
Soviet Union in collectivizing the peasantry, but Yugoslavia
abandoned that policy in the early 1950s. Nevertheless, according
to a dictum of Lenin, the petty bourgeoisie (which includes all
private peasants) is a very dangerous class, which constantly
'gives birth' to capitalism. As a consequence, postwar Yugoslav
official policy has always been hostile to the private peasants,
although it has become a little more tolerant in recent years.
There are also major ideological obstacles to the currently
favoured policy of encouraging the formation of new private non-
farm businesses as a means of absorbing the unemployed. It is, in
fact, doubtful whether this policy will ever be fully implemented
so long as the regime is committed to its present ideology.

A communist regime believes itself to be confronted by a mass
of enemies: world capitalism, imperialism, its own peasantry,
other petty bourgeois groups, religion, liberalism, anti-socialism,
counter-revolution, and so forth. In Yugoslavia this list of

enemies is extended to include Stalinism, statism, centralism, separatism, nationalism, irredentism, group ownership, anarcho-liberalism, and managerist-technocracy. Politicians' speeches and party resolutions are filled with denunciations of various combinations of these enemies (and the all-pervasive sin of 'opportunism'), and the population is expected to adjust its attitudes accordingly. The effect on public opinion of the constant repetition of such propaganda should not be under-estimated. Nevertheless, most people have probably become immune to shifts of emphasis in the speeches of politicians, and pay more attention to announcements of changes in such matters as the price of bread or electricity, regulations about incomes or pensions, or the level of interest payable on savings accounts.

Marxism is a compulsory—and generally unpopular—subject at all levels of education; and some intellectuals make considerable use of Marxist concepts and terminology in order to exhibit their loyalty to the regime. Even quite enlightened economists and sociologists often show obeisance to Marxism, trying at the same time to prove that Marx believed in a market economy, democracy, and self-management. The nervous effects of so much obligatory 'doublespeak' must be serious, above all in inhibiting clarity of thought and decisiveness of action. Neverthe-less, there is every chance that the lively and talented people of Yugoslavia will eventually break out of their present ideological shackles, and establish the real freedom of thought and action for which so many fought and died in the Second World War.

3

The Main Symptoms of the Crisis

1. The Crisis in the Economy

From 1950 to 1979, the Yugoslav economy grew at an impressive rate. The average annual rate of growth of real social product over this period was 6.3 per cent. During the first decade the rate was slightly higher, and in the last nine years slightly lower. But this rate of retardation was scarcely a reason for serious concern. Some other major indicators of growth were also very satisfactory in these years. For example, the rate of growth of real social product per capita was 5.3 per cent, and of fixed capital in the social sector (from 1954 to 1979) 8.3 per cent. But labour productivity in the social sector, which was rising at 4.3 per cent per annum in the 1960s, rose at a rate of only 1.8 per cent per annum in the period 1970–9. Many of these growth figures were high by international standards, although not as high as in some exceptionally rapidly growing countries such as Japan or the smaller economies of East Asia.

But from 1979 onwards, all of this changed. According to official estimates, real social product continued to grow, but only very slowly. The official figures suggest that the total growth of real social product from 1979 to 1985 was 5.7 per cent, equivalent to an average annual rate of 0.9 per cent. But the official figures are not adjusted for stock appreciation, which gives them an upwards bias in a period of inflation. Corrected estimates, after removing the effects of stock appreciation, suggest that in this period real social product declined by 5.5 per cent or at an average annual rate of 0.9 per cent.

Despite this decline in real social product, the number of workers employed in the productive social sector continued to increase (by 16.1 per cent over the full period, or at an average annual rate of 2.5 per cent). Consequently, output per worker in the productive social sector, measured by real social product per worker employed, fell from 1979 to 1985 by nearly 20 per cent, equivalent to an average annual rate of decline of 3.6 per cent.

In this same six-year period total real personal consumption (officially estimated) fell by 3.1 per cent, and real personal consumption per capita by 7.7 per cent. Meanwhile, real net personal income per worker in the social sector fell by as much as 26 per cent. The apparent discrepancy between these two trends is accounted for mainly by the fact that a substantial part of total personal income is derived from sources other than the social sector, such as private enterprises (mainly farms but also some small non-farm businesses), provision of tourist accommodation and services, spare-time work (moonlighting), which is now estimated to yield enough income to cover 28 per cent of personal consumption (*EP*, 24 August 1987), remittances from family members working abroad, and interest on savings deposits. Without these sources of private income, the majority of Yugoslav families would now be in a state of considerable poverty.

The most striking symptoms of the economic crisis of the period 1979–85 were the sharp falls in the volume of imports (36 per cent), real gross fixed investment (37 per cent), labour productivity in the social sector (20 per cent), and real earnings in the social sector (26 per cent). In addition, the number of registered job-seekers rose by 37 per cent to over 1 million, and the rate of inflation rose to 72 per cent. During the same period, the net foreign debt in convertible currencies, which rose from nearly $14 billion in 1979 to nearly $19 billion in 1981, was still at about the same level four years later, and the ratio of debt service liabilities to current gross receipts of convertible currencies rose from 30 per cent in 1979 to 43 per cent in 1985.

Since 1985, there has been no fundamental improvement in any of these economic indicators. Indeed, in most respects the situation in 1987 was worse than in 1985. Inflation continued to rise at an alarming rate; productivity continued to fall; unemployment was held down only by an increasing amount of overmanning in the social sector; there were growing losses in industry, which led to a disastrous fall in net enterprise saving; and the balance of payments deteriorated. Under conditions of rapid inflation, estimates of real social product become increasingly unreliable. Although the official figures show a rise in real social product in 1986, adjusted figures would probably show a fall, with further falls in 1987 and 1988. In 1988 average real personal income per worker was below its 1985 level, and falling.

2. Social Effects of the Crisis

The decline in the economy was reflected in a decline in the standard of health and educational services, in an increasing shortage of urban housing, in growing financial problems for pension funds, in a rise in corruption and economic crime, and in a growing number of strikes. In 1987 there was increasing evidence of poverty, especially in the families of low-paid workers and of workers employed in enterprises that were in financial difficulties.

Health

According to the federal secretary of the association of health organizations (*Politika*, 14 May 1987), the fall in health spending in recent years 'has brought us to the margin of existence'. In 1986 health organizations had a deficit of 65 billion dinars (about £100 million). In 1987, he said, expenditure on health services was only 3.5 per cent of national income, which was lower than ever before. Infantile mortality had been rising, and diseases that had been thought to have disappeared completely were re-emerging. The incomes of health workers were severely depressed, and there had been an increasing number of strikes in hospitals and clinics. In another report (*Politika*, 18 June 1987) the president of the association of health insurance and health services said: 'I have worked in the health service for 33 years, and I maintain that the situation has never been as bad as it is now.' Because of a shortage of resources, doctors are forced to deny patients the services and the drugs that they need.

In Sarajevo, it was reported (*Politika*, 14 November 1986), the daily financial allowance for feeding patients was so small that 60 per cent of the food consisted of potatoes, macaroni, kale, and peas; meat was served only twice a week, and then only 30 grams (about one ounce). The shortage of foreign exchange has meant that the drug firms are often unable to supply essential drugs, including insulin, and chemists' stocks of all drugs have been much depleted. In a strike at the Institute for Medical Work in Niš (*Politika*, 15 August 1987), a local trade union leader said: 'In Niš we have no money for doctors, for nurses, or for health services as a whole.'

A further symptom of the crisis in the health service is the growth of corruption. According to *Danas* (6 May 1986), 'When you go to the doctor, as is well known, you cannot have your blood pressure measured unless you push something into his white coat. (If you have only a large note, he will gladly give you change.)' In Belgrade, according to *NIN* (5 January 1986), the staff in clinics adopt an unfriendly attitude towards patients, taking them out of their proper turn and giving preference to their friends. 'It is difficult for a patient to get a bed in hospital unless he has influence, and virtually impossible for an elderly immobile patient . . . We say nothing about bribes and "blue envelopes", which are a growing practice. Knowledgeable people say that this is a regular phenomenon in some parts of the country.'

Education

The problems in education are similar to those in the health service. According to an article in *NIN* (31 May 1987), between 1976 and 1985 the percentage of national income spent on education fell from 5.9 to 3.3. The universities are now facing a desperate shortage of funds. In mid-1987 in Belgrade full professors were being paid between 136,000 and 155,000 dinars a month (about the average for all workers at that time, and equivalent to about £150 a month); lecturers ('assistants') were being paid only half as much. For years the universities have had no money for buying books and journals, and their laboratory equipment is obsolete. Among the staff there is a growing feeling of resentment, much apathy, and some strikes. At a recent meeting to celebrate the anniversary of the founding of Belgrade University the rector said: 'If we do not make a major change in policy, we shall become a backward part of Europe, a desert island like that of Robinson Crusoe.'

There is much dissatisfaction with the quality of work in

schools, although in this case more because of the reforms to the
school system, which involved the abolition of the old gymnasia
(grammar schools) and the substitution of vocational programmes.
When this reform was introduced in Slovenia in 1984, it caused
such an outcry that it had to be abandoned. In a survey made by
NIN (23 March 1986) among 500 secondary school students in
three cities in different parts of Yugoslavia, a large number of
them said that 'their secondary education had been a complete
waste of time'. Dr Marijan Korošić, a well-known Croatian
economist, wrote in *Ekonomska politika* (10 June 1985): 'I think
that our schools are producing a worse and worse product.' The
reform of secondary education gave too much emphasis to
preparing pupils for work in industry. It reduced freedom of
choice and de-professionalized teachers. 'For the first time in
history, the generations now leaving school are of poorer quality
than their parents.'

Housing

Most houses and flats in Yugoslavia are privately owned. In
1980, out of a total of 6.3 million homes, excluding holiday
homes, only 1.3 million, or 22 per cent, were socially owned.
Socially owned dwellings are built mainly by 'organizations of
associated labour' for their own employees, but some are built by
governments and by 'communities of interest'. The rents charged
for social flats are extremely low and, because of lags in
adjustment, have fallen even further in real terms during the
recent years of rapid inflation. At the same time, there is a severe
shortage of flats, especially in urban areas, and the number of
people on the waiting lists is about 500,000.

In 1979 the number of new social sector flats completed was
55,528, but, as a result of the economic crisis, the number of such
completions has dropped considerably in recent years, especially
since 1982. By 1986 it was down to 44,551. Meanwhile, the
backlog of demand for social flats has been growing, and their
distribution is often a cause of fierce disputes within organizations.
In Split, according to a report in *Ekonomska politika* (30 June
1986), every recent distribution of social flats has led to actions in
the court of associated labour. In addition, people resort to all
sorts of illegal methods to try to obtain a social flat.

Because the rents of social flats are so low, the authorities are unable to maintain the buildings and their equipment in good order. *Ekonomska politika* (3 November 1986) reports that social flats in Belgrade are in a state of decay. In one street twenty lifts are out of order; in another, a large section of the façade has collapsed. Although in the past five yers the average rent of a social flat has fallen from 5.5 per cent of household income to only 1 per cent, tenants offer strong resistance to any increase. As a result, the condition of the buildings continues to deteriorate. In another report (*EP*, 26 January 1987) it was said that in a part of Zagreb forty-seven apartment buildings out of fifty-four had leaking roofs and in some cases streams of water were coming in through the walls and windows.

The housing shortage particularly affects manual workers. According to *Ekonomska politika* (27 May 1985), only 23 per cent of social flats are occupied by manual workers, the remainder being occupied by officials, and technical and managerial employees. Consequently, most of the people on waiting lists are manual workers (*EP*, 26 January 1987). Very often they are forced to become sub-tenants at very high rents, sometimes amounting at that date to as much as 80,000 dinars a month in the large cities (more than half a worker's average monthly income). By contrast, the average monthly rent for a social flat in Belgrade was 4,720 dinars. A survey made in Slovenia presents a similar picture. People with higher qualifications and greater social influence more often live in social flats, while poorer people more often live with their relatives or in houses that they have built for themselves (*Politika*, 5 April 1987).

Another result of the housing shortage has been an increase in illegal construction of private dwellings, i.e. without planning permission. The total number of such dwellings may be as many as 300,000 (*EP*, 17 March 1986). In most cases, illegal building is done by people who cannot afford to buy through normal channels, and who are not eligible for a social flat. They are usually poor people, without political influence. But some of these dwellings are built as investments by people who are better off.

Until recently, people who were fortunate enough to obtain housing loans were paying interest rates of 10 per cent or less, while inflation was rising from 30 per cent per annum to over

100 per cent per annum. From the beginning of 1987 banks have been obliged to charge much higher rates of interest on new housing loans, although still well below the current rate of inflation, and there has been a further decline in new housing construction.

Pensions

Yugoslavia has very ambitious objectives for the level of pensions in the social sector. The aim has been to give a worker who has completed forty years of work (including credits for war service or for work in especially difficult conditions) a pension equal to 85 per cent of his final earnings, with regular subsequent adjustments for changes in the cost of living. But, for a number of reasons, very few pensioners have attained this state of bliss, and many receive very low pensions. In 1986, 19 per cent of pensioners were receiving supplementary assistance, and in Kosovo and Macedonia these proportions were 33 and 31 per cent, respectively. One reason for low pensions is that people retire without the full number of years of qualification. But the main problem in recent years has been that pensions have not been adjusted quickly enough to the rapidly rising rate of inflation. The previous rule, in precise terms, was that pensions were based on earnings in the penultimate year of work. There was also a substantial time-lag in adjusting current pensions for changes in prices. Both these defects are now supposed to be corrected but, because the cost of raising existing pensions to bring them up to the position which they would occupy in the absence of these time-lags is very considerable, the increases are to be made in four annual instalments up to 1990. Some people doubt, however, that it will be possible to carry out this plan, since its full implementation would mean raising the pension contribution rate to 23 per cent of gross personal income in 1990, and perhaps to as much as 35 per cent in later years (*EP*, 10 March 1986).

Workers who can establish that they suffer from a work-related disability can retire early, and can even receive a better pension than workers with the full number of years of work. Perhaps partly for this reason, in recent years more and more workers have been applying for disability pensions, and in 1985 more than a third of all pensioners (including survivor pensioners) were receiving such pensions. There is concern that people are increasingly being awarded disability pensions without proper justification, and steps are now being taken in some republics to tighten procedures. Unless this is done, it is thought that the proportion of pensioners to employed workers may rise to one in three, and as a result the burden of pension contributions may become unbearable.

The increasing demand for disability pensions seems to be part of a general trend to regard a job in the social sector as a means of obtaining a small, but almost completely guaranteed, income (and other benefits) in return for not too much work, together with the prospect of drawing an inflation-proof pension at a reasonably early age. While employed in the social sector, people can continue to work on their farms, or can take on spare-time jobs (moonlighting), and after they retire on pension they can devote their full time to these activities (without loss of pension). In effect, the social sector is converted into a milch cow, although in recent years it is a cow that gives a lower and lower yield of milk.

Corruption and economic crime

The growing state of economic crisis has coincided with, and probably helped to produce, a rising trend of corruption and economic crime. According to *Danas* (6 May 1986), corruption has now become quite normal:

When you are looking for a job, you must pay the director . . . . If you want a loan, and you have no political influence, . . . you will find some official and offer him a fee. You are quite mistaken if you think you can obtain a certificate or an official stamp from a commune clerk in five minutes. You must expect to be told 'Come back tomorrow', which means 'Bring some money'. Corrupt government officials usually justify their behaviour by their low pay . . . The exceptional people who are honest are laughed at as being naive.

There is widespread theft from enterprises, and the trend is upwards. Between 1976 and 1985 the number of persons sentenced for economic crimes rose from 34,481 to 58,128. But, according to *Politika* (2 November 1986), this is 'only the tip of the iceberg'. Enormous losses to enterprises in the social sector are being caused by mass criminal activity. An example comes from the section of the motorway between Belgrade and Niš, where the 350 workers who collect the fees are believed to have pocketed in 1986 20 per cent of the takings, obtaining in this way about 1 billion dinars, or more than £1 million (*NIN*, 23 November 1986).

In recent years there have been some spectacular thefts from enterprises, including tons of oil, benzine, copper ore, sheet metal, and even honey, as well as large quantities of gold, silver, and bank notes (*NIN*, 26 April 1987). But, as *NIN* points out, the number of smaller thefts and frauds is much greater. The total number of cases of economic crime reported each year has been for several years about 90,000, but some experts believe that the true figure is 1 million or more. Professor Davidović, an expert in criminology, considers that even greater losses are caused by the practice of giving jobs to relatives (*NIN*, 26 April 1987). He quotes the case of a man in Kosovo who gave responsible jobs to seventy of his relatives; 'and this happens everywhere.' People are afraid to report the misdeeds of their superiors. 'They cannot get rid of them because they did not appoint them.' Professor Davidović maintains that 'responsible people in work organizations treat social property as if it belonged to someone else. They steal it, spend it, and squander it without fear of any kind of control.' According to Dr Bora Kuzmanović, a lecturer in philosophy at Belgrade University, the prolonged economic crisis has led many workers to lose hope and to behave in an immoral way (*NIN*, 26 April 1987). The recent failures of government, together with the growing feeling that officials are corrupt, has increased the sense of alienation, which gives people a sense of justification for immoral behaviour. Since there are no direct elections, people have no means of influencing government policy; so they resort to individual action to protect their own interests.

Strikes

Officially, strikes do not exist in Yugoslavia. They are not mentioned in the Constitution, nor in the Law on Associated Labour, and they are considered to be an unacceptable phenomenon in a system of self-management. But strikes do, in fact, occur, although they are referred to euphemistically as 'labour stoppages'. Despite the fact that Yugoslavia belongs to the International Labour Organisation and subscribes to various international agreements which give workers the right to strike, no such right is mentioned anywhere in Yugoslav law. Although there is no legal prohibition of strikes, the authorities have made use of various legal and non-legal methods of penalizing strikers and strike-leaders.

Until the end of the 1970s, strikes were rather rare events in Yugoslavia. But in recent years they have become more common; and in 1987 there were two major waves of strikes. The first occurred in the first quarter of that year, at the beginning of a government-imposed six-month incomes freeze. The second followed in the third quarter, when the workers wanted to catch up with the price increases that had occurred during the incomes freeze, sometimes demanding a rise in pay of as much as 100 per cent. From 1982 to 1986 the number of strikes rose from 174 to 696, but in the first quarter of 1987 there were about 400 strikes, and the total for the year is likely to have been three or four times that number.

In almost all cases, the main demand of the strikers has been higher pay, but this has sometimes been accompanied recently by demands for improvements in other benefits or for changes in the management. In a recent strike at the rubber tyre and shoe factory of Borovo the workers asked for a 100 per cent rise in pay, a cut of 30 per cent in the number of white-collar staff, and an increase in the proportion of low-priced 'national' bread sold by bakers from 30 to 60 per cent. This is an example of the way in which the workers are beginning to use strikes as a method of presenting 'political' demands. Since June 1988 the government has relaxed price controls, while keeping a tighter hold over personal incomes and bank credits. As a result, real personal incomes have fallen sharply, while many enterprises have found themselves with insufficient funds to pay their workers even at officially approved rates. This situation has provoked a new wave of strikes, often accompanied by mass demonstrations in front of federal or republican parliament buildings.

In the early years of the 1980s, the Party and the trade unions took a firm line against strikes, and in many cases strikers and strike-leaders were victimized—some were sacked, and some were expelled from the Party. The first response of the trade union to a strike has been to call in the security services through the agency of the local Committee for National Defence and Social Self-Protection. These committees, which were established by the 11th Congress of the League of Communists in 1978, consist of leading local members of the Party and of the other socio-political organizations, officials of the workers' councils and local assemblies, directors of enterprises, presidents of government organisations, and the secretaries for internal affairs (i.e. the police). They can go into action whenever there is a state of emergency (which they themselves determine); and one type of emergency that is mentioned specifically is a 'work stoppage'. When these committees take over control, they override all normal systems of government and self-management. In a strike situation, the workers' council is usually pushed on one side and negotiations take place between the strikers' representatives and members of the management, who are supported by the trade union. Meanwhile, the Party usually organizes meetings of its members in the enterprise and calls on them to act as strike-breakers (not always with much success).

In 1985 it seemed that the trade unions might be beginning to change their attitudes a little. According to *NIN* (5 September 1985), some trade union leaders even suggested at that time that, when the workers' demands were justified and there was no other way of resolving the problem, the trade union should take the lead in organizing a strike. But no such radical step has so far been taken, or is ever likely to be taken within the existing framework. Indeed, at a meeting of the Presidency of the Council of Yugoslav Trade Unions in October 1986 (reported in *NIN*, 19 October 1986), the members took a tough line against strikes, even rejecting any suggestion that they should be made legal. Some members of the Presidency said that strike-leaders are mainly idlers and big talkers, and that there was no case for treating trouble-makers with special compassion. It was undesirable that workers should get the impression that they could achieve results by pressure, since, if this were to happen, 'we shall be unable to keep the situation under control'.

Professor Vladimir Arzenšek, who has made a special study of strikes in Yugoslavia, does not believe that the trade unions, as at present constituted, will give their support to strikes. His view, as reported in *Danas* (12 May 1987), is that the Yugoslav trade unions 'are not independent working-class organizations, because there is practically no working-class participation in them'. He says that only 10 per cent of unskilled workers are members of trade unions, and only 25 per cent of young workers are members. About three-quarters of active members of trade unions are from higher management.

It seems likely that efforts will soon be made to change the image of trade unions in Yugoslavia. As the economic crisis continues, and even intensifies, workers will increasingly resort to strike action to protect their interests. If the trade unions do not respond to such demands, they will lose members, and eventually alternative trade unions may come into existence, as in Poland. Already in a textile factory in Bosnia and Herzegovina, employing 3,000 workers, a mass meeting decided to withhold trade union dues because of dissatisfaction with the work of the local council of trade unions (*Politika*, 12 December 1986). This decision caused great concern among local trade union leaders, who used every effort to get it reversed. But the problem will not disappear.

3. Political Effects

In a country with freedom of the press and, as a minimum, freedom to form alternative trade unions and political parties, a prolonged economic crisis such as that experienced by Yugoslavia would have provoked some political changes, including a change of government and radical changes in economic policy. The absence of such freedoms in Yugoslavia, together with the saturating propaganda about the virtues of self-management, and perhaps the overriding fear that the unity of the country is insecure and that the dislodging of a single stone could start an avalanche, have so far prevented major overt expressions of political protest. In 1987, however, there were some signs of change in this respect. As already mentioned, some groups of strikers began to raise political demands; and it has been quite common for workers on strike in large enterprises to demand that leading politicians should come and meet them (demands that have so far been resisted). There have been articles in the press criticizing the Mikulić government (which took office in May

1986) for its failure to carry out its promises to reduce the rate of inflation and reform the economy. There have even been unprecedented suggestions that the government should resign, which stung Branko Mikulić to retort that his government had no intention of resigning, and would certainly not do so until it had found a way out of the crisis (*Politika*, 31 July 1987).

Professor Josip Županov, a distinguished Croatian sociologist, has said (*Danas*, 11 August 1987) that there is a growing gulf between the political and economic élite on the one hand and the mass of the population, including the middle class, on the other. Although the government was nominally committed to the introduction of a freer market economy and a reduction of the degree of government intervention, Professor Županov did not think that this would happen. 'The introduction of a market leads to a redistribution of social and political power . . . Why should those who now hold power do that?' Instead, the political élite attacks the intellectuals and tries to ingratiate itself with the workers, thus hoping to avoid social unrest. However, although this is a well-tried recipe, it is doubtful whether it will continue to work under present conditions. The effects of the economic crisis are being more and more acutely felt, especially by manual workers, who are now threatened with the closure of many loss-making plants. The main strength of the Party now lies with the white-collar workers, especially those in 'non-productive' occupations, whose numbers continue to grow and who are increasingly regarded by the manual workers as a group of parasites. If large numbers of manual workers begin to follow the example of the Borovo workers in demanding a sharp reduction in the employment of white-collar workers, the Party will be placed in an acute dilemma.

In 1985 a federal commission produced a report entitled *A Critical Analysis of the Political System of Socialist Self-management*. The report contained no fundamental criticism of the system of indirect elections, the absence of multiple candidates, the absence of the right to form alternative parties, and the absence of other elementary democratic rights such as the right to publish independent newspapers. Instead, it said that the present system is basically sound, and that any defects in its operation are due to lack of sufficient effort by the population to make it work. In 1987 the laborious process of amending the Federal Constitution was started. But this was not provoked by any desire to change the foundations of the political system, but rather by the dissatisfaction of the Serbian political leadership with their lack of direct control over conditions in Kosovo. In the course of the discussions about the suggested amendments, some people made tentative suggestions for the holding of direct elections for certain offices. But it is very unlikely that anything of this kind will finally be accepted.

Opinion on these questions is moving differently in two republics at each end of the spectrum. In Slovenia there is strong support for more democracy, more liberalism, more opportunity for freedom of expression. There is wide popularity for the idea of a 'civil society', which is interpreted to mean that there should be more tolerance, and less resort to administrative methods to counter dissenting opinions. For example, before the Mikulić government was formally installed, but when it was known that he would be nominated as prime minister, a research worker at the Centre of Marxist Studies in Ljubljana, Tomaž Mastnak, wrote an article in which he criticized Mikulić for his repressive policy in Bosnia and Herzegovina. He was prosecuted by the state attorney for infringing Article 112 of the Criminal Law of Slovenia, which prohibits insulting references to the political leaders of other republics. But this provoked many public protests, and on the second day of the hearing the attorney announced that the case would be withdrawn. This announcement was greeted with stormy applause in the crowded court (*Danas*, 22 July 1986). The Slovenian Youth Organization has been in the forefront of demands for more tolerance. It has proposed that the category of 'verbal crime' should be abolished, that conscripts should be allowed to do non-military service, that the National Youth Day should be celebrated in a more intelligent fashion than by mass rallies, and that leading figures should be subject to more public accountability. Their ideas, and some of their methods of publicizing them, have outraged conservative 'Stalinist' opinion in other republics. But so far, the Slovenian government and Party have resisted demands for firm action against them.

In Serbia, on the other hand, while there are some supporters of a civil society, especially among intellectuals, the dominant trend is an upsurge of nationalistic hostility to Albanians, especially to those in Kosovo. The situation in Kosovo will be discussed in fuller detail in Chapter 10. But at this point it must be said that current Serbian nationalism appears to be at least in part a result of the economic crisis. The Serbs of Serbia (there are substantial numbers of Serbs in other republics) are increasingly disturbed by the fact that Serbia is slipping backwards in comparison with some of the other republics. But this is joined to the fact that there is a slow but persistent emigration of Serbs from Kosovo, a historic centre of Serbian national culture. Already, Albanians represent about 85 per cent of the population of Kosovo, and the Serbs are a shrinking minority. (Even with the Montenegrins, they probably now account for only about 11 per cent of the population.) Serbs believe that the Albanians have a deliberate plan to maintain a high birth rate and to push the Serbs out of Kosovo, so as to establish an 'ethnically pure' Kosovo, which would then insist on being a full constituent republic, with the nominal right of secession. This is the belief that has prompted the Serbian government and party demand that the constitutions of both Yugoslavia and Serbia should be amended, in order to giver Serbia tighter control over the internal affairs of Kosovo. The Serbian press is carrying on a persistent and powerful campaign against Albanian 'irredentists', in which every incident is blown up and interpreted as part of a deliberate persecution of Serbs. Serbs and Montenegrins living in Kosovo have been encouraged to organize mass demonstrations of protest, both in Kosovo itself and in Belgrade in front of the Skupština. This is a very dangerous development in a country in which no one is normally allowed to organize public demonstrations except under official auspices. Moreover, these demonstrations themselves have been 'ethnically pure', which undermines a basic principle of Titoist Yugoslavia, namely, 'brotherhood and unity'.

While the demand for 'firm action' in Kosovo has official approval in Serbia, and nominally at least at an all-Yugoslav level, some Serbs have moved even further in a nationalist direction. One of the best publicized examples of this tendency was the preparation in 1986 of a draft 'Memorandum' by a committee of the Serbian Academy of Sciences and Arts, in which it was claimed that Serbia's status had been downgraded by the Comintern before the Second World War, and even by the political organs of the partisans during the war, and that postwar Yugoslavia had been largely under the control of the Croat, Tito, and the Slovene, Kardelj (*NIN* 9 January 1986). Some Serbs believe that Mihailović was falsely accused of collaborating with the German occupiers, that Serbia was seriously weakened at the end of the war by the creation of a separate republic of Macedonia and separate autonomous provinces in Vojvodina and Kosovo, and that the 1974 Constitution made too many concessions to Croatian nationalism. These are dangerous ideas in a country with a history of internal 'national' conflicts. So far, Serbian nationalism has been canalized mainly in the direction of anti-Albanian sentiment. But, if the Serbs fail to win the constitutional changes they are seeking, there will be bitter recriminations against those who have stood in their way; and this could lead to 'national' conflicts on a wider front.

While one group of Serbs is preoccupied with the question of Kosovo, another less vocal group, including some economists, is convinced that the economic crisis will not be overcome without giving greater powers to the federal government. Hence they tend to favour what people in other republics call 'centralist', or 'unitarist', policies. These ideas encounter strong resistance from Slovenia and Croatia, as well as from Vojvodina and Kosovo. So far, the economic arguments for a stronger federal government have not captured much public support, but there is a danger that at some stage they may combine with the surge of Serbian nationalism to promote the idea of Serbian hegemony, which would mean the end of 'socialist self-management' in Yugoslavia.

4

The Decline of the Economy
and the Government Response

In this chapter we shall examine in greater detail the changes in the Yugoslav economy during the 1980s, and how the government responded to them. Because of time-lags in the publication of some key statistics, most of this discussion will be based on the experience of the first six years of the crisis, 1979–85. Although the policies pursued in 1986 were different in important respects from those pursued in the previous few years, in the following year the government reverted to its previous pattern of behaviour; the spending spree of 1986 was halted, and, after a brief period of illusion, the economic crisis returned with added force. It can be said, therefore, that the experience of the period 1979–85 is representative of economic trends up to the end of 1987, and even into 1988.

1. The Great Reversal

As mentioned earlier, from the early 1950s until the end of the 1970s Yugoslavia experienced rapid economic growth. It is true that in the second half of the 1970s there were already signs of an approaching crisis—in particular, the deterioration in the balance of payments, a rapid rise in the foreign debt, and the slackening in the rate of growth of output per worker in the social sector. But the year 1979 was a climacteric: from that year onwards, the trend of economic change has been in almost all respects downwards. Some indicators of this reversal were cited in the previous chapter, but Table 4.1 gives more detail and a wider range of indicators.

The definition of social product which is used in Yugoslavia differs from the standard definition of gross domestic product

TABLE 4.1. *Growth and Decline of the Yugoslav Economy*

	Average per annum			Total
	1960–70	1970–79	1979–85	1979–85
Percentage changes				
(1) Social product, 1972 prices (adjusted)	6.0	5.6	−0.9	−5.5
(2) Personal consumption, 1972 prices	6.3	5.6	−0.5	−3.1
(3) Personal consumption per capita, 1972 prices	5.7	4.5	−1.3	−7.7
(4) Gross fixed investment, 1972 prices	6.7	7.1	−7.5	−37.2
(5) Product of the social sector, 1972 prices	7.1	6.1	−1.1	−6.6
(6) Workers in the productive social sector	2.6	4.3	2.5	16.1
(7) Real product per worker in the social sector	4.3	1.8	−3.6	−19.5
(8) Real net personal income per worker in the productive social sector	6.8	2.1	−4.7	−24.9
Position in final year of period				
(9) Registered job-seekers, monthly average (000)	320	762		1040
(10) Net foreign debt ($ billion)	4[a]	13¾		18¾

[a] 1973.

Sources: Line (1): Appendix at end of book; lines (2) and (4): YB85 (102–7) and OECD 1987, Table A); line (3): YB85 (102–8) and OECD (1987, Tables A and H), adjusted for estimated number of non-resident dependants; line (5): YB85 (102–10) and *Indeks*, adjusted for stock appreciation from Appendix; line (6): YB85 (102–5) and OECD (1987, Table H); line (7): Derived from lines (5) and (6); line (8): YB85 (102–33) and *Indeks*; line (9): YB85 (102–6) and OECD (1987, Table H); line (10): OECD (1983, 27) and OECD (1987, 16).

used in the West by excluding the value of 'non-material' services, namely, services performed by government and semi-government employees (including those engaged in education, health, culture, and social welfare) and personal services such as hairdressing. The difference in the estimated total value of the domestic product on these two definitions depends on the numbers of people engaged in these excluded services, and on their relative pay. During the 1970s this difference was 10 per cent or more of social product, but it was gradually falling, and in the mid-1980s the difference amounted to only 5–6 per cent. Official estimates of gross domestic product are given in the OECD *Economic Surveys* of Yugoslavia, but these are only in current prices. Since the official estimates of social product and its components are also available in constant prices, it is preferable to base our discussion on these.

A more serious problem is that Yugoslav official estimates of social product make no correction for stock appreciation; in US terminology, there is no 'inventory valuation adjustment'. The problem arises because, under conditions of inflation, the normal method of estimating national product from business accounts brings into business income—and hence into national product—capital gains on stocks held during the accounting period. This error cannot be removed by deflating such estimates of income or product by a price index, but can be corrected only by deflating the original stock values, and then working forwards from that point. Because inflation in Yugoslavia in the 1980s was both rapid and accelerating, the amount of stock appreciation erroneously included in the official estimates of social product was both large and increasing (see also Madžar 1985). In the mid-1980s it reached a level of 15–20 per cent of social product, and the proportion of social product officially estimated to be used for accumulation of stocks was of the same order. In an economy that was in a state of decline, this was clearly absurd, and a serious analysis is possible only if appropriate corrections are made. Details of the corrections used in this study are given in the Appendix at the end of this book.

When inflation is accelerating, the proportion of social product attributable to stock appreciation increases, and, as a result, unadjusted estimates of the rate of growth of real social product are biased upwards. Thus, in the period 1979–85, while the official estimates of real social product show an average annual rate of *increase* of 0.9 per cent, our adjusted estimates of real social product show an average annual rate of *decline* of 0.9 per cent. On an adjusted basis, the total decline in real social product in this period was 5.5 per cent, and, since in the same period the resident population increased from about 21 million to about 22 million, or by 4.5 per cent, adjusted real social product per head of population may be estimated to have fallen by about 10 per cent.

As the table shows, in the same period the decline in real personal consumption (which requires no adjustment for stock appreciation) was 3.1 per cent, and in real personal consumption per head, 7.7 per cent. But the fall in real fixed investment was very much greater. Whereas in 1970–9 real gross fixed investment, according to official estimates, rose at an average annual rate of 7.1 per cent, in the following six years it fell at an average annual rate of 7.5 per cent, or by 37.2 per cent in total.

By 1979 nearly two-thirds of 'productive' workers were employed in the social sector. (Almost all the rest were engaged in private agriculture.) Consequently, changes in the real product of the social sector, both in the 1970s and in the 1980s, were broadly similar to changes in real social product in the economy as a whole. The estimates of this series in the table are based on the assumption that the whole amount of stock appreciation is attributable to the social sector, since it is only for the social sector that the statistical authorities can make use of information taken from business accounts. The estimates show that in the periods 1960–70 and 1970–9 the real product of the social sector rose somewhat faster than real product as a whole, but that in the period 1979–85 the real product of the social sector fell somewhat faster, or by 6.6 per cent in total. Nevertheless, despite this declining trend in output, employment in the productive social sector continued to increase at an average rate of 2.5 per cent per annum, or by 16.1 per cent over the full period. The consequence was an unprecedented collapse of productivity, amounting for the full period to˙nearly 20 per cent. As we shall see in subsequent chapters, many of Yugoslavia's most acute problems in the 1980s arise from this sharp decline in social sector labour productivity.

One of the effects of this declining trend in productivity was a large fall in real earnings of workers in the productive social sector. (Other factors contributing to this result are examined in Table 4.8 below.) Whereas real net personal income per worker in the productive social sector rose in the 1960s at an average rate of 6.8 per cent per annum, and in the 1970s by 2.1 per cent per annum, in the period 1979–85 it fell at an average annual rate of 4.7 per cent, or by a massive 24.9 per cent in all. The worst year for real earnings in this sector was, in fact, 1984, when average real earnings had fallen from the peak year of 1979 by 26.7 per cent. In 1985 there was a slight recovery, of 2.5 per cent, and this was followed in 1986 by a sharp rise of 9.7 per cent. But in 1987 the workers in the productive social sector lost everything that they had gained in 1986. By June 1987 their real earnings were back to the 1985 level, and by the end of the year there were substantially lower.

The penultimate line of Table 4.1 shows how the number of registered job-seekers increased between 1970 and 1985. The number of registered job-seekers is only a rough guide to the number of unemployed, since some of those who register are still at school, and others are in less preferred jobs; on the other hand, there may be people who do not bother to register, because they see no prospect of getting a job. Because workers already in jobs in the social sector scarcely ever lose their jobs, a very large proportion of the job-seekers are young people who have never had a job, including a disproportionate number of young women. Until a worker has had a social sector job for at least a year, he is not entitled to unemployment benefit. So most of the unemployed are forced to depend on their relatives, or to do part-time unregistered private work. Also, over the past twenty years, many Yugoslav workers have emigrated to work in Western countries, especially in the Federal Republic of Germany. Despite a considerable fall since 1973 in the number of such workers 'temporarily abroad', there were still 768,000 of them in 1986 (OECD 1988, Table H).

The final line of the table gives official estimates of the level of net foreign debt in 1973, 1979, and 1985. The sharpest rise in the net foreign debt was between 1975 and 1980, when it rose from $5¾ billion to $17¼ billion. It rose by a further $1½ billion in 1981, but since that year has remained approximately steady (see the final column of Table 4.5 below). Because of foreign lending by Yugoslavia, the gross foreign debt exceeds the net foreign debt by $1–$2 billion. The 1985 the gross foreign debt was $20¾ billion, largely denominated in dollars. While, in principle, $2 billion of foreign lending can be subtracted from this (as it has been above), a substantial number of these foreign loans have been ˙made to less developed countries, and their value is uncertain. The servicing of the large gross foreign debt (equivalent in 1984 to about half of Yugoslavia's social product) has imposed a heavy burden on the Yugoslav economy in recent years. In practice, however, although a large proportion of the debt has become due for repayment during this period, there has been little net repayment of principal. Instead, debts have been reprogrammed, or rolled over, or new loans have been raised to refinance maturing debts. Until 1987, Yugoslavia paid its interest obligations punctually, but in the latter part of the year it asked for a postponement, and opened new negotiations with its creditors (and the IMF) with the aim of reducing its net servicing

TABLE 4.2.   *Changes in Major Components of Demand, 1979–1985* (annual percentage rates of change, 1972 prices)

	(1) Personal consumption	(2) Collective consumption	(3) Gross fixed investment	(4) Exports (goods and services)	(5) Imports (goods and services)	(6) Social product (adjusted)
1974–79	5.1	7.4	8.8	2.2	4.0	6.7
1979–85	−0.5	−2.1	−7.5	1.3	−7.2	−0.9
1980	0.7	−1.0	−5.9	7.5	−7.2	−1.5
1981	−1.0	−4.8	−9.8	12.0	−1.5	1.6
1982	−0.1	−0.7	−5.5	−18.5	−16.7	−0.2
1983	−1.7	−5.1	−9.7	−4.4	−14.8	−1.8
1984	−1.0	−0.2	−9.6	6.5	−4.5	−2.1
1985	0.0	−0.3	−4.0	8.0	3.0	−1.6
Addendum Total change, 1979–85	−3.1	−11.7	−37.2	7.9	−36.3	−5.5

Sources: Cols. (1)–(5): OECD (1983 and 1987, Table A); col. (6): OECD (1983 and 1987, Table A), but adjusted for stock appreciation from Appendix at end of book.

obligations over the next few years. An agreement to this effect was reached in May 1988.

2. Changes in Expenditure

Table 4.2 gives details of annual rates of change of some major components of aggregate real demand for the period 1974–9 as a whole, and for each of the following six years. It will be seen that both personal consumption and gross fixed investment fell most sharply in 1981, 1983, and 1984. Collective consumption, which is partly expenditure by enterprises on fringe benefits but mainly expenditure by government and semi-government organizations on goods and 'productive' services, also fell rapidly in 1981 and 1983, but hardly at all in 1984. Over the whole six-year period, the squeeze on collective consumption was considerably greater than on personal consumption, while the squeeze on fixed investment was greater still.

The trends in the volumes of exports and imports (of goods and 'productive' services) are instructive.[1] In the period 1974–9, the volume of imports was rising at 4 per cent per annum while the volume of exports was rising at only 2.2 per cent per annum. This was an important symptom of the maturing crisis. In the following six years the volume of imports was sharply reduced, falling at an average rate of 7.2 per cent per annum, or by 36.3 per cent in total. Meanwhile, the volume of exports fluctuated widely from year to year. In 1980–1 and 1984–5 it rose satisfactorily, but in 1982 it dropped by 18.5 per cent, and in the following year by a further 4.4 per cent. On the average, in this period of severe economic crisis, the rate of growth of real exports of goods and services was only 1.3 per cent per annum.

Experience in the years 1986–7 was no more reassuring. In 1986 the volume of exports (of goods only) fell by 1 per cent, and in 1987 it rose by 2 per cent. Meanwhile, in 1986 the volume of imports (also of goods) was allowed to rise by 8 per cent, but was cut back in the following year by about 4 per cent.

Further details on the changes in gross fixed investment are given in Table 4.3. In the years 1974–9, fixed investment in

[1] All Yugoslav data on exports and imports need to be treated with some caution. On this point, see the first few paragraphs of Ch. 9.

TABLE 4.3. *Changes in Gross Fixed Investment*
(annual percentage rates of change, 1972 prices)

	Total	Industry and mining	Social services[a]	Other
1974–79	8.8	9.6	9.3	8.6
1979–85	−7.5	−7.3	−11.7	−7.1
1980	−5.9	−1.2	−8.8	−8.6
1981	−9.8	−12.1	−13.8	−7.9
1982	−5.5	−6.9	−21.6	−3.0
1983	−9.7	−12.1	−24.0	−7.1
1984	−9.6	−11.1	5.6	−9.7
1985	−4.0	0.6	−3.9	−6.0
Addendum: Total change, 1979–85	−37.2	−36.5	−52.5	−35.7

[a] Health, education, culture, and social welfare.
Sources: YB85 (102–13) and OECD (1983 and 1987, Table A).

industry, social services, and other activities rose more or less in parallel. But in the following six years, while fixed investment in industry was cut at approximately the same rate as total fixed investment, fixed investment in social services was reduced even more severely—by more than half. The sharpest cuts in this area were made in 1982 and 1983.

Table 4.4 presents estimates of the volume of imports of goods, in 1975 and in each year from 1979 to 1985, divided into three categories: raw and intermediate materials, machinery and transport equipment, and consumer goods. Imports of raw and intermediate materials, which are essential for the maintenance of domestic production, fell in the six-year period by 17 per cent. To some extent these were replaced by local production, although often with inferior substitutes. The restriction of these imports was a major cause of the decline in Yugoslavia's rate of economic growth, and from 1982 onwards the volume of imports of these goods was allowed to level off. But the cuts in imports of machinery and transport equipment, and of consumer goods, were much more severe—approximately 65 and 75 per cent,

TABLE 4.4.   *Volume of Imports of Goods by Category, 1975 and 1979–1985*
(billion dinars at 1972 prices)

	Total	Raw and inter-mediate materials	Machinery and transport equipment	Consumer goods
1975	70.7	46.4	17.3	7.0
1979	87.9	56.0	22.4	9.4
1980	79.3	59.7	15.2	4.5
1981	75.0	57.7	13.1	4.1
1982	62.0	47.4	11.3	3.3
1983	57.1	45.4	8.6	3.2
1984	54.0	44.7	6.7	2.6
1985	56.7	46.5	7.8	2.4
Addendum: Percentage change, 1979–85	−35.5	−17.0	−65.2	−74.5

Sources: Total value of goods imports, from National Accounts tables in *Indeks*, deflated by implicit price deflator for imports of goods and services from OECD (1983 and 1987, Table A), and distributed between the three categories in the proportions shown in Babić (1987, Table 12).

respectively. Imports of machinery and transport equipment roughly stablized after 1982, but imports of consumer goods continued to decline throughout the period. The cuts in imports of machinery were closely related to, and indeed largely responsible for, the decline of investment in industry. As a result of these cuts, Yugoslav industry is now increasingly dependent on ageing and technically obsolescent equipment.

The cuts in imports of consumer goods were inevitable in the circumstances of the time. They have probably been partly offset by unrecorded imports of consumer goods purchased by Yugoslavs visiting neighbouring countries, using foreign exchange withdrawn from their foreign exchange accounts (or from their private hoards of foreign exchange). But the decline in imports of consumer goods will have had a depressing effect on incentives, and strengthened monopolistic tendencies in the domestic market.

3. The Balance of Payments

The initial cause of the crisis of the 1980s was the alarming increase in the deficit in the current balance of payments during the final three years of the 1970s. Although the federal government was not fully aware of the position at the time, this deficit was associated with a rapid increase in the foreign debt. As can be seen from Table 4.5, the current deficit in the years

TABLE 4.5.   *Major Components of Current Balance of Payments as Percentages of Social Product, and End-of-year Foreign Debt, 1975–1985*

	% of adjusted social product at current prices				Net foreign debt, end of year ($ billion)
	Net exports (goods and services)[a]	Net remittances received[b]	Net interest paid	Total current balance	
1975	−7.2	4.6	−1.0	−3.5	5¾
1976	−2.9	4.2	−0.8	0.5	7
1977	−7.0	3.6	−0.7	−4.0	8½
1978	−5.8	3.7	−0.6	−2.7	10¾
1979	−8.4	3.0	−1.1	−6.5	13¾
1980	−4.1	2.8	−1.9	−3.2	17¼
1981	−1.5	2.8	−2.4	−1.0	18¾
1982	0.1	2.1	−2.9	−0.8	18½
1983	1.1	2.1	−2.7	0.5	18¾
1984	2.2	2.8	−3.8	1.2	18½
1985	3.0	2.0	−3.3	1.7	18¾

[a] Includes 'non-material' services traded internationally, which are not included in social product.

[b] Value of money orders received from workers abroad minus withdrawals from foreign exchange accounts.

Sources: Current balance and its components: for 1975–9, OECD (1983, Table M), converted from dollars to dinars at the 'statistical' exchange rates of 17 dinars in 1975–7, 18.24 dinars in 1978, and 19 dinars in 1979; for 1980–5, *Indeks*, 1987, no. 3. Adjusted social product at current prices: Appendix at end of book. Net foreign debt: OECD (1983 and 1987), except 1976, which is interpolated from data on gross foreign debt in Grgić (1987, Table 2).

1977–9 averaged about 4.5 per cent of (adjusted) social product. In the same three years, the net foreign debt approximately doubled—from $7 billion to nearly $14 billion—and net interest payments rose in the period 1977–80 from 0.7 per cent of social product to 1.9 per cent.

The final blow was the second oil shock, in 1979. The dollar price of oil was doubled and Yugoslavia's balance of payments was subjected to a heavy new burden. Moreover, soon afterwards the Western countries began to impose stricter monetary controls, which caused a rise in interest rates, and lenders were no longer willing to extend credit to heavily indebted countries in the same relaxed manner as they had adopted after the first oil shock of 1973–4.

It was not, in fact, until 1982 that the Yugoslav government knew even approximately the extent of the country's foreign indebtedness. This was one of the results of the 1974 Constitution, which had decentralized power, especially in economic and financial matters, to the republics and provinces. Meanwhile, despite some efforts to curb demand in 1980, there was a large current deficit in that year, and the net foreign debt rose by a further $3½ billion. It was not until 1981 that the foreign balance and the foreign debt began to be brought under control. As shown above, this required sharp cuts in collective consumption and fixed investment. In the following year there was a major reduction in the volume of imports, especially of imports of raw and intermediate materials, and, although exports in that year also fell substantially, the deficit on the current balance of payments was reduced to 0.8 per cent of social product, and the net foreign debt slightly declined.

In these critical years there were two other negative influences on the balance of payments. The most important was the fall, in relation to social product, of the value of remittances from Yugoslavs working abroad. Net remittances fell from 4.6 per cent of social product in 1975 to 2.8 per cent in 1980 and 1981, and then to 2.1 per cent in 1982 and 1983. This was partly the result of the decline in the number of Yugoslavs working abroad, which fell from a peak of over 1 million in 1973 to 790,000 in 1979, and 740,000 in 1983 (OECD, 1983 and 1987, Table H). But there was also a growing reluctance among Yugoslav workers abroad to repatriate their savings, at least through official channels, because of uncertainty about government policy and a misguided government effort in 1983 to restrict the right to make withdrawals from foreign exchange accounts.

The second negative influence on the foreign balance was the rising cost of net interest payments. Expressed as a proportion of social product, these payments rose from 1.1 per cent in 1979 to 3.8 per cent in 1984, but fell to 3.3 per cent in 1985. The rise in interest payments was the result of several factors: the growth of the foreign debt (up to 1981), the rise in dollar interest rates (also up to 1981), and the rise in the effective value of the dollar (up to early 1985). In recent years, however, the net debt has stabilized, and both dollar interest rates and the effective value of the dollar have fallen.

The combined effect of both these negative trends in the early 1980s was that a net positive contribution from these two sources of more than 3 per cent of social product in most of the 1970s was converted into a drain on the social product of 1.3 per cent in 1985.

4. A Review of Government Policies to Control the Crisis[2]

A country that finds itself in the position in which Yugoslavia was at the beginning of the 1980s has to take urgent short-term measures to staunch the outflow of its foreign reserves. But it must also prepare longer-term measures designed to strengthen its underlying balance of payments and to create conditions for maintaining a satisfactory future rate of economic growth. It is important, also, that these two types of measures should not be mutually inconsistent. Unfortunately, although the Yugoslav government, as we have seen above, took a series of harsh measures to correct the country's current balance of payments,

---

[2] As in many other countries that were obliged to accept conditional assistance from the IMF during the 1980s, some Yugoslavs complain that their government was forced to implement policies dictated by the Fund which were contrary to Yugoslavia's interests. Since the IMF's conditions, and its arguments in support of them, are not publicly available, it does not seem very fruitful to pursue this line of investigation. In any case, I find it difficult to believe that the Yugoslav government would have made substantially different policy decisions in the absence of pressure from the IMF. See also Tyson et al. (1984).

these measures had a negative effect on the prospects for future growth. Despite much public proclamation of intentions to introduce reforms, including official acceptance of the Long-term Programme of Economic Stabilization in 1982, neither the Yugoslav Party nor its government ever reached the point of actually implementing any of these reforms.

The principal short-term measures carried out by the government included: severely cutting back imports of capital goods, much of which had previously been financed by foreign credits; cutting back other imports, especially imports of consumer goods, but also, from 1982 onwards, imports of raw and intermediate materials; cutting domestic spending on all goods and services, but especially on collective consumption and fixed investment; and negotiating with creditors, and with the IMF, in order to reschedule and refinance maturing debts. Apart from this last measure, all the other measures were directed essentially towards reducing the standard of living of the population, both immediately and in the future. None of these measures gave any stimulus to growth, except in so far as they encouraged import replacements, which were often costly and economically inefficient. Indeed, the cuts in imports of raw and intermediate materials struck a severe blow at domestic production and thus had a long-term depressing effect on both exports and imports.

The main weakness in all these policies was the lack of a clear strategy for stimulating exports. There were, it is true, some adverse external conditions. In the first place, the world shipbuilding industry, which is one of the few industries in which Yugoslavia had achieved a significant export specialization, was depressed from 1979 onwards; and Yugoslav export of ships suffered accordingly. Whereas in the 1970s exports of ships accounted for 6–8 per cent of the dollar value of Yugoslav exports, in the years 1979–83 this proportion fell to a little over 3 per cent. In 1984, however, it recovered to 4.9 per cent, and in 1987 to 7.7 per cent (OECD, 1983 and 1987, Table K).

Second, from 1981 to 1983 there was a serious world recession, and world imports fell. But Yugoslav's export performance was below average: its share of total OECD imports, which was 0.48 per cent in 1973, fell to about 0.34 per cent in 1974–9, and to about 0.28 per cent in 1980–2. In the next three years Yugoslavia's share of OECD imports recovered slightly, but only to 0.34 per cent (OECD, *Foreign Trade Series C, Imports*, 1985).

Another adverse factor which, although not 'external', was already in existence in 1980 was the fact that so much of the foreign loans raised in the 1970s had been misdirected or wasted. Huge sums had been poured into projects for the production of steel and non-ferrous metals which turned out to be either technically or economically inefficient. In addition to these obvious white elephants (one of which—the steel works at Smederevo in Serbia—is still absorbing a great quantity of scarce resources), there was a large amount of duplication of investment in different republics and provinces (and even in some case in different communes within the same republic). It is now said that less than one-third of the foreign debt raised in the 1970s was used for productive purposes (*NIN*, 8 November 1987); and in a speech to the Skupština in October 1987 the Prime Minister himself said: 'It is estimated that more than half of the foreign debt was invested in projects which turned out to be mistaken, or was used for consumption' (*NIN*, 25 October 1987). Thus, Yugoslav industry was faced in the 1980s with the task of servicing a large foreign debt with inadequate resources. In particular, since the emphasis of previous economic policy had been placed on developing import-replacement industries (which usually, in fact, created an even greater demand for imports of machinery and materials), Yugoslavia had practically no strong, specialized, and competitive export industries. Thus, when the need for expansion of exports became desperately urgent, there were not enough enterprises that could meet world standards of quality, cost, and marketing expertise.

Balance of payments policies

A country that is faced by an unacceptable deficit in its current balance of payments can resort to three main types of corrective policy. First, it can reduce internal demand, with the aim of reducing the inflow of imports and encouraging the outflow of exports. This policy was pursued by Yugoslavia with relentless determination from 1980 to 1984, and in the first half of 1985. Mainly by the use of administrative measures, both collective consumption and fixed investment was drastically reduced, and from time to time pressure was put on enterprises, and especially on government and semi-government organizations, to hold back increases in nominal personal incomes.

Second, a government may reduce imports by direct controls, either by imposing physical import restrictions or by rationing foreign exchange for imports. Both of these methods were used in Yugoslavia. But such methods may not be as effective in correcting a balance of payments deficit as they seem. For, if the demand for goods previously imported is allowed to continue when the supply of such goods has been restricted, this demand will be redirected towards substitute products supplied by domestic industries, and so tend to reduce the volume of exports. This tendency has undoubtedly existed in Yugoslavia in the 1980s. Not only has it offset part of the balance of payments benefits from lower imports, but it has also encouraged the production of inferior substitutes for previously imported machinery and industrial materials, and this has reduced Yugoslavia's ability to compete in world markets.

The third type of corrective policy is one that seeks to change the relative prices of tradable and non-tradable goods and services, for example, by devaluing the domestic currency. But the difficulty with a policy of exchange depreciation is that, unless it is accompanied by a strict control over the money supply, it will sooner or later lead to an inflation of domestic costs and prices, which will not only neutralize the effect of the depreciation but may even cause an 'overshoot'. Under such conditions, an exchange depreciation is only a short-term remedy. Moreover, since trade volumes usually take some time to respond to changes in relative prices, a devaluation tends to cause a temporary deterioration in the current balance of payments when expressed in foreign currencies. If, therefore, there is a relaxed money supply, by the time the devaluation begins to produce an improvement in the current balance of payments, its effects on domestic prices may have deprived it of any further beneficial influence.

Thus, the essential condition for correcting a long-term current account deficit is strict control over the domestic money supply. Indeed, if this condition is met, there will be no need to 'announce' devaluations or to use direct import or exchange controls. If a country's currency is made scarce, its citizens will strive to replenish their own supplies of that currency by more or better work, by more production, by more careful expenditure decisions, and by more sales, both at home and abroad. Exports will rise and—at least temporarily—imports will fall, and a balance of payments equilibrium will eventually be achieved, but at a much higher level of output and trade. Unfortunately, however, most governments, especially 'socialist' governments, hate to adopt a tight monetary policy, because one of the great perquisites of government is the right to borrow from the central bank at low cost (or to print money) in order to spend money on projects that satisfy its aspirations or the desires of its supporters. This reluctance is even greater in a country like Yugoslavia, where the governing party believes that it has both the right and the duty to direct the economy in detail according to its own economic and political preconceptions.

From 1972 to 1977, the Yugoslav government kept the dinar–dollar exchange rate fixed at 17 dinars to the dollar; and, despite the much greater rise during this period in Yugoslav prices than in dollar prices, the dinar was still officially valued at 19 dinars to the dollar in 1979. This was a major reason for the sluggishness of Yugoslav exports in the 1970s. With the onset of the foreign exchange crisis of 1979–80, the Yugoslav government devalued the dinar in the latter year by more than a third against the dollar, and by more than a quarter against the Deutschemark. Further large devaluations were carried out in each subsequent year. But from 1980 onwards internal producer prices were also rising rapidly (see column (3) of Table 4.6). A *real* devaluation occurs only if the fall in the foreign exchange value of the home currency exceeds the fall in its internal purchasing power in comparison with the average change in the purchasing power of foreign currencies. Babić (1987) has prepared estimates from which it is possible to derive changes in Yugoslavia's real exchange rate over the period 1976–83, and these are given in the final column of Table 4.6. The results indicate that there were significant real devaluations of the dinar in 1978, 1980, and 1983, but that in 1981 there was a substantial upward valuation.

If devaluation were a reliable remedy, on its own, for a deficit in the current account, one would expect to find some effects of the real devaluations of 1978, 1980, and 1983 on the volume of Yugoslav exports. (The effects on imports can be ignored, since imports were restricted, especially from 1980 onwards, by more

TABLE 4.6.   *Changes in Prices of Imports, Exports, and Industrial Products,
Volume of Exports, and the Real Exchange Rate, 1975–1985*

	(1) Import prices (goods and services)	(2) Export prices (goods and services)	(3) Industrial producer prices	(4) Volume of exports	(5) Real exchange rate
1975	12.9	9.1	22.0	−1.3	··
1976	2.9	5.2	6.4	9.3	−1.0
1977	14.1	12.0	9.4	−3.1	1.2
1978	12.1	17.7	8.2	−2.4	−9.3
1979	24.4	18.9	13.3	14.9	0.0
1980	71.1	71.1	27.5	7.5	−10.0
1981	10.7	8.0	44.6	12.0	9.1
1982	56.8	64.9	24.6	−18.5	0.0
1983	50.0	48.4	32.0	−4.4	−17.7
1984	105.4	88.0	57.5	6.5	··
1985	44.5	43.3	80.5	8.0	··

Sources: cols. (1) and (2): implicit price deflators, derived from OECD
(1983 and 1987, Table A), relating to imports and exports of goods and
'material' services, which are included in social product; col. (3):
OECD (1987, Table I); col. (4): OECD (1983 and 1987, Table A); col.
(5): changes in the ratio of the effective nominal exchange rate to the
relative prices of major trading partners, from Babić (1987, 20).

direct methods.) A comparison of columns (4) and (5) of the
table gives some support to this hypothesis. Although there is no
evidence that the devaluations had a significant effect on exports
in the year in which they occurred, there is some negative
correlation between exchange rate variation in any year and the
growth of exports in the following year. This can be seen
particularly in the behaviour of exports in the years immediately
following the major real exchange rate variations of 1978, 1980,
1981, and 1983. There is a suggestion, also, that the effects of
these major valuation changes persisted to a smaller extent in
succeeding years.

    As stated above, in the absence of firm fiscal and monetary
restraints, a devaluation tends to have effects not only on the
volume of imports and exports but also on internal prices. The
evidence on this point from our short time-series is not very firm,

but there is a suggestion that in this period internal Yugoslav prices responded to changes in the real exchange rate with a time-lag of about a year. It is not surprising that this relation is less clear than the previous one, because there are many more influences on internal prices than the exchange rate.

The tendency for devaluations to lead to subsequent increases in internal prices is found in all countries. But it may well be stronger in Yugoslavia than in countries with a wage system. In countries where nominal wage rates are fixed by contract for a year or more, they cannot immediately be adjusted to changes in the exchange rate. Under such conditions, a devaluation leads, at least temporarily, to a fall in real wages; and this is helpful to the solution of the balance of payments problem. But in Yugoslavia where there is no wages system (except for a very small number of private employees) there is no wage adjustment lag. Yugoslav enterprises are quick to adjust their export prices to changes in import prices (see columns (1) and (2) of Table 4.6), and this implies that a devaluation increases the profitability of exports and hence, under Yugoslav conditions, the incomes of the workers in those enterprises. Under the influence of 'solidarity', this is likely to create pressure for similar increases in personal incomes in all enterprises, and hence in all internal prices.

It seems that, under the conditions existing in this period in Yugoslavia, devaluation lost its power to improve the balance of payments within at most two years, after which all of its power flowed into inflation. Under these conditions, an attempt may be made to correct a deficit in the current balance of payments by repeated, and steadily increasing, devaluations. This is, indeed, the path that Yugoslavia has been following. But, as inflationary expectations become stronger, the response of internal prices to devaluation becomes more immediate, and the real effects of devaluation on the foreign balance steadily diminish. More and more devaluation is accompanied by more and more inflation until the whole monetary system collapses.

Prices and incomes policies

Despite its nominal commitment to a market economy, the Yugoslav government has never abandoned the use of price controls, and during the 1980s it has regularly resorted to comprehensive price controls and freezes. This is, in a sense, its answer to the problem of how to ensure that devaluation results in a continuing improvement in the balance of payments. Professor Mencinger (1987) has listed fifteen major changes in price control policy between the beginning of 1980 and the end of 1986, and his accompanying graph of rates of change in consumer prices reveals five clear cycles. The peaks and troughs of these cycles are given in Table 4.7, together with the corresponding rates of growth of prices at these turning points. (A new peak of over 250 per cent was reached in October 1987.)

TABLE 4.7.   *Cycles of Changes in Consumer Prices (Cost-of-living Index),*
1980–86

Cycle and point		Month	Annual rate of change of prices in month	
			At peak	At trough
First	Peak	February 81	74	
	Trough	January 82		15
Second	Peak	September 82	45	
	Trough	January 83		18
Third	Peak	December 83	99	
	Trough	May 84		29
Fourth	Peak	March 85	96	
	Trough	September 85		58
Fifth	Peak	April 86	119	
	Trough	December 86		75

Source: Mencinger (1987, Table 5).

In most cases the turning points in the price-series coincide with, or are close to, the dates on which new price rules were introduced. As the table shows, both the series of price changes at the peaks and those at the troughs show a strong upward trend, and there is no evidence from these data that price controls have yielded any long-term benefits. On the contrary, as Mencinger points out, price controls create price and output distortions, which the government later tries to correct by privileged price increases for particular goods or services, which in turn create further distortions. It must also be recognized that enterprises begin to anticipate the imposition of controls by increasing their prices before they would normally do. And managements begin to devote more time and energy to trying to secure price advantages than to improving the efficiency of their enterprises. Most economists would agree with Mencinger's conclusion that 'price controls in Yugoslavia, and most likely elsewhere, increase rather than decrease inflationary pressure.'

Since the 1950s, most Western countries have abandoned the use of generalized price controls as an anti-inflationary instrument. But some of them have tried to restrain inflation by incomes policies, which seem, at first sight, more feasible in countries in which the majority of the work-force is employed on wage or salary contracts. Although such policies have not proved successful, for some years the OECD *Economic Surveys* of Yugoslavia urged the need for incomes policy as an anti-inflationary instrument in that country. The government has, indeed, made occasional efforts to restrain nominal incomes, mainly by exhortation, but also by direct pressure on the incomes of government and semi-government employees. As a result of such pressure, between 1979 and 1984 the relative level of incomes in 'non-productive' activities fell in comparison with the average level of incomes in productive industries from 120 to 109 per cent. Since 1984, however, relative incomes in non-productive activities have recovered, and in June 1987 reached 119 per cent of the average in productive industries.

It is clearly very difficult for a country whose enterprises are supposed to be operated on the principle of self-management to maintain strict and long-term controls over the level of incomes paid in those enterprises. For this would be a violation of the fundamental concept of self-management, according to which it is the proper aim of each enterprise to maximize its net income (within a framework of market competition) and, in the light of its results, to pay out to its workers such personal incomes as the workers themselves may decide.

But Yugoslavia has a system of *socialist* self-management, which imposes duties on the workers in 'self-managed' enterprises as well as giving them rights. Article 15 of the 1974 Constitution prescribes that workers have the duty of 'constantly renewing, expanding, and improving social resources, for their own benefit and for the benefit of the whole community'. (See also Article 116 of the Law on Associated Labour of 1976.) This duty has been supported by 'social compacts' between governments, economic chambers, and trade unions which lay down the principles on which the net income of enterprises should be divided between personal incomes, fringe benefits, and 'accumulation'. Although these social compacts have no legal force, they do exert some moral influence, especially at times when the government threatens that, unless enterprises carry out their agreed social compacts, it will introduce legislation to compel them to do so. But these social compacts have been concerned only with the *proportion* of enterprise net income distributed as personal income; none of them has ever attempted to prescribe the absolute level, or change in the level, of nominal personal incomes. Consequently, except in so far as they may have encouraged enterprise saving (which is doubtful), they have had no effect on inflation. Indeed, it may be argued that, when workers and managers know that their incomes are governed by fixed rules relating them to the level of net nominal income of their enterprise, they will make even stronger efforts to increase the latter by raising prices.

In the first quarter of 1983, and again in the first quarter of 1987, the federal government imposed a total freeze on increases in nominal incomes. Although these freezes temporarily held back the growth of nominal incomes, they do not seem to have affected the growth of prices, which continued to rise at a rapid rate. Very probably, enterprises, which knew that the freezes were temporary, made sure that their nominal net incomes would continue to grow, so that they would be in a good position to increase nominal personal incomes at the end of the freeze. And this is what eventually happened. In 1987, for example, whereas nominal personal incomes were held during the first quarter at about 145 per cent of their 1986 level, the cost-of-living index grew in that quarter even faster than in either the previous or the succeeding quarters, and, after the end of the freeze, nominal incomes rose steeply in the following four months, by which time they had more than caught up with the rise in prices in the preceding twelve months.

If incomes policy was ineffective in restraining inflation, how was it that *real* personal incomes in the productive social sector fell in the period 1979–85, as shown in Table 4.1 above, by nearly 25 per cent? The answer, I suggest, is that real personal incomes in the productive social sector depend mainly on real product per worker in that sector (after adjustment for the share of income distributed as net personal incomes), on Yugoslavia's terms of trade with the outside world, and on industry's terms of trade with the (largely private) agricultural sector. Table 4.8 presents some figures to test this hypothesis for the period 1979–85. For the six-year period as a whole, while real earnings in the productive social sector fell by 24.9 per cent, real output per worker in this sector is estimated to have fallen by 19.5 per cent, and the earnings share by 8.2 per cent. The international terms of trade also fell by 7.9 per cent, and the industrial/agricultural terms of trade declined by 10 per cent. It seems, therefore, that each of these factors may have had some effect on the level of real earnings.

TABLE 4.8. *Percentage Changes in Real Earnings and Related Variables, 1979–1985*

End year	(1) Real earnings in productive social sector	(2) Out per worker in social sector	(3) Earnings share of product	(4) Foreign terms of trade	(5) Industrial/ agricultural terms of trade
1980	−6.7	−5.0	−2.3	0.0	−5.8
1981	−4.9	−1.5	−2.3	−2.5	−5.7
1982	−1.3	−3.5	0.6	5.1	−7.9
1983	−10.1	−3.6	−6.5	−1.0	−10.7
1984	−6.9	−4.5	−1.6	−8.5	9.1
1985	2.5	−3.2	3.8	−0.8	12.8
Total change, 1979–85	−24.9	−19.5	−8.2	−7.9	−10.0

Sources: col. (1): YB85 (102–33) and *Indeks*; col. (2): social product of the social sector at 1972 prices, after adjustment for stock appreciation: see Appendix ; no. of workers from YB85 (105–20) and *Indeks*; col. (3): social product of the social sector at current prices as in col. (2); net personal income estimated by multiplying monthly net personal income per worker in social sector production, as in col. (1), by mean number of workers in the same sector, as in col. (2), and by a factor of 12; col. (4): implicit price deflator of exports of goods and services divided by implicit price deflator of imports of goods and services, both from OECD (1987, Table A); col. (5): index of industrial producer prices divided by index of agricultural producer prices, both from OECD (1987, Table I).

When we look at the year-by-year changes, it seems that the primary influence on changes in real earnings was changes in real output per worker, but that this was modified in individual years by substantial changes in the other factors. In particular, there was a sharp decline in the share of earnings in enterprise net income in 1983, and a rise in 1985, both of which probably reflected changes in government policy. The 1982 improvement in the international terms of trade may account for the fact that real earnings in the productive social sector fell less rapidly than real output per worker in that sector in that year. Changes in the industrial/agricultural terms of trade may also have had some influence on real earnings in particular years, especially perhaps in 1983 and 1985. It would be interesting to test this hypothesis by more exact methods, but it cannot be done on the basis of such a short time-series.

Fiscal and monetary policies

The slowing down of inflation is never an easy task, especially when it has continued at an accelerating rate for a number of years. For inflation is a process by which people who have contracted to sell their goods or services for a certain sum of money, on the assumption that that sum of money will buy a definite amount of other goods and services, discover, to their dismay, that this assumption has been falsified by the subsequent rise in the prices of some or all of this latter group of goods and services. As soon as possible, the people who have been thus misled attempt to revise their own contracts upwards. If there is a relaxed supply of money, they will succeed, and others will find that the calculations on which *they* based their supply prices are now outdated. These time-lags in adjustment are a necessary condition for the continuation of inflation at a finite rate. For, if everyone were able to make an instantaneous revision in his own contract for the supply of goods or services, and if the money supply were sufficiently elastic, the rate of inflation would rapidly move towards infinity.

The consequence of these built-in time-lags is that, under inflationary conditions, there are always substantial groups of people who are deeply dissatisfied with the prices at which they are selling their goods or services, and who are preparing to redress the situation at the earliest convenient moment. This is one reason why price and income controls, and especially price and income freezes, are inherently unstable. The longer a 'freeze' lasts, the greater the sense of injustice of the people whose incomes are being held below what they believe to be their economically justified level. Eventually, this sense of injustice creates an explosion; the freeze is broken; there is a wild scramble to make the desired corrections; and prices and nominal incomes begin again to rise sharply, usually catching up, or even surpassing, the levels they would have reached in the absence of the freeze. In other words, the imposition of price or income freezes is like trying to cap a volcano. There may be a case for such a measure as a temporary component of a package of deflationary policies; but, unless those policies also ensure that the power of the volcano is reduced, they will fail.

The inner power of the volcano is the level of money expenditure or, more specifically, the excess of the rate of growth of money expenditure over the rate of growth of real output at constant prices. Unless there is some unexpected boost to real output—by, for example, the development of new petroleum or other natural resources, a favourable harvest, or an improvement in the international terms of trade—the only way to reduce inflation is to reduce the flow of money expenditure. It is well known that this can be achieved by a combination of restrictive fiscal and monetary policies. If the government reduces its fiscal deficit (or increases its surplus) and uses the proceeds to slow down its rate of borrowing or reduce its absolute level of debt, the spending power of other sectors of the economy will tend to fall. But, in order to ensure that this result follows with certainty, it is necessary for the government to combine fiscal restraint with a tight monetary policy. To a certain extent, this will happen automatically, since part of the slowing down of the increase, or repayment, of government debt will take the form of a slowing down or reduction in central bank loans to the government, which in turn will slow down the growth in, or reduce, the reserves of the commercial banks, and hence the money supply. But a government, or its central bank, may need to go further than this, especially if there is a large government debt already in the hands of the banks or the non-bank public. For, so long as the government is indebted to other sectors, those sectors have the means of forcing the government to convert some part of its debt into money, especially that part which is currently maturing. Only a tight monetary policy, with its accompanying rise in the rate of interest, will ensure that the non-government sectors are deterred from liquidating government debt and thus creating the basis for a continuation of inflation.

These elementary truths of economic policy are well known to many Yugoslav economists, to some bankers, and to some government officials and politicians. But, as in many other countries, the politicians try to push these truths out of their minds. For the short-term consequences of pursuing a genuinely anti-inflationary policy are unpleasant. As a result of the above-mentioned time-lags in adjustments, inflation has an inherent momentum which it is difficult to break. When an anti-inflationary fiscal and monetary policy is introduced, the first effect will be a decline in the expected rate of growth of nominal demand for goods and services. Those enterprises and groups of workers that had recently raised their money prices in the expectation of continued or accelerating growth of monetary demand will be disappointed. Sales of their goods or services will fall short of the levels that were previously anticipated; unwanted stocks will rise (at least temporarily); there will be a decline in value added per worker and hence, in Yugoslav conditions, in personal incomes; and an increasing number of firms will incur losses. In a capitalist economy, this will lead to a rise in unemployment, both because firms that face disappointing prices, falling sales, or rising stocks will reduce their staffs, and because some firms will be forced to close plants or to go into liquidation. Yugoslavia, however, is a communist country, in which the right of secure employment (for those already in jobs) is considererd to be a foundation stone of socialism. Indeed, Article 13 of the Yugoslav constitution explicitly gives 'workers in associated labour working with socially-owned resources' the 'inalienable' right to work. Consequently, the Yugoslav Party and government are strongly averse to the use of fiscal and monetary policies to reduce inflation. And they receive some support in this aversion from some of their central bank officials, and from a few economists who cite the anti-monetarist writings of 'Keynesian' economists in the West.

Yugoslav politicians and journalists are also inclined to point to practical difficulties in the way of implementing tight fiscal or monetary policies in their country. Under the Federal Constitution, the major role in determining budget policies is played by the governments of the republics and provinces, and—to a lesser extent—the communes. Only about one-quarter of total government expenditure is controlled by the federal government, and almost all of this is used for defence (including veterans' pensions and benefits) and for internal security. Only the federal government is allowed to run a permanent surplus or deficit; but, in practice, since the republics and provinces are very suspicious of federal financial power, they are not easily convinced that substantial federal surpluses should be permitted. In the monetary sphere, it is pointed out that the National Bank of Yugoslavia is constructed, like all Yugoslav institutions, on strictly federal principles. It consists of one federal bank and six republican and two provincial 'national banks', and the day-to-day policy decisions of the federal bank are taken by a Board of Governors composed of the governors of the republican and provincial banks. Since each republic and province is anxious to obtain as much money as possible for itself, it is difficult in such a system to ensure that federal monetary policy is fully implemented.

But experience has shown that, despite such 'constitutional' difficulties, the Yugoslav government can, when it is sufficiently determined, force the republics and provinces to carry out federal policies. This has been proved on numerous occasions in recent years, when price or income freezes have been imposed by the Skupština under 'urgent' procedures, or when laws about the allocation of foreign exchange have been imposed against the wishes of particular republics. The real reason why Yugoslavia continues to tolerate rapid and accelerating inflation is not the practical difficulties of implementing an anti-inflationary policy, but the lack of political will to face the unpleasant consequences of implementing such a policy.

Each year in the 1980s the Yugoslav government has declared its firm intention to reduce inflation, and in recent years the reduction of inflation has become 'priority number one'. In addition, the annual Economic Resolution, which sets the targets for each year, has provided for some slowing down in the rate of growth of the money supply. The government has pointed with pride to the fact that, in the outcome, although the money supply targets are not met, the rate of growth of the money supply has been lower than the rate of growth of nominal income. But this is naive. It is well known that, under conditions of rapid and accelerating inflation, everyone tries to economize on the holding of money. As a result, the 'velocity of circulation' of money increases; in other words, the ratio of the stock of money to the nominal value of the national product declines. As Table 4.9 shows, despite very large and persistent increases in the nominal stock of money, from 1980 onwards both prices and the nominal value of the social product rose even faster. From 1979 to 1985 the real stock of money fell by 50 per cent, and the velocity of circulation of money rose from 3.1 to 5.9. Such a large change in the velocity of circulation is exceptional by the standards of

TABLE 4.9. *Changes in Nominal Money Supply, Social Product and Prices, Index of Real Money Supply, and Velocity of Circulation 1977–1985*

	(1)	(2)	(3)	(4)	(5)
	\% changes on previous year				
	Money supply	Nominal social product	Cost-of-living index	Index of real money supply (1979=100)	Velocity of circulation of money
1977	35.7	17.4	15.2	92	2.9
1978	23.8	26.8	14.5	99	3.0
1979	21.9	26.1	21.0	100	3.1
1980	21.2	28.3	29.6	93	3.3
1981	25.0	42.3	41.9	82	3.8
1982	26.6	31.3	29.2	81	3.9
1983	23.0	38.2	41.2	70	4.4
1984	32.7	49.5	54.6	60	4.9
1985	45.1	74.5	71.5	51	5.9

Sources: col. (1): mean of beginning-of-year and end-of-year figures from OECD (1987, Table J); money supply (M1) consists of notes in circulation and cheque accounts at banks; col. (2): Appendix at end of text; col. (3): YB85 (102–33) and *Indeks*; col. (4): mean nominal money supply ÷ the cost-of-living index; col. (5): nominal social product, adjusted for stock appreciation, ÷ mean nominal money supply.

Western countries, and in Yugoslavia it may be attributable partly to the existence of foreign exchange accounts and hoards of foreign currency, whose dinar value automatically increases as the exchange value of the dinar falls. But the main explanation is the rate of inflation. The fact that the money supply each year increases less rapidly than the nominal value of the social product is not a tribute to the wisdom of Yugoslav monetary policy, but a proof of its failure.

5. Conclusions

After the first oil shock of 1973–4, Yugoslavia continued on a path of high spending, especially on investment. As a result, the balance of payments deteriorated, and by 1979 the current deficit had reached 6.5 per cent of social product. Meanwhile, the net foreign debt rose from less than $6 billion in 1975 to more than $17 billion by the end of 1980 (and nearly $19 billion in subsequent years). Neither high investment nor a rising foreign debt would have been a cause for long-term concern if the resources had been used for sufficiently productive purposes— more specifically, if the value of the extra production of tradable goods (and preferably of exports) had been greater than the interest payable on extra foreign loans. Unfortunately, this was not so. Much of the extra foreign debt was used to finance non-productive investment and consumption, and much of the 'productive' investment was misdirected or completely wasted. When the 1970s came to a close, Yugoslavia had accumulated a large foreign debt on the one hand and many inefficient enterprises on the other.

Sooner of later, the day of reckoning was bound to come. In fact, it came quickly, with the second oil shock of 1979. Oil prices rose sharply again, imposing a heavy new burden on the Yugoslav balance of payments. And this time, the response of Western countries was not continued expansion and the carefree recycling of petroleum dollars, but deflation and tight monetary policies. Interest rates rose, foreign loans became scarce, and soon the world economy moved into recession. The volume of world trade fell, the value of the dollar rose, and Yugoslavia's debt-service burden, along with that of many other countries.

intensified. Although US interest rates began to decline in 1982, and world trade began to recover in 1983, and although from 1985 both the dollar price of oil and the exchange value of the dollar fell, the Yugoslav economy failed to respond adequately to these improved opportunities and continued on its downward path.

By 1985, in comparison with 1979, Yugoslavia's (adjusted) real social product had fallen by more than 5 per cent, real personal consumption per head was down by nearly 8 per cent, the volume of gross fixed investment was down by 37 per cent, and labour productivity in the social sector was down by nearly 20 per cent. Meanwhile, average real earnings in the productive social sector had fallen by nearly 25 per cent, and the annual inflation rate had risen from 20 per cent in 1979 to over 70 per cent in 1985. In the latter part of 1985, in the run-up to the Skupština elections in the early part of 1986 and the Party Congress in the middle of that year, advantage was taken of the falling oil price and the falling value of the dollar to allow some expansion of demand. This expansionist policy was intensified in 1986. The money supply was increased during the course of that year by 109 per cent (compared with 47 per cent in 1985), the personal incomes of government and semi-government employees were allowed to rise faster than personal incomes of productive workers, and average real personal incomes for all social sector workers rose by 10 per cent. Despite a rise of 5 per cent in real personal consumption, it is doubtful whether real domestic product increased. Instead, there was a deterioration in the balance of payments, and probably also a sharp fall in real stockholdings. Meanwhile, the annual rate of inflation rose to 89 per cent. The price for this 'spending spree' was paid in the following year, when prices rose at a rapidly accelerating rate (reaching an annual-equivalent rate of over 200 per cent at the end of the year), while real earnings in the social sector fell back again by 7 per cent. In 1987 more and more enterprises were making losses; the total losses of such enterprises were greater than the net saving of other enterprises (so that the productive social sector as a whole was running at a net loss); and two republics (Macedonia and Montenegro) and the province of Kosovo were in a state of acute financial crisis verging on bankruptcy.

At the beginning of 1988 the outlook for the Yugoslav economy was bleaker than ever. None of the targets set for 1987 had been achieved, except the target for the growth of employment in the social sector (2 per cent), which merely meant a further addition to the degree of already excessive overmanning in that sector. The targets for 1988, offered in the Economic Resolution for that year, were set lower; but virtually no one had any confidence that they would be achieved.

Why did the Yugoslav economy go into an almost continuous downward spiral from 1979 onwards? Why did the Yugoslav government fail to halt the decline in real output and the growth of inflation? The fundamental reasons for these failures of the Yugoslav system will be considered in Chapter 5. At a more superficial level, however, it is evident that the principal cause of failure was the unwillingness of the Yugoslav Party and government to implement a policy of macroeconomic restriction—especially restriction of the money supply—in combination with a microeconomic policy designed to expand opportunities and incentives for enterprise and efficient work. What was needed was more freedom for independent decision-making by genuinely self-managed enterprises within a free market, combined with tight controls on the supply of domestic currency. Policies of this sort, although not always expressed with sufficient clarity, especially as regards the macroeconomic side, were recommended by the Commission which prepared the Long-term Programme of Economic Stabilization. The 'basic principles' of this programme, published early in 1982, were officially accepted by the Party in that year, and the full programme was endorsed, and re-endorsed, on several subsequent occasions. But it has never been carried out. (A popular saying is that the only thing that is 'long-term' about the programme is the time that it takes to implement it.) Despite the fact that social sector enterprises are nominally under self-management control, the Party has never been willing to give them freedom to take their own decisions; nor, for the reasons mentioned earlier, has the Party been willing to impose a strict control over the expansion of the money supply. Instead, the government has relied on a proliferating battery of administrative measures to control enterprise decisions—a policy exactly the opposite of that which was needed—while retaining its right to use expansion of the money supply as a cheap method of financing various government programmes and obligations.

There were ever tighter restrictions on imports, even tighter controls over the allocation of foreign exchange, and repeated attempts to improve the foreign balance by sharp devaluations, interspersed with periods of relative stability of the foreign exchange rate during which Yugoslav international competitiveness declined. Price controls of various degrees of comprehensiveness and intensity were in operation throughout the period. From time to time they were tightened into temporary price 'freezes'. But no permanent benefits ensued. Incomes policies were not normally directed towards restricting the growth in the general level of nominal personal incomes. In 1979–84 the government succeeded in holding back the rate of growth of personal incomes in government and semi-government employment relative to the rate of growth of such incomes in the productive sector; but this policy was reversed in 1985–7. Short-term income freezes were imposed in the first quarter of 1983 and in the first quarter of 1987 (in each case, during the first nine months of the period of office of a new government). But they had no lasting effects on the rate of price inflation.

In 1987 the government introduced a new system of accounting, which was to be applied in all social sector enterprises; it also proposed a new system for the determination of the personal incomes of their employees. Both these systems will be discussed in detail in Chapter 7. The new accounting system, which is already in operation, is designed to establish firmer control over enterprise income distribution under conditions of rapid inflation, for example by ensuring that assets are revalued more regularly and consistently and that material input costs are charged on a replacement cost basis. But the new system is having many unforeseen effects, and many enterprises are suddenly finding that they are trading at a loss and are in danger of being declared bankrupt. The new system for determining personal incomes, although approved by the Skupština, cannot be implemented without the agreement of the trade unions and the governments of the republics and provinces (through the establishment of new 'social compacts'). The system is intended to make the average personal income of workers in a given enterprise depend on two components: the equivalent of a 'wage', related to the kind of work performed, and the equivalent of a 'profit share', which will be determined by the firm's 'profit rate' (defined as the ratio of its current accumulation to the value of its physical assets) in comparison with the average 'profit rate' for firms in the same industry in the same republic or province. However, strong objections to this new system have been raised both by the governments of the republics and provinces and by the trade unions, and it is doubtful whether it will ever be implemented.

Both these measures are symptomatic of the sterility of government policy. Instead of freeing enterprises to compete and to make their own decisions, the government is trying to bind them ever more firmly with red tape. Ironically, the measures are an attempt to mimic the behaviour of capitalism, but a capitalism without freedom of enterprise or competition, and without the opportunities and incentives to work efficiently. Even if implemented, these measures will certainly fail, and will sooner or later be abandoned; but only after they have done great damage to the economy.

5

Underlying Causes of the Crisis

We saw in the previous chapter that Yugoslavia has been in a state of continuous and deepening economic crisis since 1979; that government policies, although partially and temporarily successful in some areas, have failed to reverse the downward trend in real output, productivity, and the standard of living, and have allowed the upward trend in the rate of inflation to continue; and that practically no one in Yugoslavia now believes that the government has found a way out of the crisis. In this chapter it is proposed to examine the underlying reasons for the crisis, and for the failure of government to overcome it. For this purpose, it is necessary to go back to the first principles of the Yugoslav system. I shall, therefore, undertake a brief review of the theory of self-management, and of its operation under Yugoslav conditions. This will bring out the fundamental difficulties in making such a system work efficiently. A description will then be given of the practical effects of this system in Yugoslavia. The chapter will conclude with a summary of some of the opinions expressed by leading Yugoslavs about the underlying causes of the country's crisis.

1. Theory of Self-Management

We shall start by examining the Western model of a competitive self-managed economy, and seeing how, when the model is adjusted to reflect real market conditions, it suggests that there are serious difficulties in making even a competitive system of self-management work efficiently. But next we confront the fact that the Yugoslav·system is not *competitive* self-management, but *socialist* self-management. In the latter type of system there arises a completely new set of obstacles to economic efficiency. Finally, we must allow for the fact that Yugoslavia is a federation of peoples of very different history, language, religion, and level of economic development. We shall find that the amalgam of socialist self-management with federalism creates a uniquely difficult environment in which to operate a successful economy.

Competitive self-management

In a pioneering article, Ward (1958) analysed the behaviour of a perfectly competitive economy which consisted entirely of industrial co-operatives, whose members both worked in the business and owned the equity. Their objective was to maximize the level of income per worker. Ward was able to show that, while the long-run equilibrium of such an economy is the same as that of an economy of competitive capitalism possessing identical techniques and resources, in the short run, co-operative firms respond to changes in prices in a perverse manner. A number of other economists have explored this model further and suggested slight amendments, but Ward's conclusions have broadly remained intact.

Yet this model is, in fact, highly misleading. There are only a few industries in a modern economy in which individual firms can sell as much as they like at a given market price, or in which the expansion of output in the long run predominantly takes the form of an increase in the number of firms of optimum size. The well-known imperfections of competition in the marketing of goods and services lead to a position in which most firms fix their selling prices, and then sell as much as they can at those prices. The level at which each price is fixed depends on the firm's assessment of the risks of long-term entry into its market by potential competitors. Moreover, while in a market economy entry is 'free' in the legal sense, imperfections in the supply of factors of production prevent it from being free in the sense that is necessary for the theory of perfect competition.

The imperfections that are crucial on the supply side are an imperfect knowledge of technique and an imperfect capital market. Both imperfections are especially important in the case of industries in which there are large economies of scale, i.e. in most of manufacturing, transport, communications, finance, and modern retailing. As a result of these imperfections, which have always been present, especially the imperfection of the capital market, new entry into business under capitalist conditions has predominantly taken the form of new one-man or family firms. Some succeed; but the majority fail. But, when there are important market opportunities, sooner or later one or more of these small firms breaks through, expands, and begins to threaten existing firms with *actual* rather than *potential* competition. Hence, the sensible firm already in existence will be careful not to raise its prices to a level at which it is confronted by such a threat.[1]

These amendments to the perfect competition model have a number of implications for the functioning of a competitive (although not *perfectly* competitive) self-management economy. The first is that firms which fix their own prices will be unlikely to react in a perverse fashion to an increase in the demand for their products. Second, this model accounts for the fact that most firms are not of optimum size. Most are of less than optimum size, and are anxious to expand as soon as (a) their technical and managerial capacity has improved to a point at which they can operate successfully on a larger scale, and (b) they are able to raise the necessary finance for such an expansion. For both reasons, but especially the latter, larger firms will tend, for a certain time, to grow more rapidly than smaller firms. Third, because of the economies of scale, larger firms (at least up to the optimum size) produce on average more value added per worker than smaller firms, after deducting interest on capital. In a co-operative economy, therefore, larger co-operatives will tend to produce and distribute more income per worker. This implies on the one hand, that there will be large inter-firm differences in earnings, and on the other, that the implicit ('opportunity') cost to the more successful co-operatives of employing extra workers will be higher than the cost to less successful co-operatives. This will give a capital-using bias to the investment decisions of successful co-operatives, and hence to the economy as a whole. All of the above phenomena are found in Yugoslavia.

The conclusion from this analysis is that, as compared with competitive capitalism, a competitive co-operative economy suffers from four main weaknesses. (1) Because workers in large

---

[1] More detailed explanation of the above arguments can be found in Chs. 9–11 of Lydall (1979) and Ch. 3 of Lydall (1984).

firms receive the rents of economies of scale, there will be excessive inequalities of earnings between firms, and little inter-firm mobility of labour. This leads to a growing sense of injustice and dissatisfaction. (2) The workers in large successful firms will be unwilling to invest in new plants, especially plants in other parts of the country, if there is a standard rule that all plants can, or must, become independent co-operatives. Hence, the mobility of capital and technology will also be much restricted. This is especially undesirable in a country such as Yugoslavia, in which there are very wide inter-regional differences in productivity. (3) The bias towards capital intensity of investment decisions reduces the capacity of the economy to absorb unemployed labour. This, again, is a special problem in a country like Yugoslavia. (4) If it is the standard rule that all enterprises must be co-operatives, and that private businesses are not permitted, a co-operative economy cannot be as competitive as capitalism (or a mixed economy), since there will, in fact, be little new entry.

There is one further characteristic of worker-managed firms which, although rarely considered by economists, is of great practical importance. In the 'co-operative dream', all workers are honest, diligent, and concerned primarily for the good of their 'collective'. While these attitudes may sometimes exist, at least for a time, and especially in small organizations, it is unfortunately not possible to rely on them as a general rule. In the real world there are always some slackers, some 'free-riders', some people willing to 'exploit the system'. These are not just 'relics of capitalism', as the communists would have us believe, but 'weaknesses' of human nature'.[2] Such people not only drag down directly the average level of productivity of the enterprise in which they are employed, but, if they go unpunished, they spread demoralization among other members of the organization. The only method of preventing this is to give managers effective powers to reward good work, to penalize bad work, and to impose the ultimate sanction of dismissal. But co-operatives are usually based on the assumption that the members are entitled to

---

[2] It is, in fact, too facile to describe them as 'weaknesses', unless one believes that it would be better if human beings behaved like ants or bees. Our egoistic 'weaknesses' are the inevitable accompaniment of individual freedom, intelligence, and initiative, without which human societies would indeed be like ant-heaps. Totalitarian and other 'utopian' regimes try to force their subjects to become precisely that.

security of employment until retirement, and that the disciplinary powers of managers must be heavily circumscribed. Under these conditions, most co-operatives will be less efficient than private enterprises of similar economic characteristics.

These considerations lead to the conclusion that, in a world of change and uncertainty, the idea that a *universal* system of industrial co-operatives would be an efficient way of producing the necessities of a good life is a fallacy. In such an economy, the degree of competition would be limited, the mobility of labour, capital, and technology would be restricted, the allocation of resources would be biased towards capital-intensive uses, inter-firm inequality of earnings would be excessive, and the level of internal efficiency of enterprise would, in most cases, be unsatisfactory. In other words, such an economy would be technically and productively backward, would have a high rate of unemployment, and would exhibit an unpleasant degree of inequality of income between regions and between workers in different enterprises.

Socialist self-management

Despite some Western assumptions, Yugoslavia has never had, and was never intended to have, a system of *competitive* self-management. Yugoslav enterprises are owned by 'society', which means in practice that they are owned by the state (which is in turn controlled by the Party). Although all enterprises in the social sector of the Yugoslav economy are nominally controlled by the workers employed in them, those workers have no rights of ownership of the assets that they use. In principle, the workers have been given the right to use these assets to generate as much income as they can, and to reward themselves accordingly. But they are not allowed to sell any of the physical assets (at least, not until they are fully depreciated), and they are under an obligation both to maintain their value by appropriate depreciation and reinvestment, and to increase them. The precise nature of this latter obligation has never been specified; even if it could be specified, which is doubtful, it would be impossible to enforce it without eliminating the last vestiges of self-management.

This conflict between ownership and management rights creates a contradiction which is embedded in the foundations of the Yugoslav system of self-management. In accounting terms, it implies a divorce between the balance sheet and the income account. Theoretically, society controls the balance sheet, while the workers in each enterprise take responsibility for the income account. But, as every accountant and every businessman knows, it is impossible to run a business efficiently on such a basis. Income cannot be separated from capital without doing violence to business decisions. Such a system also opens the door to conflicts of interest. For the workers have been told that it is their right (and their duty) to maximize the income of their enterprises, and hence their own personal incomes. This right is fairly precise, and is immediately appealing. At the same time, the workers are given a vague general responsibility to maintain and increase the equity of their enterprise. There are, inevitably, many situations in which these two objectives come into conflict. Capital can be converted into income as readily as income can be added to capital. The government, either directly or through the promotion of social compacts, has made great efforts to prevent the erosion of capital which such a system permits. But it can never succeed. As often as it blocks one loophole, another is opened. And inflation, which introduces severe distortions into balance sheets and produces illusory income in the form of capital gains, undermines all the efforts of government to compel workers to observe 'the rules of the game'.

Would it be possible to resolve this contradiction if the government, like a landowner, rented enterprise assets to the workers? Unfortunately not. Land can be rented to farmers because it is (more or less) indestructible, and the terms of the lease can require that the tenants preserve the land in its original form. But business assets are financial as well as physical; and the physical assets are (a) man-made, (b) destructible. In general, it is of no use to a business to be offered a set of physical and financial assets which have been assembled by the owner. An efficient business must be able to use its total capacity in ways that it considers to be most productive, whether by converting financial into physical assets (or vice versa), or by redesigning the set of physical assets at its disposal. Once a business has that right, the owner of the capital is at risk. But, if he is a mere *rentier*, he has no means of influencing the ways in which his capital is used, the forms that it takes, and its ultimate value.

An alternative solution might be for the government to confine itself to lending financial capital to self-managed enterprises, and collecting interest on the loans. But in that case the workers in each self-managed enterprise would own the equity. In Yugoslavia, this would be regarded as the revival of capitalism, and the end of *socialist* self-management. Ironically, the actual trend of events has already moved in a similar direction. In place of the above arrangement, whereby the government owns the financial capital and the workers own the equity, the present position is that the government nominally owns the equity while the workers in general, through their private savings, provide the financial capital. It is true that inflation is constantly destroying the value of the workers' savings and replenishing the value of 'social' equity. But this is a bizarre conception of socialism.

Socialist self-management has all the weaknesses of competitive self-management listed in the previous section, but in greater degree. For socialist self-management reduces the opportunities for free decision-making which would exist in a competitive self-management system. Under socialist self-management, at least as it operates in Yugoslavia, and would operate in any communist state, the 'self-managing' workers have much more restricted rights to use the capital of the enterprise than they would have as co-operatives within a competitive self-management system. Their rights to dispose of the income generated are also more limited. Because of the legal requirement that all enterprises in most industries must be self-managed, and hence that the workers in one enterprise cannot retain equity rights in any investment they make in another, there are almost insuperable obstacles to the mobility of capital and technology. And the ideological and legal barriers to the revival of capitalism ensure that there is virtually no new entry of small businesses. Thus, both market competition and progress in technology are seriously handicapped, or even completely blocked.

But *socialist* self-management goes even further than this. The addition of that epithet gives the state its justification to intervene in all business decisions, regardless of the nominal self-management rights of the workers. Yugoslav governments, at all levels, but especially at communal level, exercise final control over all major investment decisions in 'their' enterprises. They sanction credits from local banks, despite the fact that the banks are supposed to be controlled by the enterprises. They force local firms to take on additional quotas of workers, irrespective of whether they are needed or not. They choose the directors of local enterprises and banks, ensuring that they are politically reliable, and often give these posts to politicians who are not well qualified to fill them. And they even put pressure on local enterprises to follow a policy of autarky. For example, they block enterprise plans to invest in other communes (or republics); and they try to ensure that, so far as possible, local enterprises buy their supplies from other local enterprises.

It is an interesting question, why socialist self-management in Yugoslavia has resulted in so much devolution of power to the local authorities. We are accustomed to the idea that Marxist socialism is a system of centralized state socialism. But this doctrine was abandoned by Yugoslavia in the 1950s, and gradually the central power of the state was reduced. In principle, economic power at the enterprise level was transferred to the workers in each enterprise. But a Marxist–Leninist party cannot abdicate from its role as the 'vanguard', the sole repository of all knowledge and power. If *central* state power was to be reduced, it was necessary to shift the Party's focus of power to the local level, where it would seem to be more compatible with self-management. So, in spite of the high claims for the self-management system, the workers were not to be trusted to manage their own affairs. They were to be kept strictly under the control of the local party bureaucracy. The motives for this policy were not, of course, simply ideological. If the workers had been allowed to exercise genuine rights of self-management, tens of thousands of party bureaucrats would have lost their power and their comfortable jobs.

The effects of federalism

The state of Yugoslavia came into existence in 1918 as a result of a voluntary coalescence of several, predominantly south Slav, peoples—Serbs, Croats, Slovenes, and others. Although the Serbs were numerically the most important group, and had the advantage of already possessing their own independent state, they had not conquered the other peoples, and could not impose their own language and customs on them. The Serbs resisted federalism, but the Croats, especially, came to regard it as the only acceptable constitutional system for Yugoslavia. Matters were moving slowly in this direction when Yugoslavia was invaded and occupied by the Axis powers. When the communist resistance movement was launched, its two most popular objectives were 'liberation from the fascist invaders' and 'brotherhood and unity'. (Its third objective, although not concealed, was less prominently displayed: to carry out a communist-led revolution and to establish Stalinist socialism.)

Without their emphasis on the 'brotherhood and unity' of the peoples of Yugoslavia, it is unlikely that the communists would have won power. This was their trump card. Consequently, when the new state was established, it was clearly defined as a federation, and the constituent republics were given the nominal right of secession. There was an inconsistency here between words and deeds. Nevertheless, there was a genuine intention to remain true to the promises made during the war of national liberation.

But there was an inherent contradiction in the communist position. For the Stalinist state socialism which the Yugoslav communists wished to emulate was centralist. It required central planning, central allocation of resources, and central control of the party and state apparatus. How can such a system be made compatible with federalism? The answer is that it cannot. The nominal federal structure of the Soviet Union is nothing but an illusion, a piece of public deception like 'socialist democracy'. But the Yugoslavs were serious about federalism. The non-Serbs had had enough bitter experience of interwar domination by the Serbs. They had not fought the liberation war only to find themselves once more subjected to Serbian rule. Even if the quarrel with the Cominform had not led to a rupture between Yugoslavia and the Soviet bloc, it seems probable that Yugoslavia would have moved away, eventually, from the Stalinist model.

The introduction of 'self-management' was a convenient method of weakening the power of Belgrade, and it opened the way towards federalism. At first, power was devolved mainly to the communes. But in the 1960s there was a resurgence of 'nationalism', i.e. a desire to create a genuine federal system. And in the second half of the 1960s, during the period of the

Economic Reform, federalism was established, not only in government but, even more important, in the Party itself. The decisive turning point was the Brioni plenum of the Central Committee of the Party in 1966, as a result of which Ranković, the man who had held total control over appointments to key positions both inside and outside the Party, was dismissed. Even when, a few years later, the Economic Reform was abandoned, the federal system was preserved, and eventually consolidated in the 1974 Constitution. In retrospect, it can be seen that, although economists had regarded self-management as a means of establishing a market economy compatible with socialism, the strength of the political support for self-management came from the realization that it was a means of devolving power from the federation to the republics and provinces.

When socialist self-management is combined with federalism, it creates a whole range of new problems. For now each commune, with all its power over local enterprises, is combined with a 'national' (republican or provincial) one-party state. In Yugoslavia each of these states claims the right to direct its own economy, to formulate its own social plans, to determine its own investment priorities, to raise its own taxes, to control its own national bank, and even to establish its own balance of payments with the outside world. Each of these states is, in effect, a form of centralized state socialism, only slightly modified by the nominal right of the workers in the enterprises to manage their own affairs. The consequences of this 'feudal socialism' are disastrous for the Yugoslav economy. Investment projects are duplicated, enterprises in one republic or province are protected from competition from enterprises in other republics and provinces, there is more trade with the outside world than with other republics or provinces within the country, obstacles are put in the way of financial flows across republican and provincial borders, and each republic and province tries to hold on to as much as possible of the foreign exchange received for 'its' exports.

A small, but piquant, example of the effects of this system was given by Professor Branko Horvat in his book *Yugoslav Society in Crisis* (Horvat 1985, 80–1). When he moved his residence from Belgrade (in Serbia) to Zagreb (in Croatia) he took his Belgrade savings bank book to the Zagreb branch of his bank (Jugobanka) in order to withdraw some money. But he was told that that was impossible, because 'Serbian capital' could not be transferred to Croatia. He would have to go in person to his Belgrade bank if he wanted to draw out the money.

It is never easy to manage a genuinely federalized country. But the worst difficulties can be avoided if there is a unified market, and a unified fiscal and monetary system. Under these conditions, it would even be possible to operate some kind of self-management economy, although not a very efficient one unless there were genuine opportunities for free entry. But a federation of one-party socialist states operating on self-management principles seems to be one of the worst of all possible worlds. This is, unfortunately, the corner into which Yugoslavia has painted itself.

2. Some Effects of the Yugoslav System

This section will contain some examples of the effects of the Yugoslav system of federalized socialist self-management on three aspects of the Yugoslav economy. The topics covered are investment decisions, employment, and new entry. Other effects of the system will be described in later chapters which are devoted to other aspects of the economy.

Investment decisions

In the previous chapter I quoted the remarkable statement of Branko Mikulić, Prime Minister of Yugoslavia, that more than half of Yugoslavia's foreign debt 'was invested in projects which turned out to be mistaken, or was used for consumption'. Professor Dragoje Žarković, an economist of the Law Faculty of Novi Sad, has estimated that $6–$7 billion of Yugoslavia's foreign debt (about one-third of the total) was used to finance mistaken investments, alleging that they were the result of decisions made by politicians, without regard to the views of the self-managing workers (*NIN*, 15 June 1986). Stašimir Popović, a retired official who worked for many years in republican and federal bureaus of planning, stated in an interview with *Ekonomska politika* (29 July 1985) that, while planners could make satisfactory allocations of resources between industries, they could not allocate them efficiently to individual enterprises. 'It is not surprising', he concluded, 'that we have so many mistaken investments.'

Striking conclusions about the inefficiency of Yugoslav investment were reached by Professor Aleksander Bajt (1987), a distinguished economist of Ljubljana University. From a comparison of the productivity of fixed investment in Yugoslavia with the productivity of fixed investment in Greece, Turkey, Spain, and Portugal over the period 1960–80, he concluded that in that period Yugoslav investment was only 70–75 per cent as productive as investment in the other four countries. If, over the whole of the period 1949–80, the productivity of Yugoslav fixed investment had been as great as the average of these countries, the social product of Yugoslavia in 1980 would have been at least twice as large as it in fact was.

So much for general statements. But the reader will perhaps reach a better understanding of the kinds of mistake that were made from descriptions of some outstanding examples of mistaken investment projects. The most shameful was the giant iron ore processing plant at Kavadarci in southern Macedonia, called FENI. This was started in the 1960s with the collaboration of US and Canadian firms. Despite the fact that it was known that the local ore had a metal content of only 1.036 per cent, while the normal minimum requirement for efficient processing was 2 per cent, a decision to proceed with the project was taken by the Macedonian banks, with the help of foreign loans. Over the years, the total foreign debt of the enterprise rose to $437 million and the domestic debt to 11 billion dinars. The plant was expected to produce an annual income of $160 million, but it has produced nothing but losses, and has now been scrapped. Some of the former directors of FENI have been found guilty of fraud and sentenced to long periods of imprisonment. Many other managers and workers are also being prosecuted. But the politicians who made the faulty decisions will escape responsibility. (See *Danas*, 4 February 1986, 6 May 1986). Because of the size of the debt and the poverty of Macedonia, responsibility for repaying the foreign part of the debt has been accepted by the federal government, despite considerable reservations expressed by other republics.

Not far behind FENI in the scale of shame is the steel plant of Smederevo on the Danube in Serbia. Construction of this plant began in 1963. At the end of 1986 (twenty-three years later!) it was hoped that the main buildings would be completed by the end of 1988, and that in 1989 it would produce 1.3 million tons of steel. At the beginning of 1987 the plant was said to be capable of producing 700,000 tons of steel a year, for which purpose it was then employing 14,700 workers (*Politika*, 18 December 1986, 11 January 1987). But in October 1987 *Danas* (27 October 1987) reported that the plant was employing about 11,000 workers, of whom 3,000–4,000 were estimated to be unnecessary. The same report stated that the plant had cost $1.5 billion plus the equivalent of a further $1 billion in dinars. In the first half of 1987 it showed a loss of 55 billion dinars. To cover these losses, and to supply additional finance for the completion of the plant, all enterprises in Serbia were obliged in 1987 to contribute 0.469 per cent of their social product, while the Serbian banks agreed to defer repayments of credits due in that year. Despite the fact that this project is already responsible for one-half of Serbia's total foreign debt, the Serbian Party and government are determined to complete it. Pressure has been put on the Investment Bank to give the project an additional long-term loan of 10 billion dinars, and on the National Bank of Serbia to grant a short-term loan of 6 billion dinars (*Politika*, 4 March 1987).

Croatia also has its investment disasters. The most spectacular was the aluminium refinery constructed at Obrovac. When the Executive Committee of the Croatian Sabor (the republican parliament) decided to proceed with the project in March 1961, it was believed that supplies of bauxite in the Obrovac area could be combined with cheap electricity to produce aluminium at a competitive cost. But it took many years to raise the necessary finance, and construction of the plant did not commence until the end of 1974 (*Danas*, 21 October 1986). By that time the first oil shock had completely changed the price of energy and rendered the earlier calculations obsolete. Nevertheless, the project continued as if nothing had happened. Finally, it was discovered that local supplies of bauxite were inadequate. The plant was closed in 1983, and much of the equipment was sold to other enterprises.

Another major loss-maker in Croatia—indeed, the largest in Yugoslavia—is the firm of INA–Petrokemija, which produces artificial fertilizers. In 1986 it made a loss of 43.5 billion dinars, and in 1987 it was expected to make a further loss of 64 billion dinars. In 1978 it had been decided to expand its capacity from 740,000 tons to nearly 2 million tons, the expansion being financed by foreign loans. But at the beginning of 1987 the plant was still working at only half capacity. Of its foreign debt at that time of about $320 million, $142 million had already been 'reprogrammed', and the Croatian government was providing large amounts of special assistance to cover losses (*EP*, 9 February 1987).

Trepča in Kosovo is the largest lead and zinc plant in Europe. It employs about 25,000 workers and is responsible for more than half of Kosovo's exports. But it is in deep financial trouble. It is making a loss, and is unable to repay its maturing debts. One reason for its difficulties is that 'there was an irresponsible expansion of capacity in the 1970s'. Another is its failure to open new mines in the area, which has forced it to rely on ores of steadily diminishing metal content. As a consequence, in 1987 the management asked the federal government for permission to import 40,000 tons of lead concentrate and 60,000 tons of zinc concentrate (*Politika*, 13 April 1987). Workers' earnings are low, and the firm suffers from bad organization, 'an irresponsible attitude to work', and excessive absenteeism (*Politika*, 5 March 1987).

Another heavy loss-maker in Kosovo is the firm of Ferronikl. The plant was designed to produce 12,000 tons of nickel a year, of which 2,500 tons would be sold domestically and the remainder exported. But in 1986 the plant was operating at only 70 per cent of capacity, and its cost per ton of nickel were twice as high as the costs of a similar plant in the United States. Although two-thirds of its output was being exported, this was only possible because of an enormous subsidy from the federal government. Domestic consumers of nickel were doing their best to obtain cheaper imported supplies (*Politika*, 24 November 1986).

At Zvornik in Bosnia and Herzegovina there is an alumina plant which is said to be the largest in Europe. But throughout its existence, it has produced only losses. It employs about 4,000 workers, which is much more than in similar plants in other countries. It was financed mainly by foreign loans, the interest and repayment on which is a heavy burden. It has now been discovered that the local bauxite is not of good enough quality, and the firm has asked for permission to import 100,000 tons of bauxite of better quality from Guinea (*Politika*, 9 February 1987). Another well-known disaster project is a cellulose and paper plant in Montenegro. In twenty-four years of operation it has made a profit in only four, and it has now been closed (*Politika*, 5 March 1987). A cement plant, constructed at Golubac in Serbia, close to Smederevo, was originally designed to produce 800,000 tons of cement a year. It has now been scrapped and its equipment sold; but its foreign debt of $4.26 million still remains to be paid off (*Politika*, 1 April 1987).

As a result of autarkic republican planning, there has been much duplication of capacity in a wide range of industries. In 1984, for example, total oil refining capacity was 30 million tons, while domestic consumption of oil products was only about half as much. At that time, also, Yugoslavia had 23 sugar mills, but there was not enough production of sugar beet to keep the mills working at even 50 per cent of their capacity. For similar reasons, slaughter-houses and meat processing firms were also operating at less than half capacity (OECD 1984, 46).

A combination of socialist self-management and federalism has led to an opposite problem in the production of electricity. The major deposits of lignite are in Kosovo, and the largest remaining opportunities for development of hydroelectricity are in Bosnia and Herzegovina. Meanwhile, Slovenia, Croatia, and Vojvodina are anxious to ensure their future supplies of electricity, for which they do not have local energy resources. Reliance on imported petroleum is now out of the question, and there is increasing public opposition to an expansion of nuclear power. The logical solution would be to construct lignite plants in Kosovo and hydroelectric plants in Bosnia and Herzegovina (or thereabouts). But there are two obstacles. The first is that none of the customer regions is willing to supply the large amounts of capital that are required, because capital is scarce, and, if it is invested in another republic, the return is limited to a fixed interest, which is of little value in a period of rapidly rising inflation. The second is that the regions that possess the natural resources are reluctant to invest 'their' capital in projects that are mainly for the benefit of outsiders, and on which they can expect to earn only a low rate of return because of federal price controls on electricity. Other questions raised by the regions possessing the natural resources concern the effects of these projects on the local environment, and who will pay for the resettlement of displaced families and the costs of new infrastructure (*EP*, 14 July 1986). According to *Politika* (29 January 1987), discussions about these problems have been going on for ten years, with no agreement yet in sight. Meanwhile, the prospect of power shortages looms ever closer.

It is no accident that the best-known examples of investment disasters are in 'heavy' industries, especially in plants processing ferrous and non-ferrous ores. This is the joint result of the import-replacement bias of socialist planning (and socialist self-management), the desire of regional politicians to construct massive economic monuments (which Tito, among others, called 'political factories'), and the relics in Yugoslav minds of the Stalinist dogma of the priority of 'heavy' industries. But these are not the only enterprises that makes losses. In 1986, 2,306 organizations of associated labour, employing almost 600,000 workers (more than 10 per cent of workers in the productive social sector), made losses totalling 634 billion dinars. In the first quarter of 1987 the number of loss-making organizations had risen to 7,031 (employing about 1.6 million workers), and their total losses—for one quarter—amounted to 912 billion dinars (*Politika*, 7 April 1987, 11 July 1987). Not all these losses are due to mistaken investments, but that was a major reason.

Employment

Like many other less developed countries, Yugoslavia has a 'structural' problem of unemployment. At the end of the war, four-fifths of the Yugoslav population were peasants, the great majority very poor. In these circumstances, any development of a modern industrial sector would attract large numbers of peasants into the towns in search of better-paid work. But this problem was exacerbated by communist policies of directing available funds mainly into capital-intensive projects, discriminating against and further impoverishing the peasants, and blocking the growth of small non-farm private businesses. All of this was done for ideological reasons. So long as the Party was able to impose very high saving rates on the population, or could draw on ample foreign loans, it was able to create essentially capital-intensive enterprises which, when deliberately overmanned, were able to absorb most of the surplus labour. But when, in the period of the Economic Reform in the second half of the 1960s, enterprises were given greater freedom to work in a market environment, much of this excess labour was squeezed out. Fortunately, it was just at that time that the West European (especially West German) demand for imported labour was growing; and hundreds of thousands of Yugoslavs were allowed to emigrate in search of jobs. But after 1979 the supply of foreign capital dried up, the domestic saving rate began to fall, and the net migration of workers between Yugoslavia and Western Europe began to flow in the opposite direction.

In these circumstances, and within the limits of the established ideology, there was only one policy left: to keep putting pressure on social sector enterprises (and on the non-productive part of the social sector also) to take on unwanted workers. We have seen in the previous chapter what a disastrous effect this policy has had on productivity in social sector enterprises. It has been one of the main contributory causes of inflation, and it is the one of the principal reasons for the increasingly desperate state of the economy in 1988.

There are various estimates of the amount of overmanning in the social sector. One economist (*EP*, 2 June 1986) has put the figure at 1.5–1.8 million (out of 6.6 million), consisting of 10 per cent of workers in productive enterprises and 40 per cent of those employed in non-productive activities (mainly government and semi-government employment). Other economists put the amount of overmanning somewhat higher. From my own estimates—given in the previous chapter—of the fall in labour productivity in social sector enterprises since 1979, it would seem that over-manning in the productive part of the social sector amounts to at least one-quarter of the present work-force. Indeed, if efficient standards of management were in operation, the proportion could well be higher. When a Japanese team visited the firm of IMV in Novo Mesto to consider whether their company should invest in it, they made a careful study of the plant for two days, and then said that they would be unable to recommend the project unless the Yugoslav firm got rid of half its work-force

(*Politika*, 26 February 1987). And this firm, according to *Politika*, is generally considered to be a good one.

The greatest amount of overmanning is in non-productive activities, especially in government and semi-government administration. For example, in Croatia in the period 1977–84, while employment in the productive social sector rose by 18 per cent, employment in all governments rose by 67 per cent, and in commune governments separately by 82 per cent (*EP*, 23 December 1985). Another indication is the growth in recent years in the number of 'partially disabled' people employed in the social sector. These people usually receive full pay for working only four hours a day, and 70 per cent of them are employed in non-productive organizations (*Politika*, 16 June 1987).

The outlook for employment is now so serious that the Party is feverishly searching for a new solution. There is some talk about relaxing the 10-hectare (22-acre) limit on the size of private farms, and, in principle, both the Party and the government are committed to giving more opportunities to small enterprises, both in the private and social sectors. We shall consider this latter policy next.

New entry

A crucial condition for the efficiency of a market economy is freedom of entry. New entry may take the form of imports, decisions by existing firms to enter a new market, or the establishment of new enterprises. In the long run, if competitive pressure is to be effective, it is essential that there should be no legal obstacles to the creation of new enterprises in any industry, apart from a very few in which this may be judged undesirable on grounds of national defence or the protection of public morals. Economists who have worked on theories of self-management have usually been well aware of the need for free entry as a condition for the success of the system (see, for example, Meade 1974). But under 'federalized socialist self-management' in Yugoslavia, free entry is almost completely absent.

Competitive entry of imports into Yugoslavia has never been permitted under the present regime, and, as we saw in the previous chapter, import restrictions have become even tighter in the 1980s. From time to time the government sets aside small amounts of foreign exchange for the import of consumer goods, in the hope, it is said, that this will help to restrain inflation. But this is a futile gesture, and is in any case irrelevant to the real issue, which is how to create a threat of potential new entry.

There is also very little entry of new markets by existing firms. It would be unheard of for a firm to start competing with another firm within its own commune. That would quickly be stamped on by the communal authorities and the whole local élite. Nor is it any more acceptable for a firm in one commune or republic to start selling its products in another commune or republic in competition with established firms in the latter areas. If the goods in question were raw or intermediate materials, pressure would be put on the potential purchasers to refrain. If the goods were final consumer goods, the wholesale and retail organizations of the recipient area would similarly be put under pressure to refuse to handle them. Occasionally, manufacturers in one republic who have been confronted by such obstacles have found a way into other markets by establishing their own retail outlets. But this is a very expensive operation and can happen only rarely. Yugoslavia is like Germany before the Zollverein.

The final, and ultimately most important, source of new entry is the establishment of new businesses. But in a system of universal self-management, i.e. one such as exists in Yugoslavia in all industries except private agriculture and a few petty urban activities, the only way in which a new firm can come into existence is as an 'organization of associated labour'. While, in principle, an 'organization of associated labour' could be set up by a group of citizens, in practice this never happens. This would be regarded by the Party as a highly suspicious act, and to allow it to happen would be an impermissible concession to *laissez-faire*. New enterprises in the social sector, therefore, can be created only by decision of the local or regional political authorities. Not surprisingly, these authorities are not interested in establishing new enterprises to compete with existing enterprises in their own area, and they are particularly unattracted by the idea of setting up small enterprises, which entail a great deal of 'social' decision-making for very little benefit. In any case, Yugoslav workers in the social sector prefer large enterprises, which they regard as more secure, both economically and politically, and likely to provide them with higher personal incomes and better fringe benefits (Petrin 1986, 202–3).

Tea Petrin (1986, 192–5) has also pointed out that, in comparison with Sweden, the United States, and Japan, Yugoslavia has very few social sector enterprises employing less than 125 workers, and that only 423 new such enterprises were established in the period 1970–8. In Slovenia, according to a report in *Ekonomska politika* (11 August 1986), the number of 'organizations of associated labour' employing less than 125 workers fell from 420 in 1981 to 371 in 1985. These are pitifully small numbers, especially in a republic that is the most enterprising and dynamic in Yugoslavia.

The alternative would be to allow free entry of *private* enterprises. The Party and government are now toying with this idea, not because they want to create conditions of potential or actual competition for social sector enterprises, but because they hope that small private enterprises will absorb some of the unemployed, and especially the large number of workers who would be displaced from social sector enterprises if there were a real implementation of the Long-term Programme of Economic Stabilization. Štefan Korošec, the member of the Presidency of the Party responsible for economic policy, has said that 'small enterprises' (without specifying whether he means social or private) are 'very important', and has mentioned that according to some estimates they might emply an extra million workers (*Politika*, 14 September 1987).

Early in 1987 the Prime Minister, Branko Mikulić, held a much publicized meeting with twenty Yugoslavs who had established successful enterprises in Western countries. He said that his government was firmly committed to a policy of encouraging small enterprises, including those in the private sector, and that they would like to persuade Yugoslav workers abroad to come back and invest their savings in such firms, especially in industry, agriculture, and tourism. There is no doubt that, if such a policy could be implemented, and if such rights were given not only to Yugoslavs living abroad but also to all Yugoslav citizens, it would have a dramatic effect on the growth of the Yugoslav economy. There are tremendous reserves of private capital in Yugoslavia (in the form of hoards of foreign currency, held either at home or abroad), of skilled and unskilled labour willing to work efficiently under proper conditions of management and motivation, and of enterprise. To foreign visitors the most obvious case is tourism, where hotel facilities are entirely confined to very large and capital-intensive hotels in the social sector. The buildings are often good, but the standard of service is poor, despite (or perhaps because of) a large degree of overmanning. Returning migrant workers often build themselves villas by the sea and let rooms in the tourist season. But they are not allowed to set up private hotels, or almost any other kind of enterprise.

Despite his plea for help from Yugoslavs living abroad, the Prime Minister was not able to offer any convincing promises about the conditions they would find if they took his advance. He said that the federal government had passed a number of laws designed to facilitate foreign investments, but that their implementation would depend on establishing a social compact between the republics and provinces. He said that it was hoped to reach agreement on raising the limit for employment in private firms to ten workers, but that any new private firm would still need to obtain a permit from the local commune. It was also hoped to reach agreement with the republics and provinces about equalizing the tax treatment of private businesses, both across regions and in comparison with the tax treatment of social sector enterprises. But there has been no subsequent report of any movement in this direction.

There are three major obstacles to the establishment of private enterprises in Yugoslavia. The first is the employment limit. No entrepreneur with ambition will be willing to make the great sacrifices required to create a dynamic new enterprise if he knows that he will never be allowed to employ more than five, or even ten, workers. It is almost a complete waste of time for the Yugoslav Party and government to wrestle with the question of whether the employment limit should be five or ten. The second obstacle is the power of the communes to stop the establishment of private enterprises in their area through the use of all sorts of bureaucratic devices, including permits for this, that, and the other. So long as the communes have such powers, they will use them to prevent any competition from the private sector with 'their' enterprises. Even the few small private businesses that do manage to exist are severely penalized by taxation, to the extent of between 65 and 95 per cent of their incomes (*EP*, 23 February 1987).

The third, and most fundamental, obstacle to the entry of new competitive private businesses is the whole ideology and structure of a communist state. Deep hostility to private enterprise is embedded both in Marxism and in the Yugoslav Constitution. So long as potential private entrepreneurs know that such attitudes prevail, and that, because of the absence of genuine democratic rules, there is no chance of changing them, they will be deterred from putting their heads in a noose. In the words of an article in *Vjesnik, Sedam Dana* (25 October 1985), when anyone proposes that the private sector should be allowed to grow, 'the alarm bells start ringing on the grounds that the development of the private sector could endanger the development of socialism and the self-management character of our society, give birth to a hostile class division, and signify the beginning of the restoration of capitalist relations'. The 'alarm bells' are largely right. Freedom for the private sector would start to put competitive pressure on socialist entreprises, and would force many of them to reform or perish. Yugoslavia would become a mixed economy, and the power of the monopoly party would be eroded. But the country would emerge from its present crisis and begin to catch up with the rest of western and southern Europe.

Consider what pitiful measures the authorities resort to in order to prevent 'the beginning of the restoration of capitalist relations'. At Maribor, in Slovenia, a butcher had by 1985 built up a very successful private business by giving good service to his customers. He had taught his daughter to work in the business, and he wanted to take her on as an employee. But the law said that he could not do that without taking on two further employees (*EP*, 11 March 1985).

3. Some Yugoslav Views of the Crisis

Although Yugoslavia is a Marxist state (or, perhaps more accurately, a federation of Marxist states), in which the League of Communists controls all the media, in which there is censorship, and in which there are laws against 'verbal crimes', there has been in the past few years a growing volume of public comment on the state of the economy and the state of Yugoslav society. Some of this comment has even touched on normally taboo subjects, such as the effects of 'social ownership', the role of the Party, and the desirability of free elections. Everyone knows that these are dangerous subjects, and critics are careful to protect themselves by declaring their commitment to self-management. Self-management and 'brotherhood and unity' are the two unchallengeable ideas that are shared, at least verbally, by both critics and defenders of the present system.

We saw earlier that the Yugoslav system is a combination of three institutional arrangements; federalism, socialism, and self-management. Since virtually everyone expresses agreement with self-management, critics tend to focus their criticisms on one or other of the first two characteristics. Centralists, who come mainly from Serbia and Montenegro, criticize the excessive degree of federalism, or 'confederalism', of Yugoslavia, which they believe has not only hampered effective decision-making but also opened the door to republican and provincial 'statism'. No one openly defends 'statism', but the anti-centralists, who fear Serbian domination, accuse centralists of having their own brand of 'statism'—or, when they become especially agitated, of 'Stalinism'.

While criticism of federalism is usually expressed in the form of criticism of 'excessive' federalism, criticism of socialism is more oblique. If socialism has any generally agreed meaning, it must surely be state ownership of most productive assets, and hence state control and state planning of the economy. But the Yugoslavs rejected state planning when they moved towards a self-management system. And, in a vague sense, they rejected 'statism'. Nevertheless, they retained 'socialism', the crucial test of which was that self-management was not to become 'group ownership' but was somehow to be made consistent with 'social ownership'. The trouble is that there is no clear definition of 'social ownership'. It may be said that it means that all social sector assets are owned by 'society'; but the practical significance of this can only be that such assets are owned by the state, which is 'society's' specific agent. But this conflicts with the Yugoslav desire to reduce, or even eliminate, the power of the state over the economy.

The Yugoslav concept of socialism, therefore, is full of

contradictions. It is difficult for anyone to say so publicly. But it is perfectly in order to criticize excessive state intervention in the economy, and to attack 'statism'. Some economists and others have also focused their criticisms on the concept of social ownership itself, drawing attention to its negative effects on self-management, especially on investment decisions and the motivation of workers and managers. These critics are not usually concerned with the question of federalism, although some of them, in their desire to have something decisive done about the state of the economy, give the impression of being inclined to 'centralism'. It is, in fact, perfectly consistent to be both centralist about macroeconomic policies and decentralist about microeconomic decisions, while accepting a proper role for the republics and provinces within a federal system. But the general tendency in Yugoslavia to conduct arguments by throwing epithets at one's opponents makes it difficult to present a rational case for economic reforms.

The one view on which almost all economists agree is support for a free market, which they see as being not only desirable in itself but also a logical condition for a genuine system of self-management. Since anti-statism, self-management, and a free and unified Yugoslav market are all officially endorsed objectives of party policy, critics of the current system who support these objectives run no risk of being accused of heresy.

The crisis has now lasted so long and gone so deep that even party leaders and government officials acknowledge it. A series of public statements to this effect began to be made in October 1987. Early in that month, the vice-president of the government said: 'In the judgment of the Federal Executive Council the crisis is not only getting worse but is reaching a critical and decisive point' (*Politika*, 8 October 1987). Later in the same month, the president of the Skupština said in an interview with *Danas* (27 October 1987): 'We are in a deep and many-sided crisis, and up to now there have been many different views about how to get out of it. We have now reached the point where we have to agree on a programme of real changes, because we cannot allow the crisis to go any further.' And two weeks later *Danas* pointed out that in its Anti-inflation Programme the government had stated that 'Yugoslavia is in a deep socio-economic and political crisis'.

While there is now general acknowledgement of the existence

of a crisis, there is no agreement on what to do about it. The voice of centralism could be heard in an interview given in 1986 by Vidoje Žarković, then president of the Presidency of the Central Committee of the Party, when he said: 'The crisis of the past few years has been provoked by a great strengthening of polycentric statism, which has driven out self-management, stimulated voluntarism, autarky, and exclusiveness, and led to a weakening of the country and the Party' (*EP*, 17 February 1986). The opposition of the Party to any tampering with social ownership was expressed in a discussion at the Presidency of the Central Committee of the Party in mid–1987, when it was said that 'the defence of social ownership is an ideological and class question of the greatest significance for our self-management system' (*Politika*, 18 June 1987).

It is easy to erect or strengthen ideological barriers to thought. But meanwhile the crisis goes on; and people are becoming more and more desperate. So previously unthinkable (or at least unmentionable) ideas emerge into public discussion. The following summary of an article in *NIN* (26 July 1987) is representative of the general mood in the second half of 1987:

Despite the government's promises that inflation would be reduced, the rate of inflation has continued to rise, and is now over 100 per cent per annum. The money supply has grown at a faster rate than that which was promised at the beginning of the year, and the National Bank has told the Skupština that the extra money was needed to support illiquid and loss-making enterprises. The conviction has grown that, 'while no other federal government has been so much in favour of market criteria, no other has introduced so many measures hostile to the market operation of the economy'. The most convincing explanation for the present social crisis is the reduction of the self-management rights of workers. During the past 15 years workers have been unable to make independent decisions about the methods of creating and distributing income, and they have not been able to take risks and accept responsibility for such decisions. It has been impossible to show enterprise, either collectively or individually. The result is that we have an inefficient economic system, in which everyone has become poorer.

An even more forceful statement of similar views was expressed in an article in *Ekonomska politika* (10 August 1987), of which the following is a summary:

The government keeps saying that the system is excellent but that people fail to operate it as they should. But 'Our system is the erosion of social capital and [has led to] a fall in labour productivity, with less and less individual sense of work commitment.' This is shown by the large number of uncompleted projects, abandoned equipment, unused capacity, waste of energy, spoiling of good materials, and poor quality of final products. Economic and political functionaries are selected through connections; subordinates are obedient, while superior officials have the right to instruct the managements of enterprises what investments to make, what other loss-making firm they have to help, or with what other firm they have to amalgamate. A good system is one which makes use of individual interests. 'The only system which can function rationally is one in which those who take business decisions carry the financial risk, and those who take political decisions carry the political risk that they will be removed or not re-elected.'

Commenting on discussions in the Skupština about the reasons for the high rate of inflation, *NIN* (15 November 1987) reported that there was agreement that the main reason is the absence of a market economy, and continued:

'There is no market in Yugoslavia because the basic economic and political conditions for it have not been created.' These conditions, it argued, are: markets for goods, money, and labour; and commercial relations in place of self-management agreements and social compacts. 'Not a single enterprise in Yugoslavia is independent, not only because it is owned by the economy of its republic or province (or rather by its government), but also because it is not independent in its rights to earn and distribute income, and in commercial and investment policies, not to mention its personnel policies.' This lack of independence arises from social ownership, which gives the government the maximum opportunity to intervene, and deprives the workers of the incentive to make efficient use of capital.

Politicians are much more cautious. They no longer deny that there is a crisis, but they tend to concentrate on its superficial causes. For example, Milan Kučan, president of the Presidency of the Central Committee of the League of Communists of Slovenia, said in an interview with *Danas* (26 May 1987):

'The fact that for many years the country has been in a state of crisis has affected the attitudes of people . . . The crisis has weakened customary values. There is much anxiety; there is much less confidence in the "subjective forces" [i.e. the Party], in our ideology, and in our system.' The ambition of Slovenia, he said, is to move quickly towards the civilization of the 21st century, to forge a link between socialism and modern technology, and to develop the democratic and humane values of an innovative–informational society. This means having a market economy which is open to the rest of the world. 'We cannot go on bailing out inefficient firms . . . I think that statism is the basic problem of Yugoslavia.'

A number of economists and other social scientists have expressed much more fundamental criticisms of the present system. For example, at a discussion organized by *Politika* (23 May 1987) Dr Andrija Gams said that fear of the 'unbridled forces' of the market had led to the establishment of a 'social compact self-management' system. As a result, the managements of 'organizations of associated labour' felt no sense of responsibility for mistaken business decisions. In a true market economy, the owners of capital receive the profits from successful decisons, and bear the losses arising from bad decisions. But in Yugoslavia these losses, which are enormous, are covered by various devices, including the creation of money. In the same discussion, Professor Dragoje Žarković advocated a mixed economy as the only way out of the crisis. The concept of social ownership as non-ownership, he said, is a dogma maintained for the benefit of the bureaucracy, who can use it to hold on to its power and privileged position, without bearing any responsibility for its mistakes. Any criticism of this 'sacred cow' is denounced as counter-revolutionary. Professor Ivan Maksimović added that in Yugoslavia there is a basic contradiction of the Marxist type between the economic base and the superstructure.

Another economist, Dr Miljko Trifunović, in an interview with *Ekonomska politika* (15 December 1986), said, in summary:

Socialism assumes that nationalization solves all production problems, and that after that one can concentrate on redistribution. But if output stagnates, socialism is in crisis. The trouble is that socialism denies the individual the right to own property, and hence the freedom to make his own decisions. This deprivation of freedom results in economic stagnation. The solution is a free market. Without a market, the political authorities insist on controlling everything, and this leads in Yugoslavia to autarky and conflicts between the republics, and even between neighbouring communes. The market is, therefore, the only way to stimulate growth, to break down internal and external barriers, and to put an end to inflation.

Dr Adolf Dragičević, who is professor of political economy in the Zagreb˙law faculty, went even further, when he said in an interview with *Danas* (9 December 1986):

'We can get out of the crisis into which we have fallen only by abandoning socialism, which is an obsolete mass society, which has exhausted the finite limits of its positive action, and which completed its historic task sometime around the beginning of the 1970s.' To continue in that direction would only 'drag us even further into the misfortune of a dying world, whose visible characteristics are permanent stagflation and overindebtedness, mass unemployment, zero growth and no development, an increasing lag behind the more advanced countries, and a sterile and reactionary turn towards the past.' The way forward for technical development is to allow enterprises to get on with the job, not endless discussions and the making of compacts. The microelectronic revolution opens the door to decentralized enterprises, and it is the technical precondition for real self-management. When that revolution is complete, there will be no need for a vanguard party. It will be 'good-bye to the proletariat' and 'good-bye to a socialist society'.

Professor Jože Mencinger of Ljubljana University, in comments made to *Ekonomska politika* (6 October 1986), said:

'A mixed economy is much more efficient than any kind of "real" socialism, or self-management socialism based on the nationalization of productive resources.' In the past forty years we have created 'an economy in which there is no intiative, where we are accustomed to a comfortable life in the social sector, with various kinds of socialization which allow the less capable to exploit the more capable'. The 'social compact' economy creates cartels; the 'anarchoadministrative' economy, which is now replacing it, creates disorder. 'The contemporary world demonstrates that . . . the developed capitalist countries have no problems in devising the most efficient forms of organization, while the socialist countries are still trying to find them.' He, like Professors Dragoje Žarković and Ivan Maksimović, is in favour of giving workers in self-management organizations shares in the equity of their enterprise.

In an article in *Danas* (1 December 1987), Slavko Goldstein and Marijan Korošić, two well-known Zagreb personalities (the former a retired director of the university publishing house, and the latter a senior economist at the Economics Institute), put forward a ten-point programme for radical economic and political reform. The main principles of this programme can be summarized as follows:

The basic principle is that there should be freedom of competition within a mixed economy, with complete freedom of entry for new private businesses, without restriction of size. All detailed controls over self-management enterprises, including the Law on Associated Labour, should be lifted. This would mean rescinding all social compacts which restrict independent self-management decision-making, as well as controls over prices and foreign trade. All barriers to internal trade and the internal movement of capital should be eliminated. There would be a strict control over the money supply, with the abolition of the right of the government to borrow from the National Bank. The expenditures of all government and semi-government bodies should be reduced. The mass of laws, many of which are unnecessary and even contradictory, should be rationalized and greatly reduced; and those that remain should be rigorously enforced. Yugoslavia, while remaining socialist, should join the European Economic Community and act as a bridge between East and West, and between the more advanced and the less advanced countries. There are also proposals for halting the present discussions about the revision of the Federal Constitution, for holding new elections to the Skupština, for setting up a new government, and for creating the conditions for a genuinely pluralistic and democratic society.

Such a programme is unlikely to be accepted voluntarily by the League of Communists, because it would eliminate its monopoly of power and privilege, as well as being an affront to its ideological prejudices. But the preparation and publication of this programme is a courageous attempt to map out what needs to be done if Yugoslavia is to be rescued from its present state of crisis. These ideas are now part of the agenda. They could be suppressed, and then at most temporarily, only by a resurgence of the most reactionary kind of communist practice.

6

Enterprise Self-management

In the previous chapter we considered the general economic efffects of a self-management system, and in particular the effects of the Yugoslav system of *federalized socialist self-management*. But self-management is a method of internal organization of enterprises; and we need to consider it from that aspect also. In this chapter I shall start by discussing the aims of a self-management system of organization. It will be suggested that these aims are democracy and efficiency; and we shall proceed to consider whether they can be expected to be achieved in any self-managed economy, and in particular whether they have been achieved in Yugoslavia. This will be followed by an examination of the implications of the increasing number of strikes in Yugoslav enterprises in recent years. Finally, we shall consider some recent proposals for revision of the Yugoslav system of enterprise self-management.

1. Aims of Self-management

I am not aware of any official statement of the original aims of the Yugoslav system of enterprise self-management. But it seems reasonable to assume that the principal aims were as follows. First, there was a desire to establish 'industrial democracy', i.e. the right of workers in an enterprise to exercise the same sort of control over the policy of that enterprise as citizens are believed to exercise over the policies of their governments. Democracy is considered by communists to be a desirable aim in itself, and an essential constituent of socialism (provided, of course, that it is not 'bourgeois' democracy but 'socialist' democracy). Second, it was probably believed that self-management is a more *efficient* method of organizing enterprises than either capitalism or state socialism. Some people certainly make this claim; and even those who do not must believe that self-management is at least not much worse than other methods. For one of the principal aims of socialism is to increase real social product. If it were believed that the cost of operating a system of self-management in terms of loss of real social product was substantial, this might persuade many socialists that the gains from the system in terms of democracy were not sufficient to make the establishment of such a system desirable. (This was certainly Stalin's view and, if he had lived, would probably have been Lenin's view also.) It seems probable, however, that most supporters of self-management comfort themselves with the belief that the system has advantages both in terms of democracy and in terms of efficiency.

In the previous chapter it was suggested that a principal initial reason for the Yugoslav move towards self-management was the desire to weaken central control from Belgrade, and to open the door to genuine federalization. At the time when the first decision was taken—in 1950—it would have been impossible to have won support for an immediate devolution of economic and political power to the republics and provinces. But self-management, although adopted for 'democratic' and 'anti-statist' reasons, did in fact clear the way for such a devolution of power in the second half of the 1960s. While I believe that this was the major motive for the move towards self-management, I shall not discuss it further at this point. For self-management is advocated in other contexts; and it seems clear that the two main criteria by which it must be judged are its effects on democracy and efficiency.

2. Self-management and Democracy

People like democracy because they want to have some influence on social decisions that affect their interests. The major struggles for democracy have been concerned with control over the composition and policies of governments. By analogy, it is often suggested that a similar set of objectives should be sought within enterprises. In a capitalist economy, such a proposal comes into conflict with the rights of individual owners or shareholders to make (or influence) the final decisions about the use of their capital. But in a co-operative constructed on the principle that all its worker-members are also shareholders, this conflict of interest would be less acute (although it would not be completely absent). This is not, however, the situation in Yugoslavia, where the equity in enterprises is owned by 'society'. As we have seen in the previous chapter, and as we shall see further in this chapter, this division of interest is at the heart of Yugoslavia's problems with the efficient operation of a system of self-management.

The naive view of self-management, which has always been dominant in official descriptions of self-management in Yugoslavia, is that, if workers are given the rights to elect a workers' council and other bodies, to hold regular assemblies to discuss major questions of policy, and to be consulted by referenda on special issues, they will use those rights to safeguard their interests and to further the interests of the whole 'collective', while at the same time paying due regard to the interests of 'society'. What is missing from this utopian view is a recognition not only of conflicts of interest between the workers in an enterprise and 'society', but also of conflicts of interest between different groups of workers within an enterprise. There is also an unrealistic assumption that all workers want to be involved in all levels of decision-making.

In any enterprise there are several levels of decision-making, and they may not all be of equal interest to all workers. Consider the following four main types of decision: (1) decisions about the constitution, structure, and rules of the enterprise; (2) major business decisions, such as those about investments, technology, location, employment, products, markets, and prices; (3) decisions that more directly affect the interests of individual workers, such as the allocation of jobs, promotion, rewards and penalties, and allocation of special privileges (e.g. houses and cars); (4) decisions about the appointment and dismissal of managers. In a small co-operative all the workers may wish to be directly involved in all these types of decision. But in an enterprise that employs a hundred or more workers, and even more so in an enterprise employing thousands, it is neither practical for all workers to be involved in all these decisions, *nor is it normally their wish to be so involved.*

While, in a loose sense, people like to be able to take decisions about matters that are of concern to them, no one believes that he (or she) should be involved in *all* such decisions. For the making of decisions imposes costs on the decision-maker: costs of time, information, skill, and worry about the outcome. Thus, people usually leave decisions about medical treatments to their doctors, and about legal matters to their lawyers. For similar reasons, it seems likely that most workers in a self-managed enterprise would prefer to leave major business decisions to their professional managers, subject only to the (largely formal) approval of the workers' council or a general assembly. But, if such a system is to work satisfactorily, two conditions must be met. The first is that the workers, or their representatives, should have a decisive say in the appointment or dismissal of their top managers; and the second is that these managers should have a compelling interest in the success of the business.

In the Yugoslav system of self-management, of the four levels of decision-making listed above, the first is excluded from worker control because the rules about the structure and methods of operation of self-management enterprises are prescribed in detail in the Law on Associated Labour (and in subsequent social compacts). The second level—major business decisions—is theoretically under the control of the workers, but in practice has been kept almost exclusively in the hands either of the management or, especially in recent years, of the local or regional politicians. The influence of the politicians may be justified by the argument that they represent 'society'; but in any case Yugoslav workers have no choice in the matter.

The appointment of top managers ('directors') to Yugoslav enterprises is also, in most cases, firmly in the hands of the politicians. Even on paper, the workers' council has only one-third of the representatives on the selection committee. The remainder are nominated by the commune and the local trade unions—both of which are controlled by the Party. And, of course, the members of the workers' council itself are nominated by the trade union. Officially, the workers' council makes the final choice of director from the short-list sent to it by the selection committee. In practice, this list usually has only one name. According to *Danas* (19 November 1985), there is no confidence in the job competitions, which are considered to be corrupt and manipulated. 'It is no secret that, before the public advertisement of a director's job, people know exactly who will be appointed. Of course, the same applies to appointments in government and the socio-political organizations.' No one in Yugoslavia tries to pretend that the workers have any real say in the appointment or dismissal of directors. The few cases where there is apparently a successful internal move to replace a director are the result of external decisions, which are then implemented by pretending to use the internal self-management machinery.

The only decisions on which Yugoslav workers try to exert a significant influence are those that affect the immediate interests of individual workers, or groups of workers. To quote from my previous book (Lydall 1984, 114):

There is abundant evidence from empirical studies of self-management enterprises, by both Yugoslav and foreign investigators, that at meetings of the workers' councils most proposals for major business decisions come (as one would expect) from the management; that the discussion of these issues is dominated by managers and technicians, with some participation by the chairman; that manual workers, who are usually under-represented in relation to their numbers in the enterprise (especially the unskilled), confine themselves mainly to raising detailed points about the likely effects of any change on the group which they represent; and that the discussions only come alive when they focus on a question such as the treatment of an individual worker or the allocation of a flat.

The irrelevance of the workers' councils when major problems arise was shown during the waves of strikes in 1987. In all cases, the workers were demanding large increases in incomes; but in no case did they put these demands to their workers' council. Their demands were directed at their managers and at governments, and it was the latter that finally found the means to settle the disputes. After a settlement had been reached over the head of the workers' council, it was rubber-stamped by the council, which thereby demonstrated its subservience to outside forces.

Most workers' assemblies have become a formality and a waste of time. Goldstein (1985, 57–60) describes a typical monthly assembly meeting in the enterprise of which he was director for twenty years. The following is a summary:

Out of 250 workers about 150 will be present. The meeting usually starts at 6 a.m., at the beginning of the work day, but it sometimes starts 20 minutes before the end of the work day. The accountant gives a report full of figures; but no one listens. Everyone knows that all of this has been considered on the previous day at the workers' council, and that the only reason for holding an assembly is to satisfy the law, which requires that the accounts must be endorsed by the assembly. In principle, the assembly also decides how to distribute available income. But, in fact, all of it has already been paid out or set aside for obligatory payments. So the assembly decision is merely a rubber stamp. During the past 30 years the accounting system has become more and more complicated, with a steady accumulation of restrictions, obligations, resolutions, social compacts, and new methods of calculating income. Only the accountants know how to make the calculations, and these even have to go to special seminars to receive instruction. 'It is not surprising that the self-managed worker feels himself manipulated, not to say deceived. He does not even know who is doing the manipulating—the accountant, the lawyer, the director, or some unseen person who designs all these compulsory forms.' At the end of the meeting there are formal votes on various points which have already been discussed and agreed several times before, but which have to be given official endorsement. No one asks any questions; no one votes against anything; no one abstains. After 20 minutes people leave the meeting and hurry to their work. These sorts of meetings happen 15 times a year.

A 1986 study of the attitudes of 672 workers in a firm at Pančevo reported that only one-third of the workers had a positive attitude towards self-management. This attitude was more often held by the better educated and by the more highly skilled workers. Two-thirds of the respondents said that self-management activists are not particularly highly regarded. Two-thirds also considered that they themselves had no influence on important decisions, and 73 per cent said that they had no influence on the composition of self-management bodies (*NIN*, 17 August 1986).

In an interview with *Ekonomska politika* (28 October 1985), the general director of the firm of PIK said that:

The management teams, with the support of the socio-political structure, draw up development programmes according to their own unrestricted judgments, and these are formally accepted by the self-management organs. If these decisions lead to losses, the managements quietly go to the workers and say: 'You are not to blame, nor are we. The fault lies in objective conditions, the international market, the government, the economic system, economic policy.' And since the workers' personal incomes do not depend essentially on whether the enterprise makes a loss or a substantial profit, the workers accept this account, and also accept that the management teams who conceived these programmes, both inside the economy and outside it, should stay on in their jobs, and even be given promotion.

It is questionable whether, even in a strictly independent self-managed enterprise (which could exist only in a *laissez-faire* competitive environment), it would be possible to establish a truly 'democratic' system of workers' control, except in the case of a very small enterprise in which it is easy to keep everyone informed and to make collective decisions. But in the Yugoslav system, in which the state, in effect, retains the ownership of enterprise equity, and in which the one-party communist system drives the state to intervene in every important aspect of enterprise decision-making, internal democratic control of enterprise policy 'withers away'. The workers still have the right to attend innumerable meetings and to listen to interminable speeches. And, occasionally, they may be able to raise some problem which concerns them. But their power to correct injustices and to safeguard their immediate interests is probably less than it would be in a private enterprise with an effective trade union.

3. Self-management and Efficiency

At this point we are not concerned with the general economic efficiency of a system of self-management. This topic was explored in the previous chapter. But the efficiency of an economic system depends not only on its method of allocating resources, its degree of reliance on the market mechanism, and similar macroeconomic institutions and policies: it depends also on the internal, *organizational*, efficiency of its enterprises. This is the question which it is proposed to discuss here.

The organizational efficiency of an enterprise depends on three main characteristics. It depends, first, on its internal structure, i.e. on such matters as its own internal division of labour, the relations between its departments, and the structure of internal decision-making. In order to maintain its efficiency under changing external conditions, an enterprise must be able to adjust its internal structure to those conditions. Second, the efficiency of an enterprise depends on the quality of its management. This raises such questions as the methods of selection and training of managers, their incentives, their rights, and their duties. Third, the success of an enterprise depends on the quality of its work-force, and on the incentives and opportunities for that work-force to work efficiently. In a situation where the composition of the work-force is largely given, the problem resolves itself into how to make the best use of that work-force by good management, and by providing incentives for good work, and penalties for bad work. This implies that there must be an effective system of discipline. We shall, therefore, proceed to consider the organizational efficiency of self-managed enterprises in Yugoslavia under three headings: enterprise structure, management, and incentives and discipline.

Enterprise structure

The internal structure of Yugoslav enterprises is regulated almost entirely by law, primarily by the Law on Associated Labour of 1976. The broad outlines of this system have been described in Chapter 2, but the 671 Articles of the Law on Associated Labour are much more intricate and detailed. Enterprises need to employ large numbers of lawyers to interpret this and other laws, and there are special 'courts of associated labour' to decide the thousands of cases that arise out of this legal regulation of the internal organization of enterprises.

The effect of the Law is that every enterprise has to conform strictly to a standard pattern, and that there is scarcely any scope for 'self-managed' enterprises to adjust their structure and methods of operation to meet the requirements of their business and the ideas of their managers and workers. Apart from the general disadvantages of this state of organizational rigidity, two specific ill-effects of the Law have been frequently mentioned by directors of enterprises and others. These are the forcible fragmentation of enterprises into basic organizations, and the power given to those organizations to veto enterprise policy decisions.

An extreme example of irrational fragmentation is the railway system. The situation was described in an article in *NIN* (23 November 1986), of which the following is a summary:

The Yugoslav railways are divided into eight 'completely separate organizations'. Until recently these were further divided into 365 basic organizations, each of which, according to the Law on Associated Labour, had the right to select its own managers, irrespective of the views of the managers of the larger organizations. Moreover, each basic organization had the right to make its own disciplinary decisions, without regard to any damage caused by bad work to the railway system as a whole. With great difficulty, the number of basic organizations in the railways has now been reduced to between 40 and 50. But this still leaves many occasions for conflicts of interest. For example, trains run late; and one reason for this is that each basic organization keeps control over its own rolling stock, which is often returned empty. There are seven or eight different types of locomotive, and some variations also in the passenger coaches. This imposes the need to maintain a large stock of spare parts and tools. Repairs are done four or five times, and during all this time the rolling stock is out of action. As a result, 'The Yugoslav railways have become the incarnation of disunity and bad work.' Locomotives, trains, and crews stand idle, waiting for work for their own basic organization, and every day hundreds of wagons clatter empty around the country.

In an interview with *Ekonomska politika* (8 July 1985), Vinko Kaštelić, of the Federal Council for Social Organization, pointed out that the Law on Associated Labour required that every basic organization should be commercially independent. This means that it has to have its own price list, which may be subject to price control. But the relations between basic organizations in an enterprise are not, in fact, on a commercial basis, with transfer prices, but are determined by income agreements. The requirement to construct independent price lists 'means the destruction of the enterprise'. Another effect of the Law is that, when an enterprise has factories in different communes, the communes insist that each factory should be a separate basic organization. In this way they aim to raise the maximum tax revenue for themselves, even when this is contrary to the economic efficiency of the enterprise as a whole or the wishes of the workers. The fragmentation of enterprises into basic organizations has given each basic organization the power to veto decisions of the whole enterprise. At a discussion organized by *Politika* (12 December 1986), the director of a large 'complex' enterprise, which contains 77 work organizations and 280 basic organizations, distributed over 40 communes, said that, before they could reach a decision on any matter of general policy, it was necessary to obtain the agreement of every component organization. If even one organization refuses to agree, the whole process of organizing meetings and taking referenda has to be repeated, which is very time-consuming and expensive. The same point has been made by many other directors of large enterprises. Amendments to the Law on Associated Labour are now being discussed, and one proposal is that work organizations should be given much greater powers at the expense of basic organizations. But any change in the status of basic organizations would require amendments to the Federal Constitution. It remains to be seen whether such changes are likely to be accepted.

Management

The efficiency of an organization depends crucially on the quality of its management, and especially of its top manager (in Yugoslavia, the 'director'). In the words of Goldstein (1985, 65). 'No one can so quickly ruin an enterprise as an incapable director, and no one can bring it so much success as a capable one.' But the Yugoslav system is biased against the appointment and training of good directors. When the Party decided to convert Yugoslavia to self-management, it probably did not realize all the implications of the decision. It is true that it very soon accepted that self-management required the abolition of central planning and a greater role for the market. But the success of self-management enterprises operating in a free market depends on the quality of their management. This became abundantly clear during the period of the Economic Reform in the second half of the 1960s. But when the Party saw how much the role of the managers expanded in these conditions, it took fright. It saw power over the economy slipping out of its hands; the Party was in danger of becoming redundant. So, in 1971 the Party launched a 'counter-reformation' to weaken the power of the managers and the so-called 'technocracy' (or the 'manager–technocracy'). This led to the 1974 Constitution and the Law on Associated Labour which fragmented enterprises, gave small groups of workers a veto on enterprise policy, and established the 'social compact' economy.

While the official doctrine is that the workers, through their representatives on the workers' council, choose their director, in practice most directors, especially those of large or medium-sized enterprises, are chosen by local politicians. In the words of *Ekonomska politika* (6 October 1986), 'Statistical analysis demonstrates that the people occupying leading positions in many of the most important economic organizations have been appointed because of political services to the government, the socio-political organizations, and the like.' Such people, the paper believes, would have trouble in finding jobs in enterprises in a mixed economy. Goldstein (1985, 67) remarks that in choosing directors too much attention is given at present to educational qualifications, and especially to previous experience as a political organizer. 'I dare say that this latter mistake has caused more damage to our economy than all the mistaken investments put together.' In a discussion with *Ekonomska politika* (6 October 1986), Professor Janez Jerovšek stated that there is no system for training managers, and that politicians without special training are given managerial positions. The director of a successful small Slovenian firm which produces industrial designs said, in an interview with *Ekonomska politika* (23 November 1987) that, while in Slovenia directors are mainly recruited from industry, in Serbia they are mainly politicians, who are not interested in production or design but only in how to complete their period of office.

Once appointed, directors are not given the right to select their closest colleagues. In a discussion organized by *Politika* (12 December 1986), a director said: 'I have no right to choose my senior staff, no right to allocate jobs, no right to make any changes, yet every day I read in the press that directors are responsible.' Instead of being able to organize an efficient management team and concentrate on their real job, directors spend most of their time either in negotiations with outside bodies, trying to obtain bank credits, allocations of foreign exchange, or permission to increase their prices, or in a variety of internal and external meetings. The director quoted above added that he is obliged to attend innumerable meetings of the Party, the trade unions, and all sorts of other organizations, and that this prevents him from getting on with his real job. When the Presidency of the Central Committee of the Party invited the directors of seventy large enterprises to come and discuss their problems, it discovered that most of the directors spend four-fifths of their time outside their firms at meetings of the economic chambers, the communities of interest, the communes, and committees of the Party. According to the director of a successful engineering firm in Vojvodina (*EP*, 6 April 1987), while directors in other countries spend 90 per cent of their time on buying, selling, increasing production, and planning development (and the rest in 'talking about girls'), in Yugoslavia directors spend only 10 per cent of their time on the first set of jobs and 90 per cent of their time in 'quasi-self-management meetings'. He added that, when he returns from a visit to a developed country, he feels so depressed by the conditions in Yugoslavia that it takes him several days to recover.

In these conditions, it is not surprising that many (or even most) directors try to avoid taking risks. The director of the Slovenian firm quoted above said flatly that Yugoslav directors are not interested in taking risks. They try to maintain the status quo, while seeking to obtain good financial results by methods other then increasing output. An enterprising director has a hard life. When things go well, it is the workers' council that gets the credit; when things go wrong, the director gets the blame. As pointed out by *Ekonomska politika* (9 February 1987), managers can use the self-management system to protect themselves from criticism, since, if they get the approval of the workers' council for any proposal, their own responsibility is 'diluted'.

The post of director is no longer as popular as it used to be. According to *Danas* (19 November 1985), conditions have changed greatly since the mid-1970s. At that time, directors were exceptionally important, privileged, well paid, and respected. Many sigh for the 'good old days', when it was enough to 'bang the table' to get things done, and a telephone call could decide who should get a flat or a job. But 'The problem today is that the job of director is not accepted as being a professional job.' According to some estimates, there were in Croatia at that time as many as 900 unfilled vacancies for the post of director.

In an interview with *Ekonomska politika* (25 February 1985), the director of TOZ, a firm producing pencils in Zagreb, said:

'The director has been overthrown and no longer exists. In practice, it is a wretched job involving manipulation. In one of my books I wrote that in this country we look for directors who are mediocre, narrow-minded, and obedient . . . At the present time 50 per cent or more of directors are unequal to their jobs.' If the director has no authority, nothing happens. But the trade unions want to deprive directors of their power. At the same time, the director is expected to be very well qualified. He must understand the economic system and the political system, and the 700 laws which govern his behaviour. He is also expected to set a personal example of honesty and good work. In Western countries, managers are given special education, but there is no such provision in Yugoslavia. 'For many years we have taken power away from directors, with the slogan that they had usurped the rights of self-management, and that everything would be in order if the workers managed. In 1974 we inaugurated direct self-management, and since then we have been in a state of crisis.'

Incentives and discipline

It was pointed out earlier that no self-managed enterprise can be expected to operate efficiently unless there are incentives for good work and penalties for bad work. It is especially important that there should be an effective method of dealing with people who abuse their membership of the organization by persistent absence from work, idling, poor workmanship, creating disturbances, drunkenness, refusal to carry out management instructions, and so on. This means that someone must be given the authority to grant rewards for good work and impose penalties for bad work or infringements of discipline. Industrial co-operatives are usually reluctant to give such powers—over their own members—to their managers. Yet, except in very small organizations, this is the only practicable way in which incentives can be given and discipline maintained.

Since 1974, the powers of Yugoslav managers to reward good work and penalize bad work have been sharply curtailed. Despite the fact that managers have the responsibility to make their enterprise work efficiently, they have been deprived of most of their power to carry out that responsibility. At the same time, enterprises have been obliged to take on more and more unnecessary workers, especially since 1979. This combination of emasculated management and a growing army of redundant workers has led to a disastrous decline in discipline. A leading director said in 1985 (as reported in *NIN*, 30 December 1985): 'The effects of the collapse of work discipline and responsibility are terrible.' Another director said: 'It mostly comes down to this: if you feel like it, work; if not, you need not; no one can do anything to you. Every day we have more and more workers who, knowing that no one can do anything to them, decide to do little or nothing.'

Goldstein (1985, 72–3) maintains that a director needs to be able to define jobs, to choose his closest colleagues, to reward good workers, and to discipline bad ones. But the Law on Associated Labour allows the director only the first of these rights. So the director is given responsibility without power. Some of the older directors have continued to run their enterprises in an authoritarian manner, contrary to the law. But many of these have since retired or given up in face of increasing outside intervention. Their younger successors rarely acquire the same authority, and are constantly frustrated by the opposition of internal groups. Things are steadily getting worse. Meanwhile, workers are becoming increasingly reluctant to serve on workers' councils and other self-management committees. They realize that these jobs impose responsibilities and often cause unpleasantness. They are particularly averse to serving on disciplinary committees (Goldstein 1985, 85–6).

The director of a successful Slovenian firm said in an interview with *Ekonomska politika* (18 December 1985) that there is too much income-levelling in Yugoslavia.

As soon as someone rises above the average there is talk about it. People try to find some fault or some hidden explanation. Instead of encouraging people and firms to earn more by producing better results, we discourage them. On the other hand, I consider that our laws give too much protection to idlers and inefficient workers . . . the workers who do the least work are those who have the most say. They know all their 'rights' and hang on to them by all means. In fact, a firm cannot do anything about a person who does not do his job.

According to Kos (1986, 43–4), the 'egalitarian syndrome' is responsible for the fact that enterprises hardly ever pay any rewards to their workers for inventions. In the largest machine-building firm in Slovenia, which employed 3,600 workers in 1978, not a single reward was paid between 1961 and 1976. Politicians raise objections to paying rewards on the grounds that the inventions are produced in working hours. Inventors who try to claim rewards are often victimized, and risk losing their jobs.

Some of the results of the lack of incentives and discipline were revealed in the report of a survey of a Belgrade factory (*EP*, 28 January 1985). The factory had 100 metal-working machines, each of which employed one worker. The working day started officially at 6.30 am. At 7.15 am on the day of the survey, only 12 machines were working; 27 machines were being prepared for work; 27 workers had not yet arrived; and the rest of the machines were not working for other reasons. At 7.45 am 17 machines were working; and at 1.40 pm 16 were working, with 23 workers still absent. The shift ended at 2.15 pm. In that shift and the following one, out of fifteen working hours, the machines were working for only two. The same article reported that in another Belgrade firm, which makes wood products, the amount of idleness and carelessness was such that output was less than 10 per cent of its proper level. Many of the skilled workers in this firm were busy with private work.

It is widely said that attitudes to work have changed. For example, Dr Slaven Letica, who is Professor of Medical Sociology and Health Economics in the University of Zagreb, has said: 'In this country the "couldn't care less" attitude has assumed the form of a special psychosocial epidemic.' Yet Yugoslav workers employed abroad are 'responsible, industrious, and successful'. A delegate to the Congress of the League of Communists of Croatia in 1986 said (*EP*, 2 June 1986): 'Today, conscientious and consistent work for seven hours a day in a work organization provokes surprise, and very often a sneer.' There is also widespread use of enterprise facilities for private work and outright stealing of materials and tools. In an interview with *Danas* (31 December 1985)], Stane Dolanc, a prominent party member, former close associate of Tito, and at present a member of the Presidency of the Federation, said:

> We have gone so far that people do moonlight work during working hours, in the factory with factory materials, and no one says a thing about it. Everyone knows about it, every president of a commune, every policeman. I myself know the position in Ljubljana, but I don't report it, simply because I wouldn't get anyone to come and mend a leak in my home.

In a recent visit to an enterprise he asked them, 'Do people steal from you?' They replied, 'They don't steal any more. They have already stolen so much that they cannot sell what they steal on the market. The market, the town, and the surrounding area are completely saturated.'

There is a vast amount of absence from work. For example, in 1986 Radio-Split reported (*Danas*, 6 May 1986) that the employees of the local self-management community of interest for pensions (i.e. the people who process pension applications) were spending time in office hours playing billiards in a nearby inn. 'There is nothing unusual in that. Commune management workers can more easily be found in nearby coffee bars than in their offices.' The scandal was all the greater in this case because there were more than 4,000 applications waiting to be processed. People often have to offer bribes to get their cases considered.

An article in *NIN* (7 September 1986) remarks that a visitor to Belgrade who noticed the crowds of people walking about in the centre of the city might think that there was a strike. 'But it is only the workers taking advantage of the blessings of self-management in order to go about their private business in working hours.' Recently, the disciplinary committee of the basic organization which operates the airport buses for the Yugoslav airline in Belgrade recommended that a worker who had gone off in working hours to drive his private bus should be dismissed. But the workers' council rejected the proposal. More generally, it is a well-known fact that many workers take sick leaves in order to work on their family farms at peak periods.

Apart from such illegitimate absences from work, a great deal of working time is lost because of meetings, both for self-management and for other purposes. A delegate at the Congress of the League of Communists of Bosnia and Herzegovina said (*Danas*, 3 June 1986) that he was shocked to hear that each day in Yugoslavia there were 500,000 workers away at meetings and 700,000 absent because of sickness (in all, about one-fifth of all workers in the social sector). Despite repeated resolutions that self-management meetings should be held outside working hours, the standard practice seems to be to hold them in working time. For example, *Danas* (19 August 1986) states that 'we all know that assemblies of workers, trade union, party, and other meetings start at least one hour before work finishes'. Many workers also leave work to get a permit from the commune or to get a driving licence.

Because of all the absences from work and the time wasted during working hours, it is widely reported that on the average the number of hours worked per working day of 8 hours in the social sector is only 3½. As *NIN* (25 January 1987) points out, this contrasts sharply with the private sector, where people work as much as 16 hours a day. Alternatively, one can consider the average number of days in the year when the workers are away from their place of work. According to *Politika* (30 December 1960), this amounts to 150 days, including Saturdays and Sundays, annual holidays, 15 days of sickness, public holidays, 5 days of voluntary absenteeism, and special leaves for births, weddings, honeymoons, and funerals.

As indicated earlier, this general state of slackness in the social sector is partly the result of the deliberate and persistent overmanning of that sector. The director of a firm that makes electric motors (and exports half its output) has compared his firm with an Italian firm which does similar work (*EP*, 21 July 1986). The Italian firm employs only one-quarter of the number of workers in his firm, but produces four times as much. While the Yugoslav firm has fifty engineers, the Italian firm has only one. Instead of the one hundred workers in his firm who have higher educational qualifications, the director would gladly manage with only twenty, and pay them three to four times as much. Then everything would go better. 'Naturally, I cannot do this because, as director, I have no influence on appointments, discipline, or rates of pay. At least, no effective influence.' That year he was obliged to take on another 150 workers, which, he said, was impossible unless he converted his factory into a charitable institution. A great deal of the overmanning, both in the non-productive sector and within productive enterprises, consists of unnecessary white-collar workers. The director of a Yugoslav factory which makes motocultivators has compared his operation with that of a similar West German factory. He found (*EP*, 20 July 1987) that output per manual worker is the same in both factories, but that, since his factory employs ten times as many office workers, output per worker overall in his factory is only about two-thirds of the West German level.

The state of inefficiency of Yugoslav self-managed enterprises has been summarized by the director of a factory in Split, in an interview with *Danas* (9 February 1988):

'We have the lowest productivity in Europe; our products are of very poor quality; . . . one-fifth of our workers are away sick; we use our resources in work organizations to do private work; we spend an unbelievable amount of time at meetings, which are our main productive activity; we probably have the largest number of invalids in Europe; production is hindered by bad interpersonal relations; lack of discipline at work has been brought to perfection; it is quite normal to have all kinds of theft, carelessness, and corruption—both by workers and by managers.' He believes that the Law on Associated Labour is the main cause of all these problems. Under its influence, 'we have forgotten how to work efficiently, we have eliminated all initiative, prevented proper management, driven the best qualified workers out of our enterprises, and given citizen's rights to dogmatism, demagogy, and idlers.'

Before we leave this subject, it is important to remark that there are still some well organized and successful firms in Yugoslavia, especially, but not exclusively, in Slovenia. Unfortunately, however, it is becoming steadily more difficult to find them.

4. Strikes

No phenomenon so clearly reveals the collapse of self-management in Yugoslavia as the growing number of strikes. This upward trend has been visible for several years. But the year

1987 witnessed an explosion of strikes in all parts of the country. According to *NIN* (29 November 1987), in the first nine months of that year there were more than 1,000 strikes involving about 150,000 workers. Some strikes in Macedonia had not been reported officially and were not included in those figures.

In a competitive (or *laissez-faire*) system of self-management, in which there was no detailed government intervention in enterprise affairs, it would be hard to think of reasons for the workers to go on strike. It makes no sense for the self-employed to strike against themselves, or against the managers whom they themselves appoint. But the Yugoslav system is one in which there is persistent detailed government intervention in enterprise affairs, including the appointment of most directors of enterprises. When, in these ways, the workers' rights of self-management are removed, they have only one remedy against perceived injustices: to go on strike. Such a strike will be directed not against the workers' council, which is the body nominally responsible for determining enterprise policy, but against those who really determine that policy, namely, the government (and the trade union leaders who act as its agents). This is precisely what happened in 1987.

There were two waves of strikes that year. The first was occasioned by the incomes freeze in the first quarter of the year; the second by the attempts of the workers to adjust their incomes after the end of the freeze. Since the strikes were directed primarily against the freeze and its consequences, the body on which the workers were trying to put pressure was clearly not their own workers' council, but the government. In at least two cases, the workers marched to demonstrate in front of their republican parliament building. In Skopje, according to a report in *NIN* (22 November 1987), 3,000 workers from the local steelworks marched to the centre of the city and occupied the square in front of the Macedonian parliament building. In Ljubljana (in Slovenia) also, as reported in *Danas* (15 December 1987), more than 4,000 workers employed at a machine-building firm went on strike and marched to their parliament building.

The principal demand in all these strikes was for a massive increase in personal incomes—often as much as 100 per cent. But it is significant that the additional demands were often of a 'political' nature. For example, in the Ljubljana strike just mentioned the workers demanded a 50 per cent increase in pay, the dismissal of their trade union leaders, and the replacement of all top management except their recently appointed general director. At a strike in Borovo of a large rubber tyre and shoe-making plant the demands were for 100 per cent increase in pay, a 30 per cent reduction in the number of white-collar staff, and a guaranteed supply of imported raw materials. Some other demands which were mentioned at one of the mass meetings included a larger supply of low-price bread and lower prices for meat, milk, fruit, and vegetables (*Politika*, 24 August 1987).

A much publicized strike at two coal pits at Labin, on the Istrian peninsula, started in April 1987 and lasted for 33 days. The strikers' original demands (*Danas*, 21 April 1987) were for 100 per cent increase in pay for the manual workers, the dismissal of the management, the provision of housing loans which could be used in their home areas by the large number of migrant workers from Bosnia and Herzegovina, replacement of the trade union leaders in the pits, and a reduction of the administrative staff. These demands were only partially achieved, although there was a substantial increase in pay, and two of the most unpopular members of management were removed. But the comments of *NIN* (26 April 1987) are significant. The Labin strike, the paper said, has given a revealing picture of the failure—even the irrelevance—of self-management. The strike was organized by the workers at mass meetings. They ignored the workers' council, and addressed their demands mainly to the politicians, and to a lesser extent to the trade unions. The workers' council played no part in any negotiations, except to pass resolutions condemning the strike. Negotiations from the side of the authorities were in the hands of an emergency committee of the local élite, completely cutting across the self-management system.

One of the demands raised during several of these strikes has been for a reduction in the number of office employees. We have seen above that it is the white-collar element that has been particularly swollen in recent years, both inside and outside productive organizations. All of these 'white-collar parasites' have to be maintained by the productive workers; and the latter are beginning to realize this. But the strength of the Party increasingly lies among white-collar and administrative workers.

Unless something is done to correct the situation, the day may come when there will be a revolt by the manual workers against this 'new class'.

5. A Proposal for Reform

A detailed proposal for the reform of the present self-management system was put forward by Slavko Goldstein in a short book in 1985. Goldstein, who was director of the University of Zagreb's printing and publishing business for more than twenty years, has abundant first-hand experience of the operation of the present system, and a large part of the book consists of a critique of that system.

Goldstein believes that the failures of the Yugoslav economy arise mainly from weaknesses in the internal organization of enterprises rather than in macroeconomic policy, although this gets most attention, especially from politicians and from academics with no first-hand experience of industry. Since the adoption of the 1974 Constitution and the Law on Associated Labour of 1976, he maintains, enterprises have been broken up and disorganized; directors have lost the power to impose discipline and to give rewards for good work, and are not allowed to choose their closest colleagues; enterprises are subject to constant outside intervention; and the workers have little real power over the appointment and dismissal of their directors. There are too many rules, social compacts, and norms; many managers have left industry; there is a bad system of income determination; and there are bad personal relations within enterprises.

Goldstein proposes that 500 selected 'organizations of associated labour' of varying size should be given the right to choose their own methods of internal organization. If the experiment proves to be a success, as he believes that it would, the same choice should then be extended to all organizations. To encourage practical thought about these matters, he outlines a model statute for a medium-sized firm of 150–500 workers. The main rules are as follows. The firm is a single organizational unit with five departments. Its income will be calculated according to existing rules. But each worker's personal income will have four components, based on (1) the nature of his job, (2) his qualifications, (3) the total income of the enterprise, and (4) the quality of his work and his attitude towards it. The amounts to be paid in respect of the first three components will be determined by the rules of the enterprise, which have been approved by the workers' council and the assembly. But the fourth component will be at the discretion of the director and other top managers. This component will represent between 20 and 25 per cent of total personal income.

Final authority will rest with the workers' assembly, which must meet once a year, but may be called, if really necessary, more frequently. At the annual assembly there will be a review of the year's work; the net income of the enterprise will be distributed; the plan for the coming year will be discussed and approved; changes can be made in the statutes of the enterprise; workers' appeals will be considered; proposals for substantial investments and loans will be approved; the workers' council and other committees will be elected; rules for the allocation of flats and housing credits will be formulated, and any other matters that are referred by the outgoing workers' council may be discussed. The annual assembly will also elect the director, by secret ballot, and may terminate his employment if it so wishes.

The rights and duties of the workers' council will be essentially the same as at present, but there will be important changes in the composition and responsibilities of two committees. One of these will be a personnel committee, consisting of three full members and two substitutes. This committee will consider proposals from the director or from line managers for dismissals. Grounds for dismissal will include idling, damaging enterprise property, sabotage, repeated absence from work or from the job, fighting, theft, and repeated drunkenness. This committee can also recommend the amount of discretionary income—component (4) above—that should be paid to a particular worker, although the manager has the final decision on this. In conjunction with the director, this committee will decide on the income to be paid to other senior managers. It also decides, in the absence of the director, the amount of the director's income and his expense allowances.

The procedure for the appointment of a director will be supervised by the workers' council, with the assistance of a candidates committee. This committee, like others, is to be elected by the annual assembly, and will contain no direct representatives, as at present, of the commune or the trade unions. The vacancy for a director must be advertised, and the workers' council will draw up a short-list of eligible candidates, preferably containing at least two names. The workers' council submits the whole short-list to the assembly, but it recommends only one candidate. Each candidate on the short list will address the assembly, giving his plans for the future of the enterprise. The workers can ask questions and make comments. Any group of ten workers can also nominate an independent candidate for the post. Voting will be by secret ballot, with successive eliminating rounds if necessary until one candidate gets an absolute majority of those present. A director will be appointed for four years, and can be reappointed as often as desired. But the assembly has the right to remove him before the end of his term of appointment.

The above is only a bare summary of Goldstein's proposals. But it will be seen that their main purpose is to give the director of an enterprise greater independence from the local political establishment, and greater authority within the enterprise, not only legally, through the right to reward good work and recommend dismissals, but through his direct election by and sense of responsibility towards the annual workers' assembly. Goldstein suggests that the annual assembly should last for a whole weekened, so that all aspects of the enterprise's past performance and future plans may be thoroughly discussed, and the election of the director, the workers' council and other committees may be carefully considered.

In the years that have elapsed since the preparation of Goldstein's book, he has become more pessimistic about other aspects of the Yugoslav system of self-management. In his joint article with Marijan Korošić in *Danas* (1 December 1987), which was referred to in the previous chapter, Goldstein recommended much more radical reforms, including the repeal of the Law on Associated Labour and the opening up of the Yugoslav economy to free competition by all types of enterprise, including purely private businesses. The problem is, however, that both his first set of proposals and the more recent set are likely to encounter strong resistance from the party establishment. While competition is undoubtedly the only long-term remedy for the weaknesses of the Yugoslav economy, it will be more difficult to win popular support for it than to win support for a more effective system of internal self-management. It might be better, therefore, for reformers to concentrate on the latter point for the time being.

7

Enterprise Income and its Distribution

One of the fundamental problems of the Yugoslav system is the separation between ownership and control of social sector enterprises. The equity capital of each enterprise is owned by 'society', which means the state, or more precisely the party–state bureaucracy which controls the state, while the workers in each enterprise have been given the nominal right to use that capital for their own benefit without any immediate financial obligation. Of course, the state has not yielded such rights to the workers without imposing other costs on them. The first kind of cost is the imposition of a rigid framework of laws and regulations designed to prevent the workers from dissipating the equity capital of their enterprises. Clearly, it is essential for the state that the workers should not convert 'society's' capital into their own income. So there are complex and detailed regulations about the definitions of various kinds of income and the exact procedure for calculating these. These definitions try to ensure that the workers pay all operating costs and fiscal and financial obligations, and make proper provisions for depreciation, before they determine the amount of income that they can draw from the enterprise. Capitalist countries, of course, also have accounting rules, which are designed to prevent business operators from 'milking' their business at the expense of its creditors. But in an industrial co-operative, in which the members are also share-holders, there is, in any case, a strong incentive for the members to maintain the value of their equity. In Yugoslavia the workers have no such direct interest; and this encourages them to make decisions that are contrary to the wishes of the state. Hence, the state attempts to use laws and 'social compacts' to try to prevent the workers from abusing their self-management rights.

But this is only the negative side of the problem. The socialist state is also anxious to maintain a high rate of investment; and it has a strong preference for financing that investment, so far as possible, by the 'accumulation' of existing enterprises. For, in that case, investment is financed out of an increase in the equity of socially owned enterprises and becomes part of social capital. So the second type of cost that is imposed on the self-managing workers is that they are expected to save as much as possible of their enterprise's net income. But this objective is more difficult to attain. To prescribe that workers should pay themselves only a standard 'wage' would deprive the self-management system of all meaning. The incentive to maximize enterprise income would disappear; and there would, in fact, be no guarantee that there would be any increase in enterprise saving. In addition, in the absence of a labour market, it would be impossible to determine the appropriate wage for each job. Until recently, the state has relied mainly on the goodwill of workers to give some priority to saving, supplemented by the rhetoric and influence of party members in management, the trade unions, and workers' councils. But the collapse of enterprise saving in the last few years has created a crisis in this area. Hence, the government is trying to win acceptance for a new system of personal income determination, which will guarantee that due weight is given to saving. We shall consider these proposals in a later section of this chapter.

The third type of cost that the workers are obliged to pay for their right to 'self-manage' social property is the constant intervention of the socialist state in every aspect of enterprise policy and operation. The forms and degrees of intensity of these interventions have been described in previous chapters, and it is not necessary to repeat that description here.

In the conditions of economic crisis that have developed in Yugoslavia during the 1980s, all three types of cost have much increased. In particular, the combination of rapid inflation with falling productivity and real income per worker in the social sector has (1) enormously increased the opportunities for shifting resources from capital to income, (2) drastically reduced the workers' willingness to accumulate enterprise income, and (3) encouraged the government in its natural propensity to try to find solutions for all economic problems by multiplying its interventions in enterprise affairs.

1. The Effects of Inflation on Income Accounting

There is a long history of discussion about the effects of inflation on income accounting (see, for example, the book of readings by Parker and Harcourt, 1969). Normal accounting practice is based implicitly on the assumption that the value of money is approximately constant. But, when the annual inflation rate rises above 5 per cent, and especially when it rises above 20 per cent, normal accounting rules produce distorted results. Some of the principal distortions are caused by the failure to revalue fixed capital and stocks. For example, if the annual rate of inflation is 20 per cent, and this applies to all prices, the value of fixed capital (and hence the allocation for depreciation) should also be raised by 20 per cent. If this is not done, there will be inadequate provision for depreciation, the apparent net income of the enterprise will exceed its true income, and the expenditure of apparent income on wages, dividends, and taxes (or in Yugoslavia on personal incomes, collective consumption, and taxes) will be excessive. Gross saving by the enterprise will usually be less than it would be if correct accounting figures were available, and net true saving may even become negative.

The effects of inflation on stock values, and hence on apparent income, are more complex. The problem arises from the normal, and convenient, accounting practice of calculating the value of stocks consumed by adding the beginning-of-year value of stocks to material purchases and subtracting the end-of-year value of stocks. When prices are approximately constant, this method yields quite satisfactory results. But, when prices are changing, there is an inconsistency between the three prices: those ruling at or near the beginning of the year (which affect the initial value of stocks), those ruling during the year, and those ruling at or near the end of the year (which affect the end-of-year value of stocks). When prices are rising, the standard method of calculating the cost of materials used is biased downwards, because the price at which initial stocks are 'bought in' is too low, and the price at which final stocks are 'sold out' is too high, compared with the current cost of buying such materials during the year. As a result, the amount of apparent value added is overestimated. This overestimate, or 'stock appreciation', also inflates enterprise profits, saving, and apparent investment in stocks. The entire enterprise accounting system is distorted; and, if no corrections are made, the same types of distortions will occur in the national accounts. This problem is discussed further in the Appendix at the end of this book, which also presents estimates of the aggregate amount of stock appreciation in Yugoslavia in recent years and its effect on the value of the social product.

Table 7.1 gives some estimates of the effects of these distortions on aggregate values in the accounts of social sector enterprises. It

TABLE 7.1.   *Net Saving of Social Sector Enterprises, before and after Stock Appreciation Adjustment, 1977–1985*
(percentages of adjusted social sector product at current prices)

	(1) Net saving before stock appreciation	(2) Stock appreciation	(3) Net saving after stock appreciation	(4) Under-provision of depreciation	(5) Net interest paid
1977	7.9	11.1	−3.1	0.7	. .
1978	7.8	6.8	1.0	0.5	. .
1979	8.6	9.9	−1.3	1.0	. .
1980	13.0	14.9	−1.9	1.6	5.2
1981	14.9	14.7	0.1	1.7	5.2
1982	13.5	16.1	−2.6	3.0	6.3
1983	13.2	16.9	−3.7	4.4	8.6
1984	16.8	22.6	−5.9	4.4	11.5
1985	14.6	25.4	−10.8	4.2	16.1

Sources: col. (1): National Accounts tables in Yearbooks and *Indeks*; includes allocations for accumulation and reserves of social sector enterprises, but excludes their expenditure on investment component of collective consumption (mainly workers' housing); col. (2): Appendix, which also gives estimates of adjusted social sector product, used as denominator throughout; col. (3): col. (1) − col. (2); col. (4): correct depreciation assumed to be 5.2% of value of fixed capital at end of previous year, as in 1974, both expressed in 1972 prices; data for fixed capital from YB86 (102–12) and for actual depreciation from YB86 (107–1 and 107–2); estimates of correct depreciation at 1972 prices inflated by implicit price deflator for gross fixed investment from OECD (1987, Table A); actual depreciation in current prices from Table 107–7 of various Yearbooks; col. (5): *Ekonomska politika*, 15.9.86, p. 26.

should be noted first that, according to the official figures, the net saving of social sector enterprises, when expressed as a percentage of adjusted social product, *increased* in the 1980s. Yet, as we know, this was a period when real social sector product was scarcely rising even before adjustment, and after adjustment was falling. The explanation for this statistical illusion is the growing amount of stock appreciation, resulting from the accelerating rate of inflation. This is shown in column (2) of the table. These figures also indicate the extent of overestimation of social sector product in each of these years. When the share of stock appreciation is rising, the growth of social sector product will be overestimated in the official series.

When net social sector enterprise saving is adjusted for stock appreciation, it is possible to obtain more realistic estimates of the extent to which these enterprises were adding to, or subtracting from, their net worth. As can be seen from column (3) of the table, there were only two years in the period 1977–85 when aggregate adjusted net saving of social sector enterprises was positive, and then only to a very small extent. Even in 1977, net social sector enterprise saving was negative; but from 1982 onwards the net saving ratio was increasingly negative, reaching a net dissaving ratio in 1985 of more than 10 per cent.

It is more difficult to estimate the extent of under-provision of depreciation. The figures in column (4) have been calculated by comparing aggregate allocations for depreciation in social sector enterprises at 1972 prices with the value of fixed assets held by those enterprises at the end of the previous year, also at 1972 prices. A series starting in 1974 shows the average percentage rate of depreciation, calculated on this basis, falling steadily from 5.2 in the first year to 4.0 in 1984. The estimates in column (4) have been made on the assumption that this rate should have remained at 5.2 per cent throughout the period. But it is possible that the 1974 depreciation rate was already too low. In fact, the rate was 5.4 per cent in the years 1969–71, and there have been many complaints in the press that the revaluation of fixed assets has fallen badly behind the rate of inflation. For example, *NIN* (4 January 1987) has quoted the estimate that 'in recent years' inadequate depreciation has led to capital being run down to the extent of about $20 billion.

Even if asset values are correctly adjusted for inflation at the end of each year, the amount of depreciation allocated in the following year will be inadequate if inflation continues during that year. For example, in 1985, when the cost-of-living index, for the average of the year, was about 30 per cent above its level at the end of 1984 (and if we assume that the same figure is appropriate for the increase in the value of fixed assets), depreciation provisions of 5.2 per cent of the dinar value of fixed assets held at the end of 1984 would represent only 4 per cent of their value in real terms.

The correct figures of under-provision of depreciation, if they were available, should be subtracted from the figures of net saving, adjusted for stock appreciation, in order to obtain a realistic estimate of the extent to which social sector enterprises were maintaining their capital. Even if we assume that the figures in column (4) are sufficient for this purpose, it is clear that the extent of social sector enterprise dissaving in Yugoslavia since at least 1977 has been very considerable, reaching as much as 15 per cent of social product in that sector in 1985. (Preliminary figures for 1986 suggest an even worse position.)

Since 1982, partly under pressure from the IMF, the Yugoslav government has raised interest rates on both bank deposits and bank credits. Although these rates have scarcely ever risen to the level of the current rate of inflation, and in any case the higher loan rates have been charged only on new loans, in recent years social sector enterprises have been obliged to pay considerably larger amounts of bank interest. Column (5) of the table shows the amount of net interest paid by enterprises, expressed as a percentage of their adjusted social product. It will be seen that net interest paid has been of the same order of magnitude as net dissaving, after adjustment for under-provision of depreciation. It could be argued that, instead of raising interest to offset the effect of inflation on the real value of debt, the capital value of debt should be indexed. In that case, most of the interest paid in recent years by enterprises would be excluded from the expenditure side of their income account, and this might lead to a similar rise in their net saving. This is perhaps the line of reasoning that is responsible for the change in the treatment of interest in the new accounting rules introduced in 1987 (to be discussed further below).

Paradoxically, despite negative net saving by social sector

enterprises, their aggregate net worth has continued to increase (see Table 7.2). This is the result of a combination of inflation and non-indexed net enterprise debt, mainly in the form of bank credits. For inflation reduces the real burden of non-indexed debt to the borrowing enterprise, and thus compensates, in whole or in part, for its failure to maintain its net worth out of current income. In effect, the lenders (who in Yugoslavia are mainly citizens holding cash or dinar bank deposits) are forced by

TABLE 7.2. *Net Saving, Changes in Assets, Liabilities and Net Worth, and the Ratio of Net Debt to Net Physical Assets, Productive Social Sector, 1977–1985*

	(1) Net saving (after depreciation and stock appreciation)	(2) Change in net value of physical assets	(3) Change in net liabilities	(4) Change in net worth	(5) Net debt as % of net physical assets (end of year)
	(billions of dinars at current prices)				
1977	−18	319	72	247	27.3
1978	7	229	53	176	26.7
1979	−12	449	146	303	27.9
1980	−23	681	314	367	32.4
1981	2	1,155	243	912	29.1
1982	−57	1,590	342	1,248	26.9
1983	−109	2,094	1554	540	39.9
1984	−259	4,376	1359	2,837	36.7
1985	−843	11,107	2307	8.980	29.0
Total 1977–85	−1312	22,000	6390	15,610	
Addendum: end-of-year values:					
1976		1,082	−310	772	28.7
1985		23,082	−6700	16,382	29.0

Sources: col. (1): net saving and reserve allocations of social sector enterprises: National Accounts tables in Yearbooks and *Indeks*; stock appreciation adjustment: Appendix; col. (2): net value of physical assets, from Mates (1986, Table A6); net financial liabilities, from flow-of-funds tables in National Bank of Yugoslavia *Quarterly Bulletin*; col. (3): as for col. (2).

inflation to transfer part of their real net worth to social sector enterprises.

If the net flow of new lending to enterprises in each year from 1977 to 1985 (see column (3) of Table 7.2) is inflated to 1985 values by the implicit price index of gross fixed investment (from OECD 1987, Table A), and if to this is added the stock of net debt already existing at the end of 1976, also revalued at 1985 prices, the total real supply of loans to enterprises up to 1985 amounts to 21,600 billion dinars at 1985 prices. This represents 94 per cent of the net value of physical assets of social sector enterprises in 1985, which was slightly more than 23,000 billion dinars.[1] But the aggregate balance sheet of social sector enterprises in that year showed a net debt of only 6,700 billion dinars, and a net worth of nearly 16,400 billion dinars. In effect, inflation had caused the sum of approximately 15,000 billion dinars at 1985 prices to be transferred without compensation from the population at large to social sector enterprises. But this process of 'expropriation' cannot continue indefinitely. For, as a population becomes more convinced that inflation will continue, and even accelerate, they begin to take all possible measures to economize on money and non-indexed bank deposits; the velocity of circulation of money increases; the real value of the net debt of enterprises falls towards zero; and the scope for extracting further transfers of resources from the population by inflation eventually disappears.

As Table 7.2 shows, the net inflow of loans to social sector enterprises in the period 1977–85 of 6,390 billion dinars was the sole source of current finance for the expansion of their physical assets in every year except 1978 and 1981. In the other years, part of external finance was used to enable enterprises to dissave, i.e. to pay out more in personal incomes, fringe benefits, taxes, and contributions than the total net income available. But, as a result of inflation, both the net value of physical assets and the net worth of enterprises increased much more than the increase in their net debt. The ratio of net debt to the net value of

[1] Since most of the net debt of enterprises in 1976 was accumulated over previous years, the 1985 value of that debt should be greater than the amount used in the above calculation. But these estimates are, in any case, subject to a number of possible errors, and since they are intended only to provide orders of magnitude, it is not worth trying to make more precise adjustments.

physical assets remained fairly stable, and in 1985 it was almost exactly the same as it had been in 1976. On the basis of similar calculations, Yugoslav official statisticians (*Jugoslavija 1945–1985*, 1986, 241) claim that this is proof that during this period the productive social sector maintained an approximately constant rate of 'self-financing'. But this is no more than a statistical illusion.

2. The New Accounting System

Description

The new accounting system has three main purposes. The first is to ensure that the net value of fixed assets is regularly revised in proportion to changes in prices, and so to ensure that social sector enterprises make depreciation provisions that are adjusted in the same proportion, or in other words that they make indexed depreciation provisions. The second is to oblige enterprises to cost materials consumed at prices close to replacement cost, and thus to remove a substantial part of stock appreciation from enterprise net income. The third is to exclude from enterprise costs almost all of net interest paid, together with the cost of providing for the net increase in the value of foreign debt directly owned by (or to) social sector enterprises as a result of the fall in the value of the dinar (so-called 'foreign exchange differences'). We shall give some estimates below of the effects of these changes on aggregate social sector net income. But we must first discuss the changes in the rules in a little more detail.

Under the new rules, as from the beginning of 1987 net fixed assets must be revalued at the end of each year by indexes relating to the purchase prices of such assets on the previous 30 September. The Federal Statistical Office will calculate such indexes for eight groups of assets, one of which will refer to all kinds of mechanical equipment. The use of broadly based price indexes for all assets falling within each group will yield unsatisfactory results in some cases; but it will be better than having no clear rules, especially in a period of rapid inflation. The new system will, apparently, not make any correction for past undervaluation of fixed assets. But it will ensure that, on the average, there will be no further undervaluation; and, gradually, as old assets are fully written off and new assets are introduced, the new system should raise the total amount of depreciation to the real amount intended by the depreciation rates in operation. The rule for stocks is that they must be revalued at the end of each quarter with the use of a single price index, and that materials used during the following quarter must be charged accordingly. The use of a single index is arbitrary and will produce some very misleading results in particular enterprises and industries. Over the whole economy, however, the new system should lead to a substantial reduction in the amount of stock appreciation at present included in enterprise net income and saving. It will not eliminate all stock appreciation, because there will be no offset to capital gains on work in progress and stocks of finished goods. At the same time, the requirement that all stocks must in future be revalued at sale prices ruling at the end of each year will tend to increase the amount of stock appreciation included in enterprise accounts in comparison with the methods previously in use.

In future, the amount of net interest paid by enterprises, plus the net cost of 'foreign exchange differences', arising out of their holdings of assets or liabilities expressed in terms of foreign currencies, can be offset against capital gains on their net physical assets during the year. The amount of this offset is limited by the size of the capital gains, but for most enterprises this will be no restriction. Enterprises that have large net interest payments and few physical assets will be unable to obtain the full offset; but it is difficult to think of many such cases. The elimination of net interest as a cost to enterprises will be much welcomed, especially at a time when they are being forced to increase their accounting costs of materials and depreciation. But it will not improve their cash flow, or liquidity, problem, since they will still have to pay interest, even although it is no longer charged as a cost. An unfortunate side-effect of the system is that it may reduce the influence of the rate of interest on investment decisions, and to that extent undermine the effort to bring down the rate of inflation by introducing positive real rates of interest. But it is doubtful whether, under present Yugoslav conditions, where enterprises scarcely care any more about changes in their nominal costs and liabilities, investment decisions are much affected by the real rate of interest. All that they really care about is their cash flow, and that, as already pointed out, is not affected by the new accounting system.

Estimate of effects of the system on net income

According to *Ekonomska politika* (28 December 1987), the increase in material costs of social sector enterprises in the first three quarters of 1987 as a result of the new accounting system was 7,526 billion dinars, while the amount of net interest paid and the cost of 'foreign exchange differences' in the same period was 6,324 billion dinars. Between the same two periods, depreciation provisions rose (*EP*, 11 January 1988) from 1,430 to 3,438 billion dinars, and, since prices approximately doubled, depreciation provisions in the first three quarters of 1987 may have been about 600 billion dinars higher than they would have been without the new accounting system. The overall effect on the net income of social sector enterprises would therefore appear to have been approximately 6,300–7,500–600 billion dinars, or a reduction of 1,800 billion dinars. It is interesting to note that between the same two periods the amount of aggregate net saving by social sector enterprises fell by 1,600 billion dinars in current values, or by approximately 2,600 billion dinars in 1987 prices.

The decline in reported enterprise net saving in the first three quarters of 1987, much of which was probably due to the change in the accounting system, was reflected in a large rise in the value of reported losses. Enterprises making a loss in this period employed one-fifth of all workers in social sector enterprises, and, when their losses are deducted from the net saving of other enterprises, aggregate net saving in the period was *minus* 600 billion dinars (*EP*, 11 January 1988). Losses continued to grow rapidly in the first half of 1988 as a consequence of the price freeze, which lasted until May of that year, and the tight monetary policy of the second half of the year will probably lead to further difficulties for many enterprises.

Assessment

In one sense, the new legislation is a courageous attempt to bring reason and order to the accounting methods used in the social sector. But insistence on uniform practices in such a complex field is dangerous. We have already noted the distortions that are likely to be introduced by the application of general price indexes to a wide range of goods. The clamour for adjustments and exemptions will certainly grow. Already some highly capital-intensive industries, such as electricity and railways, have been exempted from revaluing their fixed assets until at least 1989; social housing has been completely exempted (despite the fact that in this sector current depreciation represents less than 0.25 per cent of its capital value); and enterprises making losses will be allowed to cover them in whole or in part by using up to half of their legally prescribed depreciation provisions (*EP*, 13 April 1987).

As the effects of the new accounting system become more and more clear, enterprises will seek to find new ways to circumvent them. Prices will tend to rise faster than they would otherwise do. Even in the conditions of 'price freeze' imposed in early 1988, some firms, such as the manufacturer of the 'Yugo' car, have introduced new models at much higher prices than for their previous models. Yugoslav managers are often very resourceful, especially in finding ways around laws and social compacts. According to the vice-president of the government (*Politika*, 22 November 1986), the new accounting rules were introduced 'because at present every chief accountant can choose whether or not to show a loss'. He may well be over-optimistic in thinking that the new rules will fundamentally alter this situation.

Some major new distortions will be introduced by the system of *partial* indexation of balance sheets. While physical assets are to be revalued, and net interest is to be treated as if it were a form of capital gain, financial assets and liabilities are not to be indexed. This will have unequal effects on the equity (or 'business fund') of different enterprises, depending on their proportion of net liabilities to physical assets. In Croatia, where the levy on enterprises for aid to the less developed republics and Kosovo is based on the 'business fund', instead of on the net income of the enterprise, there will certainly be cries of distress. In general, the new system will give a strong incentive to all firms to maximize their net debt ratio. Both the revaluation of physical assets (but not of financial assets) and the elimination of most interest from the cost side of the operating account will push firms in the same direction.

Does this mean that the government should not have tried to bring some order into the accounting system? If the purpose of the question is to ask whether the government has a responsibility to do something about the chaotic state of enterprise finances, the answer is clearly that it does have such a responsibility. But to make changes in accounting rules without tackling the underlying causes of the economic troubles will not achieve very much, and may even make things worse. Despite all efforts to evade the regulations, more and more enterprises will be plunged into accounting losses, and this will only encourage an even greater feeling of irresponsibility. The 'self-management' system will be increasingly discredited, and the workers (and their managers) will place the blame for all losses and failures on the government. As a result, the new accounting system will be a major step towards a confrontation between the workers and the state in Yugoslavia.

3. The Proposed New Personal Income System

The second part of the Party's plan to restrain personal incomes and increase enterprise saving is the proposed new personal income system. The new accounting system goes only part of the way towards this ultimate objective. While it is designed to give a more realistic picture of enterprise net income, and, in so far as this results in many enterprises showing a loss or a very low net income, may be expected to put some pressure on enterprises to limit their payments of personal incomes, there is no guarantee that this restraint will be sufficiently effective. So long as enterprises have no incentive to save, personal incomes will be essentially out of control. Hence the second part of the plan is an attempt to design regulations that will give enterprises such an incentive.

The essence of this plan was recommended in the Long-term Programme of Economic Stabilization, but the first practical move in this direction was apparently made in July 1985, when a draft paper was submitted to the Central Committee of the League of Communists at the federal level (*EP*, 22 July 1985). The proposal has been discussed and amended many times since then, but, although it was finally meant to be introduced in July

1987, it is still in limbo. Some aspects of this process of discussion and amendment will be described below. At this point, however, we shall concentrate attention on the nature of the problem, and of the solution offered.

The essential idea is that, whereas at present net personal income is a single item in enterprise accounts, in future it should consist of two parts. The first would be the equivalent of a wage, and the second would be the equivalent of a profit share. The proposal is that the first part of each worker's personal income should be determined by the average personal income paid (presumably in the previous year) in the industry and the republic or province to which the enterprise (or, more precisely, the basic organization of associated labour) belongs, and by the level of the worker's own skill and the conditions of his work. The second part would depend on the 'rate of accumulation' in his basic organization, calculated as follows. The net saving of the organization (as defined in the new accounting system, after deducting the first component of personal income) will be divided by the net value of physical assets employed (revalued according to the new regulations). When this rate is higher than the average for enterprises in the same industry in the same republic or province in the previous year, the workers' income will have a positive second component; and vice versa. (No rules have yet been announced on how this total will be distributed between individual workers.) These positive or negative components will absorb only part of the positive or negative saving revealed in the initial calculation. The remainder will constitute the final contribution to saving or dissaving by the organization.

The logic of this proposal is obvious. It is essentially an attempt to mimic conditions in a capitalist economy, where workers in prosperous firms usually receive higher wages than those that would be payable in a purely competitive labour market, i.e. where there is an element of explicit or implicit profit-sharing. But the difficulty with trying to introduce such a system in a socialist self-management economy is that several of the crucial conditions are absent. First, there is no competitive labour market to give a benchmark for the first component of the 'dual-income' system. The proposal is to use existing average personal incomes in the industry and the republic or province to which the enterprise belongs as the indicator of that competitive wage. But there are wide differences between incomes in different industries in Yugoslavia, and even wider differences between the various republics and provinces. No one can seriously claim that these differences are a reflection of competitive wage differences; indeed, one of the purposes of the new personal income system is to get rid of 'non-competitive' influences on personal incomes. The proposal, as it stands, would tend to perpetuate these non-competitive differences between industries and regions, although it would reduce inter-enterprise differences within given industries and regions.

Second, since there is no capital market, and because there are many kinds of arbitrary interventions in the determination of prices, the availability and cost of loans, supplies of foreign exchange, employment quotas, and so forth, neither the benchmark rate of accumulation for a particular industry in a particular republic or province nor the rate of accumulation achieved by a particular enterprise can be regarded as a reflection of the degree of efficiency of that industry or enterprise. Apart from this, there have already been arguments about whether interest paid should be included in saving (as it will be in the new accounting system) and whether the denominator for the rate of accumulation should be net physical assets or the 'business fund'. It has now been decided that interest will be excluded. In that case the denominator should logically be the business fund. But it seems that the denominator will continue to be physical assets.

There are bound to be many other disputes about the definition of industries, the benchmark period, the effects of price controls, both in the benchmark period and the current period, and other matters. The basic problem is that, in the absence of free markets, it is impossible to invent parameters for determining such a sensitive variable as personal income, without becoming embroiled in endless arguments. These arguments will be all the more intense because of the close involvement of two powerful institutions—the republican and provincial governments, and the trade unions—the agreement of both of which is necessary if the new system is to be embodied in a set of social compacts. A federal compact between all these parties was signed in March 1987. But the criteria for determining the first income component were left to be decided by each republic or province separately, and a month later the republics and provinces passed the problem on to their enterprises. Consequently, as Branko Mikulić, the Prime Minister, complained at a meeting of the Central Committee of the Party, there will be 9,500 different systems of income determination (*Politika*, 1/2 May 1987). Meanwhile, the trade unions had begun to press for the postponement of the introduction of the scheme from 1 July 1987 to 1 January 1988.

Confronted by rapidly rising inflation in the second half of 1987, and frustrated in its attempt to get the new personal income system into operation, the federal government finally imposed a price freeze, which was due to continue until May 1988. But at the beginning of the freeze the prices of some basic goods and services (such as electricity and railway transport) were allowed to rise sharply, and the dinar was steeply devalued. As a result, most enterprises were caught between frozen prices for their products and a large increase in their input costs. The effects on the net income of enterprises in the first half of 1988 will have been both arbitrary and, in many cases, catastrophic. The rates of accumulation achieved in this period will turn out to be quite unrepresentative of past rates, as well as of hypothetical equilibrium rates. It seems virtually certain, therefore, that the introduction of the new personal income system will be further postponed; and there is every possibility that it will be completely abandoned.

4. Conclusions

The new accounting system has some logical features. But, as a method of adjusting enterprise accounts to a state of rapid inflation, it is incomplete. While physical assets are to be revalued regularly, the price indexes used will in some cases produce arbitrary and contentious results, which will tend to undermine confidence in the system. Moreover, failure to revalue financial assets and liabilities (except in a roundabout fashion by permitting the deduction of net interest from current costs) will open up opportunities for new forms of financial manipulation designed to improve the net income position of enterprises, as well as to evade the controls on personal incomes.

Although the government has been able to impose the new accounting system by federal legislation, it will not achieve its ultimate aim of increasing enterprise accumulation unless the new personal income system is also implemented. But the latter depends on obtaining the agreement of the republics and provinces, and the trade unions. As so often in Yugoslavia, while these bodies have signed a social compact which accepts the new system in principle, they have so far prevented its implementation in practice by the procedural device of passing responsibility for determining a vital element in the agreement to the individual enterprises. Unless this decision can be reversed, the whole purpose of the scheme will be defeated, since every enterprise will be able to determine its own distribution rules. But any attempt to formulate a general rule applicable to all enterprises will cause so much argument and so many disputes that a successful outcome along that route seems equally unlikely.

The prospect is, therefore, that this whole Sisyphean effort to compel the self-managing workers to obey strict rules in the distribution of enterprise income will collapse, and that the confusion which will thereby be created will leave matters in a worse state than they were before. The fundamental problem is the divorce between ownership and control, and the lack of natural incentives for the self-managing workers to make decisions that are in the interests of society at large. In the absence of such an 'invisible hand', the Party is trying to attain the same result by using the 'visible hand' of the state. But it will not work. All intelligent Yugoslav observers, including most economists, are well aware of this. But they dare not say so. Powerless, they simply have to wait for the inevitable failure of the new system.

The Yugoslav system of self-management succeeded in generating a modest amount of enterprise saving up to the early 1970s. At that time, real incomes were rising and there were good opportunities for obtaining foreign loans and foreign technology. There was, therefore, an incentive for the workers in progressive enterprises to 'plough back' part of enterprise net income, especially since the provision of internal finance was often a precondition for obtaining additional external finance. But these conditions have disappeared in the 1980s. Real incomes in the social sector have fallen precipitately, the flow of foreign lending has dried up (or has been stopped by the Yugoslav government), and rapidly rising inflation has generated illusory enterprise income and savings. The new accounting system will eliminate the last factor. But it will not alter the underlying lack of incentive to save. Only under conditions of genuine self-management, and preferably with worker participation in the ownership of the equity of their enterprises, is there any prospect of raising enterprise efficiency, real income, and real saving.

8

Taxation and Money

This chapter is concerned, first, with the fiscal activities of government and semi-government agencies, and second, with the banking system and monetary policy. Section 1 will start with a description of the main sources of government revenue, transfers between different levels of government, and the main forms of public expenditure. This will be followed by a review of fiscal policies. Section 2 will follow a similar pattern in relation to banking and the monetary system. Since it will become apparent that in Yugoslavia the division between fiscal and monetary policies is even less well defined than in many other countries, this latter section will contain a discussion of the combined effects of fiscal and monetary policies on the state of the economy.

1. Fiscal Structures and Policies

The structure of revenues and expenditures

Taxes are collected at three levels of government in Yugoslavia: by the federal government, by the governments of the republics and provinces, and by the communes, including some multi-commune cities. (Some small levies by 'local communities' can conveniently be included with miscellaneous sources of revenue.) The other main source of public revenue is 'contributions', collected by 'self-management communities of interest'. These 'communities' are of two kinds. The first group, and by far the most important, consists of agencies for financing and managing the social services: education, health, pensions, child benefits, and some other minor services. The second group consists of agencies that the residents of a commune may decide to establish for the financing of local housing, utilities, roads, and other

TABLE 8.1.   *Revenues of Governments and other Agencies as Percentage of Adjusted Social Product, 1979–1987*

	1979	1981	1983	1985	1987
Governments					
Federation	5.5	4.8	4.5	4.5	5.6
Republics and provinces	6.4	6.6	5.5	4.8	4.0
Communes and cities	3.3	2.9	2.5	2.5	2.6
Total	15.2	14.3	12.5	11.7	12.1
Self-management communities of interest for social services					
Education	5.0	4.2	3.5	3.7	4.1
Health	6.3	5.6	5.0	5.2	5.8
Pensions	7.3	7.1	7.1	7.7	10.6
Child benefits	1.4	1.2	1.0	1.2	1.4
Other	2.0	1.8	1.4	1.9	2.3
Total	22.0	20.0	18.1	19.6	24.2
Other[a]	9.2	8.3	9.7	8.9	7.7
Grand total	46.4	42.6	40.3	40.2	44.0

[a] Includes self-management communities of interest for other purposes, the fund for the development of the less developed regions, and local communities.

Sources: revenue data from *Indeks*, various issues; adjusted social product: Appendix.

purposes. Table 8.1 gives a picture of the relative importance of these different sources of revenue in alternate years of the period 1979–87. For convenience of comparison, the original data in current dinars have been expressed as percentages of adjusted social product in the corresponding year.

During this period, total revenues of these agencies amounted to between 40 and 46 per cent of adjusted social product. But there is some duplication in the figures of government revenues, because in the years covered by the table about half of the gross revenues of the republics and provinces was transferred to the federation (where it again appears as revenue). There was also a smaller counterflow of grants made by the federal government to the republics and provinces. Consequently, as will be seen below, the consolidated revenue of these agencies represented a share of adjusted social product which was between 2 and 3 per cent less than the totals shown in Table 8.1.

Some of the noteworthy features of the figures in Table 8.1 are as follows. In the first place, although Yugoslavia has a low per capita product (about $2,000), the government takes a large share of its total product. The costs of defence and administration are heavy, and the scale of social services is large for a fairly poor country. Second, the share of total (gross) revenues fell from 1979 to 1983, but rose sharply in 1987. The latter change seems to have been mainly the result of a large rise in revenues collected (and disbursed) by pension funds, which was partly the consequence of an improvement in pension benefits. Third, from 1979 to 1983 there was a considerable fall in the proportion of social product collected to finance education and health services. (As Table 8.2 will show, *expenditure* on education was higher in each year than the figures shown in Table 8.1, but it also had a declining trend as a proportion of social product up to 1983.)

Data on consolidated government revenues and expenditures come from a different source, and are differently classified. Table 8.2 shows these data as percentages of adjusted social product in alternate years from 1979 to 1987. The figures show a similar fall in the share of social product taken by government between 1979 and 1983, of somewhat more than 6 per cent, followed by a substantial recovery in 1987. On the expenditure side, the fall from 1979 to 1983 was an even greater 6.7 per cent; but the recovery to 1987 brought the percentage budget surplus back in the latter year to almost the same insignificant level obtaining in 1979. Moreover, as will be shown below, since much of government spending was financed outside the budget, by expanding the money supply, the government continued to run a very large overall deficit.

The table shows the unusually large share of social product used for national defence and administration. The fall in this share from 1979 to 1983 was mainly the result of the nearly 10 per cent decline in that period in the personal incomes of government employees in comparison with incomes of employees in productive industries. Expenditure on education was affected by the same influence, although this accounts for only part of the large decline in its share from 1979 to 1983. Since 1984 the

TABLE 8.2. *Consolidated Public Sector Revenue and Expenditure as Percentage of Adjusted Social Product, 1979–1987*

	1979	1981	1983	1985	1987
Revenue					
Direct taxes[a]	26.0	23.4	20.5	21.6	27.7
Indirect taxes[b]	14.7	13.9	12.8	11.9	11.4
Other tax and non-tax revenue	3.1	3.4	4.1	4.1	2.5
Total	43.8	40.6	37.4	37.6	41.5
Expenditure					
National defence and administration	9.7	9.7	8.7	9.3	9.8
Education	6.3	5.6	4.7	4.9	5.6
Social security and welfare	16.6	14.6	14.7	14.7	19.7
Interventions in the economy	3.9	3.4	4.1	4.2	4.0
Other[c]	7.2	6.6	4.9	4.2	2.2
Total	43.7	39.9	37.0	37.2	41.3
Balance (revenue less expenditure)	0.1	0.7	0.4	0.4	0.2

[a] Includes taxes on income and property, and social security contributions to self-management communities of interest.

[b] Includes taxes on goods and services, and customs duties.

[c] Includes expenditure on housing and local amenities, and consumption subsidies.

Sources: budget data: OECD (1982, 1984, 1988, text tables); adjusted social product: Appendix.

relative incomes of workers in the non-productive sector have been allowed to recover; and by 1987 they were back to the position which they occupied in 1979.

Separate figures are available in the OECD reports of the revenue and expenditure of the federal government; and these throw some further light on the sources and uses of federal government revenue, and of the fiscal relations between the federal government and the governments of the republics and provinces. In 1985, for example, of total federal revenue of 686 billion dinars, 150 billion dinars was derived from customs duties, 264 billion dinars from basic sales tax (of which the federal government was entitled at that time to one-half), and 251 billion dinars from transfers from the republics and provinces. While all customs duties accrued to the federal government, it received only about one-third of total sales tax revenue in 1985. The other two-thirds of sales tax revenue (about 481 billion dinars) was taken by the republics and provinces and the communes and cities (of which the communes and cities appear to have received about 130 billion dinars).

Out of an initial tax revenue of 442 billion dinars in 1985, the republics and provinces transferred 251 billion dinars to the federal government, but received back grants to the value of 60 billion dinars. This implies that the disposable income of the republics and provinces in 1985 was about 251 billion dinars. The income of the communes and cities in that year was 229 billion dinars.

On the expenditure side, the federal government allocated 460 billion dinars to defence, and a further 106 billion dinars to pension funds, much of which was probably in respect of pensions of military personnel and veterans. Federal expenditure on administration was 48 billion dinars, and, apart from the grants to the republics and provinces of 60 billion dinars, only 19 billion dinars was used for other purposes. Direct expenditure by the federal government on investment has been virtually eliminated since the adoption of the 1974 Constitution, but, as we shall see below, the federal government continues to have an important indirect influence on investment through its control over the level of bank credits.

Although expenditure on administration by the federal government appears to be modest, total expenditure on this item by all government and semi-government agencies is considerable. In 1985, total expenditure on defence and administration was 863 billion dinars, of which defence expenditure by the federal government was 460 billion dinars. This implies that the cost of administration was 403 billion dinars. Since federal expenditure on administration was only 48 billion dinars, expenditure on this item by all other agencies appears to have been 355 billion dinars, or about 3.8 per cent of adjusted social product in that year. This is one indicator of the extent to which Yugoslavia is 'over-administered'.

Fiscal policies

This topic falls under four main headings. First, we shall consider the aggregate effect of fiscal policy on the balance of the economy, which is especially relevant to the problem of inflation. Second, some issues arise in connection with the tax structure, i.e. of the kinds of taxes imposed. Third, we shall consider some aspects of the redistributive effects of the tax system. Fourth, we need to take note of the multiplicity of taxation and expenditure agencies.

Macroeconomic policy

We have seen that the bulk of taxation in Yugoslavia is raised by governments or communities of interest which are outside of the direct control of the federal government. It is also the standard rule in Yugoslavia that these bodies are not entitled to run surpluses or deficits, except for short periods as a consequence of unforeseen events. Any macroeconomic fiscal policy would, therefore, have to be carried out through the federal budget. But the republics and provinces are strongly suspicious of federal financial power. They have the final authority, through the Chamber of Republics and Provinces, over all economic and financial policies, and it would be difficult in normal circumstances to get their agreement to substantial federal surpluses or deficits.

However, a determined federal government could overcome this difficulty. At present, even when government sector budgets appear to be approximately in balance, government policies exert a powerful inflationary influence on the economy through their instructions to the banking system to cover various forms of expenditure by increasing the volume of credit. One of the most important examples of such expenditure is the payment of interest on loans originally raised in foreign exchange and re-lent to domestic borrowers, mainly social sector enterprises, in dinars. As the value of the dinar sinks, the interest paid by the final borrowers in dinars becomes less and less adequate to pay the foreign exchange interest. The 'solution' found for this problem has been to finance the uncovered interest by expanding the money supply. In other words, when the dinar interest payments by final borrowers are insufficient to cover the interest paid on these loans, the National Bank simply buys additional foreign exchange with new money.

Other expenditures that are dealt with in a similar fashion will be described in the second section of this chapter. It is obvious, however, that the decision to make the banking system responsible for covering such expenditures out of new credits has a major inflationary effect on the economy. This effect would be avoided if the responsibility for these expenditures was taken into the budget, and the necessary taxation was raised to cover them. Instead of collecting these resources by disguised taxation, through inflation, they would then be collected by open taxation, and the public sector would no longer be exerting a substantial inflationary influence.

Tax structure

Some Yugoslav economists and politicians believe that an important cause of the country's poor economic performance is the inappropriateness of its tax structure. For example, the Long-term Programme of Economic Stabilization recommended that there should be a shift away from indirect taxation towards direct taxation. But there are no convincing reasons for believing that this would have a beneficial effect on economic performance. In many Western countries, in fact, the majority of 'informed opinion' favours a shifts in the opposite direction. Underlying this argument there may well be a different one, namely, that there is a need for a more progressive tax structure, and that this cannot be achieved without a greater emphasis on direct taxation.

Up to now, the republics and provinces (or at least the more prosperous ones) have shown a strong resistance to allowing the federal government to enter the field of income tax. In Yugoslavia, as will be seen in Chapter 10, there is a wide dispersion of incomes between different regions. At the extremes, per capita income in Slovenia is about five times as large in real terms as per capita income in Kosovo. If the federal government were allowed to levy an income tax, there would always be a risk that it would move towards introducing some degree of progression in the tax structure; and this would automatically cause a large redistribution of resources between the richer and poorer republics and provinces. That is probably the (unspoken) reason why federal government tax powers have been kept strictly within the field of indirect taxation, which is mainly proportional in its incidence. The only government authorities that collect income tax at present are the republics and provinces. They have imposed a small amount of progressiveness; but it is related strictly to the average level of income within each republic or province.

Some economists have also suggested that the present sales taxes should be replaced by a valued added tax. Existing sales taxes vary somewhat between republics and provinces, and even between communes, but probably not enough to cause significant economic distortions. A small part of these sales taxes is raised from industries other than wholesale and retail trade, but in 1985 74 per cent was collected from retail organizations and nearly 13 per cent from wholesale organizations. So it seems that these sales taxes are not very different in their incidence from a value added tax. The taxes now levied on enterprise net income are essentially equivalent to value added taxes, although they are not completely uniform across republics and provinces.

The federal government is trying to persuade the communes to give up their existing sales taxes and rely in future either on transfers from the budgets of the republics and provinces or on revenue raised by taxes on local incomes and property. It is scarcely feasible for the communes to set up the apparatus to assess local household incomes; this is a matter that is best left to the republics and provinces. Taxation of local property, on the other hand, would be a useful addition to commune revenue. But the local bureaucracy would not be pleased by a proposal to impose significant taxes on their villas, flats, and weekend houses. It would also be inequitable if taxes were levied on houses built by modest households, while the occupiers of 'social flats' were allowed to enjoy the privilege of heavily subsidized accommodation, which they often—illegally—rent to sub-tenants at very high rents. There may, after all, be something to be said for allowing the communes to retain their sales taxes, which at present account for about 60 per cent of their revenues.

Another proposal, which has been included in the set of draft amendments to the Federal Constitution, is that the income of 'organizations of associated labour' that arises from monopoly power, or from other special advantages, should be transferred to the federal government. This is an old story. Under the Law on Associated Labour, 'organizations of associated labour' are not supposed to distribute 'extra' income arising from these sources among their workers. Instead, all of such income is meant to be saved and reinvested in the enterprise. But no one has yet been able to identify 'extra' income, and enterprises do not show it as a separate category. If any government were to try to force them to do so, there would interminable arguments about its definition and measurement, especially at a time when price controls and other government interventions are causing enormous distortions in enterprise incomes. Indeed, in the current situation, many enterprises would have a good claim for reimbursement on account of the receipt of 'sub-competitive' incomes. As many economists have pointed out, the first priority is to reduce government intervention and permit real competition. After that, if differences in income per worker in different enterprises still seemed to be excessive, it would be reasonable to introduce a progressive tax on enterprise income within each republic or province, based on the level of the enterprise's net income per worker.

Redistribution between income groups

All republics and provinces have progressive income taxes on total personal income, but their present coverage is quite small. The usual rule is that the tax is imposed only on income exceeding about three times the average net personal income per worker in the social sector of the given republic or province. According to *Danas* (9 September 1986), in 1985 the number of persons subject to this tax was a little over 13,000 (compared with about 9 million persons in employment or self-employment in that year), and the tax raised was about 13 billion dinars (compared with a total gross public revenue in that year of 3,736 billion dinars). The marginal tax rates on these incomes rise to as much as 80 per cent in some republics, but there is a great deal of evasion. It would be much more sensible if, as a staff writer in *Ekonomska politika* (15 February 1988) has suggested, the minimum point for assessing personal income tax were to be brought down to approximately the average income of each republic or province, and the scale of progressivity were to be less steep. There is also a case, as mentioned above, for an effective tax on house property. The present taxes are inequitable, and largely evaded. But this would be a minefield for any Yugoslav government, and it might be better to accept the fact that, at least under present conditions, house property is largely immune from taxation in Yugoslavia.

The multiplicity of tax authorities

In addition to the federal government, the eight republics and provinces, and over 500 communes, Yugoslavia has more than 5,000 'self-management communities of interest'. Every one of these agencies is a tax authority. Although, in principle, the communities of interest are allowed to raise in 'contributions' only the amounts agreed by the delegates from their member 'organizations or associated labour', in practice, such organizations have little option but to agree with proposals presented to them by the community managers.

There seem to be two main disadvantages of this system of fragmented tax authorities. The first is that, since it is difficult for each authority to make its decision within the framework of a general view of social needs and social capacity to pay, the total amount of taxation tends to be raised above what it would be in a more unified system. The second is that the multiplicity of authorities increases the number of administrators and clerical workers, so imposing a heavy cost on an economy that can ill afford to use its resources in this way. According to *Ekonomska politika* (11 March 1985), the creation of the self-management communities of interest has often amounted to no more than the conversion of a previous government bureau into a new organization. 'So society has been burdened with one more bit of government.' The result has been a duplication of administrative personnel in a society that is 'already exhausted by the increase in its apparatus of officials'. Opinion, the paper reports, is moving in favour of the idea that in future self-management communities of interest should be regulated by general laws instead of by social compacts, which have practically no authority, legal or otherwise.

2. Monetary Institutions and Policies

In Yugoslavia, as in other countries, the structure of monetary institutions, rules, practices, and flows of funds are extremely detailed and complex. Moreover, each of these characteristics tends to change rather rapidly over time, as the monetary authorities try to establish controls that are more or less effective. It is beyond the scope of this book to enter deeply into these problems, a full understanding of which would demand of the reader a specialized knowledge of monetary economics. Nevertheless, since it is impossible to obtain a clear picture of the Yugoslav economic system, and of the origin of its present economic difficulties, without giving attention to its monetary institutions and policies, this section will contain an outline of the main characteristics of these institutions and policies. We shall start with a description of the banking system, and then proceed to consider the types of monetary policies that have been used in recent years, and their effects. The section will conclude with some remarks on two topics of special interest: the effects of exchange depreciation on the balance sheets of Yugoslav banks, and the revealing light thrown on the Yugoslav financial system by the recent collapse of the Bosnian firm of Agrokomerc.

The banking system[1]

Banks are virtually the only financial intermediaries in Yugoslavia. The Post Office Savings Bank is of little importance, and other savings banks, although permitted to exist in principle, are negligible. There are no building societies (or savings and loan associations), no private pension funds, and life insurance scarcely exists. Virtually all financial assets and savings are held in banks, or kept in cash in the form of dinar or foreign currency notes. In principle, therefore, the banks are in a very strong position to influence decisions about consumption, saving, and investment, both by households and by enterprises.

Day-to-day banking business in Yugoslavia is carried on by 'basic' banks, of which there are about 170. Some large

[1] In this sub-section I have drawn on the useful summary of the Yugoslav financial system given in OECD (1987, Part III and Annex IV).

enterprises with many component 'organizations of associated labour' also have 'internal' banks, which are largely a means of pooling enterprise liquidity. In addition, most basic banks are members of an 'associated' bank, almost always within their own republic or province, whose main function is to arrange finance for major projects and to handle foreign exchange transactions. 'Basic' banks are essentially local or regional organizations. Their legal status is that they are controlled by their 'founders', which are local enterprises and, in some cases, local communities of interest. The founders send delegates to the bank's assembly, which is supposed to exercise ultimate control over the bank's affairs and to elect its director and its 'credit committee'.

In practice, however, banks are primarily the agents of the local and regional political bureaucracy. No one in Yugoslavia disputes that this is now the position. For example, an article in *Ekonomska politika* (27 July 1987), after pointing out that, according to the law, banks are independent organizations and carry the risks of their own decisions, continues: 'But it is not so in practice. All the more significant credit decisions are made under the orders, or with the approval, of politicians, who maintain their "strongholds" and influence in the banking system through their control over appointments (no management position in a bank can be obtained without political approval).' The director of a bank in Ljubljana has said (*Politika*, 8 October 1987): 'It is clear that none of us has become a director without the approval of the Party's cadres section. Hence, resistance to various pressures has its limits.' What are we to do, he asked, when the local political assembly has approved a particular investment? A banker from Skopje, capital of Macedonia, when asked whether banks can carry on their work independently, replied (*EP*, 22 June 1987) that they can make an independent assessment of a proposal but that, after that, there are pressures from various quarters to alter the assessment. These pressures come from the 'organizations of associated labour', from the top management of the banks, and from governments. 'Then there starts a game whose aim is to reverse the bank's assessment.'

Since the total volume of bank credit is restricted by federal government regulation, and the real rate of interest on bank loans has almost always been negative, and since, in any case, socially owned enterprises are not too worried about their level of indebtedness, there is an enormous excess demand for credits. Some credits are earmarked by federal policy for particular industries or purposes (e.g. for agriculture or for exports), but the rest of the permitted amount of credit has to be allocated by *ad hoc* decisions. In this process, great influence is exerted by the larger local enterprises, which are usually also the larger debtors, and by the local political bureaucracy. Since virtually all credits are given to local or regional enterprises, much of the money thereby created returns as deposits to the credit-giving banks. In the words of the vice-president of the Associated Banks of Belgrade (*EP*, 24 February 1986), 'We have shut our banks up within the boundaries of the republics and provinces, and each bank finances the projects of its own members.' There is, however, inevitably some leakage to other regions and to the rest of the world, so that allocations of net new credits do not fully determine the increase in the local or regional money supply. Despite great efforts to 'bottle up' sources of funds within regional boundaries, some banks find themselves with excess liquidity which they are not allowed to use for expanding credits to local enterprises, and this has led to some inter-regional flows of bank funds (and to the uncontrolled expansion of bank lending to firms such as Agrokomerc).

Deposits at basic banks can be made on various conditions and at correspondingly different interest rates. 'Giro' deposits, which can be transferred by cheque, yield no interest. Other dinar deposits are classified according to their period, ranging from 'sight' to two years or more, and their interest rates vary accordingly. There are other varieties of deposit, which are made for special purposes, e.g. for housing, and which are subject to special conditions. Of great and growing importance are foreign exchange deposits, which can be made both by enterprises and by persons in any foreign currency. They earn interest in dinars, calculated at the current exchange rate, and the principal can normally be withdrawn at any time in the given foreign currency. The existence of these foreign exchange deposits has created some unusual problems for the Yugoslav banking system, which will be considered further below.

The other main part of the Yugoslav banking system is the National Bank of Yugoslavia. Although this is a central bank, it consists in fact of one federal bank and eight national banks, one for each republic and province. To a considerable extent, each republican or provincial national bank acts autonomously, and keeps a watchful eye on the financial position of its own republic or province. The Board of the National Bank of Yugoslavia consists of the governors of the national banks of the republics and provinces, each of whom has an equal vote. Unanimity is required for all important decisions, although in cases of disagreement the matter may be referred to the federal government for decision.

There is much evidence that the federalization of the National Bank has been an obstacle to implementing a coherent monetary policy. According to the vice-governor of the National Bank (*EP*, 22 February 1988), the governors from the different republics and provinces prevent the formulation of effective regulations to put a stop to illegal, or 'grey', increases in the money supply, which has been a persistent problem in Yugoslavia. 'Grey' issues of money occur whenever enterprises that are short of funds to pay their obligations insist that the banks should make them the necessary advances to restore their 'liquidity'. Under political pressure, and in part because the banks are in any case controlled by their customers, the banks usually comply. As a result, the state of illiquidity is partly shifted from the enterprises to the banks. It was recently estimated (*EP*, 22 February 1988) that 80 out of 170 basic banks in Yugoslavia are 'illiquid' or, strictly speaking, bankrupt.

It is not really clear what is the role of the National Bank of Yugoslavia. Monetary policies are determined by the federal government, and targets for increases in credits, decisions about 'selective' priority credits, and the levels of different interest rates are included in the annual Economic Resolution adopted by the Skupština. In principle, the National Bank has the function of implementing these policies. In practice, it gives the impression of being feeble and ineffective. It shows no evidence of resisting the demands either of the federal government or of the national banks (and hence the governments) of the republics and provinces. From the point of view of policy, it might just as well not exist.

Basic banks are obliged to maintain certain reserves, which consist of cash in hand and deposits at the National Bank. Although there is a 'reserve ratio' and a 'liquidity ratio', these are mere formalities which have no practical bearing on the credit policies of the banks, whose credit targets are determined by the federal government. There are also targets for the growth of the money supply (M_1, defined as cash in circulation and deposits in cheque accounts), but these are invariably adjusted upwards during the year, and then exceeded.

Monetary policies

According to the 1984 OECD survey of Yugoslavia (p. 19), 'In Yugoslavia, monetary policy has typically played an important role in demand management.' If this were really true, it would be difficult to account for the fact that, in the ten-year period 1977–87, the total money supply (M_1 at the end of the year) rose approximately thirty-fold, and the cost-of-living index (average for the year) rose more than fifty-fold. In spite of this experience, there are still some people who try to argue that increases in the money supply have no effect on the rate of inflation. In November 1985, for example, a round table of 'eminent monetary experts' in Novi Sad (in Vojvodina) agreed unanimously that under Yugoslav conditions monetary restriction would have no effect on inflation (*EP*, 11 November 1985). They argued that enterprises would not reduce their prices but simply would accumulate stocks of finished goods, financing this by the issue of bills of exchange.

The Mikulić government, which took office in May 1986, was clearly influenced by such attitudes when it set out to curb the rapidly rising inflation of that year by it policy of 'programmed inflation'. According to Professor Aleksander Bajt (*Danas*, 14 April 1987), who was economic adviser to the previous government, the idea behind 'programmed inflation' (to which he was totally opposed) originated in the National Bank in the autumn of 1985. The idea was that, if the government simply 'announced' that the rate of inflation in the coming year would be such and such, and reduced the rate of interest in line with that forecast, public expectations would adjust accordingly, and the rate of inflation would come down to that level. It was this comforting idea that was put to the test by the Mikulić government. On assuming office, it stated that the curbing of inflation was its first priority (*EP*, 11 May 1987). One month later, it raised taxes on some products and put a four-month freeze on the prices of a further 42 per cent of products. At the same time, interest rates were reduced, the supply of money was relaxed, and the National Bank forecast that by the end of the year the annual rate of inflation would be down to 55 per cent. The actual outcome was that in the twelve months ending in December 1986 the money supply rose by 109 per cent (the highest on record) and the cost-of-living index rose by 90 per cent. When at last the government saw how matters were developing, it began to reproach industry for failing to respond to its 'anti-inflationary' measures.

More than a year later, in an interview with *Politika* (14 August 1987), the Prime Minister was still of the opinion that the responsibility for curbing inflation lay with 'everyone', not just with the federal government. 'How', he asked, 'can the Federal Executive Council [the government] be solely responsible for reducing inflation when there are thousands of self-management and government agencies making decisions about economic development, consumption, their market share, the level of prices, and so on?' He pointed out that the federal government was directly responsible for determining the prices of only 11.5 per cent of industrial products and 14.5 per cent of retail prices, and concluded from that that the government played only a minor role in generating inflation. It is no wonder that most Yugoslav economists consider the Mikulić government to be a disaster.

But the economists are not entirely blameless. They are so afraid of the label of 'monetarism' that most of them (with some honourable exceptions) avoid facing up squarely to the role of expansion of the money supply in generating inflation. Quite rightly, they place much emphasis on the importance of introducing genuine market relations in Yugoslavia; and increasing numbers of them are including in this the right to establish competing private enterprises and self-managed enterprises in which the workers own shares. But many give the impression that, if only such market reforms were implemented, the problem of inflation would disappear. They do not seem to have noticed that many predominantly market economies suffer from inflation, and often very rapid inflation. The market is of crucial importance for efficiency, but the control of inflation is a separate problem.

An alternative line of defence offered by the National Bank for its failure to curb inflation (*EP*, 10 November 1986) is that it does not have the power to prevent the money supply from growing faster than its planned rate. Among the reasons mentioned are that enterprises fail to pay their debts to the banks, and that they fail to deposit dinars when they purchase foreign exchange. These reasons throw a revealing light on the level of financial irresponsibility of the Yugoslav system. Another reason given by the National Bank is also instructive. During the last few years, Yugoslavia has been running a substantial surplus in its trade with the Soviet Union because, while there has been a sharp fall in the quantity of oil imported from the Soviet Union, as well as a fall in its price, the Yugoslavs have been unable to find other products worth buying from the Soviet Union. Moreover, since roubles are inconvertible, the National Bank has been obliged to issue dinars to Yugoslav exporters in exchange for blocked roubles, and thus to increase the domestic money supply. This is a penalty that Yugoslavia pays for the large share of its foreign trade which it carries on with countries having inconvertible currencies.

But these excuses for over-running the planned rate of increase of the money supply do not touch the central problem, which is the planned rate of increase itself. This exists primarily because of the government's desire to finance a substantial part of its expenditure by cheap money rather than by taxation. When the federal government wants to give 'selective' credits—at a cheap rate—to 'priority' industries, or for 'priority' purposes, it does not raise the taxes necessary to finance these credits: instead, it instructs the banks to give the credits. Similarly, when the government discovers that a large part of the loans raised from abroad has been used to make dinar loans to Yugoslav enterprises, and that the dinar service payments on the latter loans increasingly fall short of the amounts required to meet the interest and principal on these foreign debts, it instructs the National Bank to cover the difference by issuing new money. At a meeting of a committee of the Skupština in December 1986, the Federal Secretary of Finance said: 'We must face our reality— that we have in this economy and in this country a very serious state of financial disorder . . . In this country debts are not paid; in some cases not even is the interest paid.' But the state of financial disorder starts at the top, in a federal government that

TABLE 8.3. *Nominal and Real Interest Rates, 1975–1985*
(per cent per annum)

	National Bank discount rate (annual average)	Real interest rate using change in cost of living in:		
		Current year	Mean of current and following year	Mean of current and following two years
1975	6	−14.9	−10.4	−9.6
1976	6	−5.4	−6.7	−7.0
1977	6	−8.0	−7.7	−9.3
1978	6	−7.4	−10.0	−12.9
1979	6	−12.4	−15.4	−19.0
1980	6	−18.2	−21.9	−20.6
1981	6	−25.3	−21.8	−22.9
1982	18	−8.7	−12.7	−16.7
1983	26	−10.8	−14.8	−19.1
1984	53	−1.0	−6.2	−10.9
1985	66	−3.2	−7.9	−14.2

Sources: National Bank discount rate: Babić (1987, 17); cost-of-living index: YB85 (102–33) and *Indeks*.

continues to assert its right to print money to pay its bills.

The government's accommodating, or 'soft budget', approach to monetary policy is illustrated by its attitude to interest rates. Throughout the 1970s, even when prices were rising quite rapidly, interest rates were kept low, and real interest rates were negative. This policy was maintained even after the onset of the crisis in 1979. As Table 8.3. shows, the discount rate of the National Bank, which is a fairly good indicator of the whole structure of interest rates, was held fixed throughout 1980 and 1981 at 6 per cent. This was at a time when prices were rising at 30–40 per cent per annum. As a result, the real interest rate in those two years, on any of the three estimates shown in the table, was about −20 per cent. It was not until 1982 that, partly under pressure from the IMF, rates were finally raised. They continued to rise in the next three years, and in 1984–5 they were nearly equal to the current rate of increase of the cost of living.

However, if lenders and borrowers can be assumed to look further ahead than the immediate moment, and if their guesses about the future are anywhere near what eventually happens, the level of real interest rates in 1984–5 may be better represented by one of the last two columns of Table 8.3. In that case, not even in 1984–5 were real interest rates positive.

In 1986 and 1987 the real interest rates again became heavily negative. In the middle of 1986, under the influence of the doctrine of 'programmed inflation', the discount rate was cut to 56 per cent, but the year-on-year increase in the cost of living rose to 89 per cent. In the first quarter of 1987 the discount rate was fixed at 61 per cent, but the cost of living for the full year increased by 120 per cent. The plan for 1988 was that the discount rate was to be fixed each month at 1 per cent above the eqivalent annual rate of increase in industrial prices in the previous month. This system has produced violently fluctuating interest rates, and one suspects that it is either the result of incredible stupidity or designed to discredit monetary policy. At the beginning of the year the government forecast that the rate of inflation for 1988 would be only 32 per cent. But no one believed it. In December 1987 the cost-of-living index was 170 per cent above its level in December of the previous year, and even under the 'price freeze' of the first few months of 1988, prices continued to rise at a rate equivalent to an annual rate of about 100 per cent. As mentioned previously, the agreement made with the IMF in May 1988 sets a target rate of inflation for the end of the year of 95 per cent. The actual outcome will almost certainly exceed this by a substantial amount.

Although the persistent maintenance of negative real interest rates is an indication of the government's underlying attitude to monetary policy, it is by no means certain that, under the conditions existing in Yugoslavia, high interest rates have a great deal of influence on expenditure. So far as enterprises are concerned, their accounts are now in such a state of confusion that most of them no longer care about increases in their costs. Nor do they even care very much about their state of liquidity, so long as they think that they can force the banks to bail them out. All that they really care about is how to find the cash to pay their taxes, their imports, and the monthly incomes of their workers. Until recently, they took it for granted that their supplies from domestic sources could be obtained on credit and that, when these bills matured, any shortage of funds would be made good by the banks. This was the *reductio ad absurdum* of socialist self-management.

This discussion of Yugoslav monetary policy is concluded with a summary given in Table 8.4, of the changes in the cost of living and the money supply in the period 1977–87. From the second column of the table it can be seen that in 1977–8, before the crisis year of 1979, the money supply was growing faster than the cost of living. Indeed, it had been rising much faster than the cost of living for a number of years. For example, from 1973 to 1978 the

TABLE 8.4. *Changes in Cost of Living and Money Supply, 1977–1987*

	(1)	(2)	(3)	(4)
			Increase in money supply[a] as % of:	
	Change in cost of living[b] (%)	Money stock at beginning of year	Consolidated government expenditure	Adjusted social product
1977	15.2	21.6	14.3	6.6
1978	14.5	25.6	16.5	7.5
1979	21.1	19.0	12.7	5.6
1980	29.6	23.1	14.5	6.3
1981	41.9	26.6	15.6	6.2
1982	29.2	26.6	15.9	6.0
1983	41.2	20.1	11.3	4.2
1984	54.5	43.1	19.5	7.2
1985	71.5	46.5	17.1	6.4
1986	89.0	109.1	27.2	11.6
1987	120.0	92.5	23.0	9.3

[a] Change in money stock from end December of previous year to end December of given year.

[b] Change from average of previous year to average of given year.

Sources: cost-of-living index: YB85 (102–33) and *Indeks*; money stock (M1, = cash in circulation and cheque accounts): *Indeks*; consolidated government expenditure: 1977–85, as in Table 8.2; 1986–7: 92.4% of gross government and semi-government revenues as given in *Indeks* (approximately the same proportion as in 1981–5); adjusted social product: Appendix.

money supply rose by 306 per cent, while the cost of living rose by 123 per cent; thereafter, for five or six years the rate of growth of the money supply was less than the rate of increase of prices, especially in 1981 and 1983–5. But in 1986 the brakes were taken off, and in the twelve months ending in December of that year the money supply was allowed to rise by 109 per cent. In the following year, as already noted, the cost of living rose by 120 per cent (average for the year), and by the end of the year the rate of increase for the previous twelve months had reached 170 per cent.

The third and fourth columns of the table indicate the importance of increases in the money supply as a source of funds for extra-budgetary government expenditure. In the years 1977–83 the ratio of the increase in the money supply to consolidated government budgetary expenditure was about 15 per cent. Thereafter, this ratio increased rapidly, rising to as much as 27 per cent in 1986. When the increases in the money supply are expressed as percentages of adjusted social product, it can be seen that between 1977 and 1985 the government normally took about 6–7 per cent of the social product for extra-budgetary purposes (1983 was the major exception). But in the following two years this proportion rose to an average of more than 10 per cent. These figures show that the small surpluses and deficits that appear in government budget accounts (see Table 8.2) are quite misleading indicators of the inflationary or deflationary stance of the Yugoslav public sector. The Yugoslav government has always used its control over the banking system to cover expenditures in excess of its revenues, and this is a major cause of the current economic crisis.

The effects of exchange depreciation on the banks

One of the principal effects of inflation is to redistribute wealth between lenders and borrowers. Unless both parties successfully anticipate inflation by fixing the terms of loans in such a way as to compensate for inflation, the lenders find that the real value of their loans declines, and the borrowers find that the real value of their debts declines to the same extent. Moreover, everyone who holds cash or non-interest-bearing deposits in banks finds himself in the camp of the wealth-losing lenders. One way in which lenders (but not the holders of bank notes) can safeguard their position is to index the value of their loan against an appropriate price index. An alternative is to make the loan in terms of a foreign currency which is expected to retain its real value. If the borrowers accept the loan on either of these conditions, neither party has any basis for complaint if events turn out differently from what they originally expected.

Financial intermediaries, predominantly banks, are not particularly concerned about the effects of inflation on their balance sheets, so long as their loans and deposits are all made on a similar basis. If both deposits and loans are non-indexed, the losses that the banks make on their loans are compensated by the losses that their depositors make on their deposits. If, however, both loans and deposits are indexed, or are expressed in a foreign currency, the banks are equally protected. (Indeed, they will make a gain from the issue of notes in domestic currency, which cannot be indexed.) Banks in most countries, therefore, are careful not to make loans on one basis and to accept deposits on another. But in Yugoslavia the situation is different.

During the period 1974–81, the Yugoslav banks borrowed, or gave guarantees for, a very large foreign debt, mainly expressed in dollars. A considerable part of these funds was passed on as *dinar* loans to domestic enterprises. This meant that the banks were accepting the exchange risk on these loans. And the risk has turned out to be a disaster. In 1974 the official rate for the dollar was 17 dinars; by early 1988 it was over 1,300 dinars. Since the average rate at which the foreign debt was raised was probably about 25 dinars, its dinar value in early 1988 was about 50 times as great, approximately the same as the change in the cost of living over the same period. Consequently, the enterprises that received the dinar credits have seen their real values fall to about 2 per cent of their original value. Correspondingly, the banks have seen their dinar assets in respect of these loans fall to about 2 per cent of the dinar value of their foreign liabilities.

A further source of bank losses has been the acceptance of foreign exchange deposits from domestic residents, which have also been used to make dinar loans. While, in the case of the loans raised from foreign sources, only part has been converted into dinar bank loans, the whole amount of the foreign exchange deposits has been converted in this way. At the end of 1985 it was estimated (OECD 1987, Diagram 5) that the value of bank debts to households in respect of foreign exchange deposits was about $9.5 billion. These deposits were accepted by the banks and were lent, interest-free, to the National Bank in exchange for interest-free loans in dinars. In principle, the banks are entitled to withdraw these foreign exchange 'loans' when necessary to repay their depositors. But, so long as the net inflow of foreign exchange deposits is positive, as it has been up to now, there is no net withdrawal of funds from the National Bank. Nevertheless, the banks still have to find the interest payable on these deposits. Against the $9.5 billion of deposit liabilities outstanding at the end of 1985, the banks had at that time only about $1.5 billion of assets in the form of dinar credits. Since the average rate of interest paid on the deposits was about 9 per cent (Mates 1986), the banks would have needed to charge an average interest rate on their counterpart dinar loans of over 50 per cent in order to cover themselves. This they were not doing. Although interest rates on bank loans have increased considerably in recent years, the higher rates are charged only on *new* loans, and the average rate charged lags well behind.

In the following two years the dollar value of the dinar fell to a quarter of its end-1985 value, and the proportion of the value of foreign exchange deposits covered by the counterpart dinar loans will have fallen to about 4 per cent. Thus, in early 1988 the banks would have to charge an *average* rate of interest on their dinar loans of over 200 per cent to cover themselves. This is probably the reason why the cost of the interest payments on foreign exchange deposits has now been accepted by the National Bank. But since, as *Ekonomska politika* (18 January 1988) points out, the National Bank does not have a source of funds to cover this, it will be obliged to pay this interest also out of new money. Another problem arises from the fact that most of the foreign exchange desposits have been made in Deutschemarks, and that the value of the Deutschemark has risen considerably in recent years compared with the value of the dollar. Consequently, in spite of the fact that the net inflow of deposits in 1986–7 was quite small, the dollar value of the stock of deposits rose in those two years by nearly $2 billion to about $11.5 billion (*EP*, 7 March 1988).

While the uncovered debts of the banks in respect of residents' foreign exchange deposits are known more or less precisely, the amount of the banks' other uncovered foreign liabilities is a matter of guesswork. The *gross* foreign exchange liabilities of the banking system at the end of 1985 were estimated (OECD 1987, Diagram 5) to be about $23 billion, of which $9.5 billion was owed in respect of foreign exchange deposits. These estimates also suggest that $9 billion of the remaining $13.5 billion was owed to the banks by enterprises, which would leave the banks with net foreign exchange liabilities of $14 billion (of which $4.5 billion would be in respect of liabilities other than foreign exchange deposits). But, as Mates (1986) has pointed out, there is considerable doubt as to whether the banks have a legal right to such large claims against enterprises, since much of the foreign exchange supplied to enterprises by the banks was sold to them, not given on credit. Mates estimated that the total uncovered foreign exchange liabilities of the banks at the end of 1985 amounted to $12.5 billion, and this suggests that at that time their total gross liabilities were substantially larger than $14 billion. In a statement to the Skupština in July 1987 (*Politika*, 25 July 1987), the vice-president of the government mentioned that the total foreign exchange losses of banks and 'organizations of associated labour' (presumably at that time) amounted to 10,000 billion dinars, which would have been equivalent to about $15 billion at the current rate of exchange. Whatever the exact amount of uncovered bank liabilities may be, it is clear that the financing of these debts will impose severe fiscal and monetary problems.

A side-effect of the right of citizens to make foreign exchange deposits has been that, as inflation has continued and accelerated, the dinar value of these deposits has grown much more rapidly than the value of dinar assets held by households. While the net inflow into foreign exchange deposits in recent years has been fairly modest, the dinar value of the stock has risen enormously. For example, from the end of 1982 to the end of 1986 the net inflow was less than 1,000 billion dinars, but the value of the stock of deposits rose by more than 4,000 billion dinars (*EP*, 14 March 1988). In these four years the dinar value of these deposits multiplied by a factor of nearly 10, and by the end of 1987 this factor must have been more than 20. Since the stock of dinar assets held by households has risen much more slowly than this, the proportion of household assets held in foreign exchange accounts has steadily grown: while in 1980 this proportion was less than 40 per cent, by the end of 1986 it had reached nearly 70 per cent. As this process continues, the scope for further squeezing of the wealth of households through inflation is being reduced, and, so long as the authorities rely on inflation as a method of financing government expenditure, they will be obliged constantly to speed up the rate of inflation in order to achieve the same real effect.

The Agrokomerc affair

Agrokomerc is a large 'complex' organization, which in 1986 contained fourteen work organizations and thirty-four basic 'organizations of associated labour', mainly engaged in the production of food products. In 1986 it employed about 11,500 workers, and a year later, when its affairs were the subject of wide comment in the press, it was said to be employing 13,000, or even 14,000, workers. Its headquarters are in a small town in north-west Bosnia, a relatively poor region. Twenty years ago, when the firm was of negligible size, Mr Fikret Abdić became its director and proceeded to build it up into a giant enterprise. In 1986 Agrokomerc ranked, in terms of its turnover, as the twenty-ninth largest enterprise in Yugoslavia (*EP*, 7 September 1987).

The first mention of trouble in this previously highly regarded enterprise appeared in the press in August 1987. Thereafter it gradually emerged that the firm had been issuing 'uncovered bills of exchange' to the tune of at least 250 billion dinars, but perhaps as much as 400 billion dinars (*Politika*, 20 August 1987). According to a report in the London *Times* (3 November 1987), these uncovered bills were 'promissory notes without collateral', and their total value was $500 million. It seems that for some time the firm had been issuing such promissory notes and having them endorsed by its local bank in Bihać (where, incidentally, the partisans held the first meeting of the Anti-Fascist Council for the Liberation of Yugoslavia). The bank was completely under the control of Mr Abdić and his colleagues, and apparently complied with all their wishes. Indeed, it even handed over several copies of its official stamp to Agrokomerc, so that the notes could be endorsed without the bother of sending them to the bank. Not only was this clearly illegal, but the bank was breaking the law by endorsing a quantity of 'bills of exchange' far in excess of its limit. There is also some doubt about whether enterprises are entitled to issue promissory notes at all, and whether banks are entitled to endorse them.

Agrokomerc's promissory notes were sold to sixty-three banks in different parts of Yugoslavia, mainly in Slovenia, Croatia, and Serbia. Apparently, it is permissible for banks to buy bills of exchange without limit, and they also have the right to discount such bills at the National Bank. Normally, banks are unwilling to use their funds for financing enterprises in other republics and provinces, but it seems that in this case the banks in the more prosperous parts of Yugoslavia had funds in excess of the amounts they were permitted to use for giving credits to their own customers (*Politika*, 27 August 1987). Moreover, the rate of interest offered on the Agrokomerc bills were 'attractive' (presumably well over 50 per cent). However, when these banks learnt, in the late summer of 1987, that the Agrokomerc bills were unsafe, perhaps even worthless, they were furious.

A campaign was immediately started to punish the people responsible for the swindle, and to discover who had abetted them. Mr Abdić, who was a member of the Central Committee of the League of Communists of Bosnia and Herzegovina, and also a member of the federal parliament, was soon dismissed from both these positions and placed under house arrest. Meanwhile it emerged that the vice-president of Yugoslavia, Mr Hamdija Pozderac, who comes from the same part of Bosnia, had close connections with Mr Abdić and the firm of Agrokomerc. His brother and many other relatives were employed in the firm, and there were suspicions that Mr Pozderac had used his political influence in its favour. After a few weeks of agitation in the press, Mr Pozderac resigned from his high government office, although still declaring his innocence. (He has since died.) According to the London *Times* (3 November 1987), at that time more than a hundred party members were under investigation, and scores more had been arrested. Meanwhile, the bank accounts of the firm were blocked, its workers were not being paid, thousands of turkeys were dying of starvation, and the whole enterprise was in danger of destruction. Some Slovenian bankers pointed out that it would have made better sense to have carried out a 'consolidation', which would have preserved more of the assets of the firm than the policy of attacking it from all sides (*Politika*, 1 October 1987).

The Agrokomerc affair has undermined public confidence in almost all of the political and financial institutions of Yugoslavia. It has thrown a revealing light on the close relations between the local political establishment, the directors of major enterprises, and the banks. It has also shown that these groups of people and institutions have been involved in widespread breaches of the law. The vice-governor of the National Bank, for example, has said (*Politika*, 27 August 1987) that the issue of uncovered bills of exchange is illegal, and that the Bihać bank broke the law by endorsing bills far beyond its entitlement. The manager of the Ljubljana branch of the Belgrade Bank has revealed that he was asked by a high official of the National Bank of Bosnia and Herzegovina to purchase 3 billion dinars of Agrokomerc bills of exchange (*Politika*, 27 August 1987). Apparently, he refused.

Petar Dodik, who is a member of the Presidency of the republic of Bosnia and Herzegovina, said (*Danas*, 10 November 1987) that a main cause of the Agrokomerc scandal was the connection between the management of the firm and powerful politicians, especially the Pozderac brothers. In this way, the firm's managers were able to obtain influence over the banks, not only in Bihać but also in Sarajevo. They were also able to establish control over the Social Accounting Service, which is the official body through which all enterprises have to make their bank payments, and which has the specific responsibility of checking on the validity of bills of exchange. A leading Slovene politician, Jože Smole, who has held many high positions, including a period as governor of the National Bank and another as federal minister of finance, maintained (*Politika*, 25 August 1987) that the directors of Agrokomerc would not have issued such a large number of uncovered bills of exchange without the approval of the local commune, the Bihać bank, the Associated Banks of Sarajevo, the National Bank of Bosnia and Herzegovina, and the Social Accounting Service of Bosnia and Herzegovina. He did not specifically mention the Party, but, since all the top personnel of these organizations are party members, its involvement is clearly implied.

Other commentators have pointed out that the lessons of the

affair do not apply only to Agrokomerc, its management, or the politicians of Bosnia and Herzegovina. Aleksandar Singer, who is a retired Belgrade banker, has said (*NIN*, 4 October 1987) that all the top bankers and politicians must have known that Agrokomerc was overspending. What Abdić did, he said, is done everywhere. His only mistake was in going too far. And Professor Davor Savin, of Maribor University, has pointed out (*Danas*, 25 August 1987) that there are hundreds of 'organizations of associated labour' which have issued illegal 'uncovered bills of exchange'. In other countries, he said, such organizations would immediately be subject to severe penalties.

Although the laws will doubtless be tightened, no cure for the current state of financial laxity will be found so long as Yugoslavia has a 'soft budget' approach to monetary policy, and persists in its attempts to combine self-management with the doctrine of 'social ownership'. No increase in laws, compacts, and penalties can succeed in overcoming the fundamental contradictions of the system.

9

Foreign Trade

While general problems of balance of payments policy were discussed in Chapter 4, in this chapter attention will be concentrated mainly on commodity trade. Section 1 will be concerned with trends in real exports and imports, the importance of commodity trade within the general balance of payments, and the structure of this trade, both by area and by commodity composition. Section 2 will consider the methods that have been used to allocate scarce foreign exchange and their effects on export performance.

1. Trends and Structure of Commodity Trade

Yugoslav statistics of foreign trade are rather unsatisfactory and difficult to interpret. There are two major problems. The first is that until 1983 all exports and imports were valued in so-called 'statistical' dollars, by converting the original valuations into dollars at the rate of exchange ruling at the beginning of the year. The consequence was that, when the value of the dollar against the dinar or other currencies changed during the year, the reported values of trade in dollars did not correspond to their values at the time of entry or exit from Yugoslavia. When the dollar was rising, the reported values were too high, and vice versa. If all exports and imports were originally declared in terms of dinars and then converted into 'statistical' dollars, it should be possible to reconstitute the original dinar values by multiplying up by the 'statistical' value of the dollar in terms of dinars. This has been the procedure followed by the Yugoslav statisticians for many years. But it seems that the assumption underlying this method is incorrect.

For the years 1984–6, the statistical authorities have published

(*Indeks*, 1987, nos. 3 and 9) the values of exports and imports both according to the traditional method and in terms of current dinars, i.e. at the rates of exchange ruling at the time of the export or import of the goods. And these latter values are very much higher than the values obtainable on the old system. The increase in value, for both exports and imports, in 1984 was 18 per cent, in 1985 43 per cent; in 1986 53 per cent for exports and 58 per cent for imports. These figures suggest that there was also some degree of undervaluation of exports and imports in terms of dinars in previous years, although the amount may well have varied with the rate of depreciation of the dinar.

The second problem is that Yugoslav trade values appear to be substantially understated, even in terms of dollars. This was clearly demonstrated in a special analysis made by OECD (1983, 51) of trade between Yugoslavia on the one side and West Germany, Italy, and all OECD countries combined in the years 1978–81. In all cases, the reported values of imports into Yugoslavia were lower than the export values reported by the partner countries, despite the fact that the Yugoslav values were c.i.f. and the partner country values were f.o.b. As regards Yugoslav exports, the values reported by Yugoslavia were usually lower than the values of imports from Yugoslavia reported by the partner countries—but frequently so much lower as to be implausible. This difference was most marked in the case of Yugoslav exports to West Germany. There seems to be no doubt, therefore, that Yugoslav trade values are (or at least were at that time) underreported in terms of dollars, and that the difference was especially large in the case of Yugoslav imports. One can only guess at the reasons for such underreporting; but it seems possible that exporters understate values in the hope of retaining part of the foreign exchange that they would otherwise be obliged to surrender to the authorities, while importers may wish to minimize their import duties (and also avoid enquiries into the source of the foreign exchange used for imports).

For both these reasons, it is necessary to treat Yugoslav foreign trade statistics with a certain amount of scepticism. Special difficulties of interpretation arise in the analysis of trends in trade expressed in dinar values, and hence in the relations between current dinar values of exports, imports, and social product. It may be for this reason that Yugoslav official statistics of trade are frequently expressed in terms of dollars or, strictly speaking, in 'statistical' dollars. However, while these dollar values are better than dinar values for the years up to 1983, they are still not satisfactory, both for the reason given above and because the real value of the dollar has fluctuated considerably during the past ten years.

Despite these reservations, four tables based on Yugoslav official statistics of foreign trade and payments are presented for the reader's consideration. Table 9.1 shows the dollar values of exports and imports in the years 1977–87, and the corresponding official volume indexes for the same period. It will be seen that the dollar value of exports more than doubled between 1977 and 1981, but remained fairly stable thereafter, at least until 1986. But these values were much influenced by the changes in the value of the dollar, both in relation to other currencies and in relation to world prices. The export volume series shows a rather different pattern, with a more modest rise from 1977 to 1981 and a greater degree of fluctuation in the following years. If the

TABLE 9.1. *Values and Volumes of Commodity Trade, 1977–1987*

	Value ($US billion)			Volume indexes (1979=100)	
	Exports (f.o.b.)	Imports (c.i.f.)	Balance	Exports	Imports
1977	5.3	9.6	−4.4	96.7	85.7
1978	5.7	10.0	−4.3	95.8	85.0
1979	6.8	14.0	−7.2	100.0	100.0
1980	9.0	15.1	−6.1	110.7	89.9
1981	10.9	15.8	−4.8	116.0	78.5
1982	10.2	13.3	−3.1	105.1	67.5
1983	9.9	12.2	−2.2	105.1	62.6
1984	10.3	12.0	−1.7	116.7	61.5
1985	10.6	12.2	−1.6	125.5	62.8
1986	10.9	12.9	−2.0	121.7	66.5
1987	11.4	12.6	−1.2	121.7	62.5

Sources: values: 1977–85, OECD (1987, Table M); 1986–7, *Indeks*; volume indexes: YB85 (102–27) and *Indeks*.

volume index is to be trusted, the average annual rate of real growth of Yugoslav exports from 1979 to 1987 was nearly 2.5 per cent, although almost all of this occurred between 1983 and 1985, after which there was a slight decline. On the import side, the dollar figures show a substantial fall from 1981 to 1983, followed by a fairly stable level until 1985 and a substantial rise in 1986 (the year of 'programmed inflation' and the Party Congress). The volume series shows a much greater decline from 1979 to 1983, and a similar rise in 1986.

TABLE 9.2. *Structure of Balance of Payments, Selected Years, 1973–1985* (percentages of total payments)

	1973	1976	1979	1982	1985
Payments					
Imports (c.i.f.)					
Petroleum	7.6	14.1	15.3	23.8	23.1
Other goods	88.5	82.3	80.4	64.5	64.9
Net interest	3.9	3.6	4.3	11.7	12.0
Total	100.0	100.0	100.0	100.0	100.0
Receipts					
Exports (f.o.b.)	60.8	63.8	46.4	67.8	76.5
Transport and travel (net)	19.4	15.1	12.0	15.4	13.5
Remittances (net)	24.6[a]	18.5	11.7	8.4	7.2
Other services (net)	5.5[a]	4.8	5.0	5.4	8.8
Total	110.3	102.2	75.0	96.9	106.0
Surplus or deficit	10.3	2.2	−25.0	−3.1	6.0

[a] Estimated by allocating the total for these two items in the same proportions as in 1974.

Sources: petroleum imports: YB85 (102–29) and *Indeks*; other data: OECD (1983 and 1987, Table M).

Table 9.2 is designed to indicate the relative importance of commodity trade within the framework of the general balance of payments of Yugoslavia. For this purpose, the values of imports and exports have been expressed as percentages of total payments for imports and net interest. For simplicity, the data are given only for every third year from 1973 to 1985. This table reveals a number of striking features. First, there was a very large increase in the share of petroleum imports from 1973 to 1976, mainly as a result of the first oil shock; and again from 1979 to 1982, as a result of the second oil shock. (Since 1985, as Table 9.3 will show, the cost of oil imports has fallen substantially, although not completely back to the 1979 level.) Second, the cost of net interest payments rose considerably after 1979, reaching 12 per cent of total payments in 1985. (This, again, will have fallen somewhat in the following two years.) Third, on the receipts side, there was a large fall in the relative size of net remittances. In 1973, net remittances from Yugoslav workers abroad covered about one-quarter of total payments for imports and net interest, but by 1985 this proportion had fallen to 7.2 per cent.

The combined pressure of the rise in the price of oil, the rise in net interest payments, and the fall in net remittances forced Yugoslavia to make other adjustments in its balance of payments. But the response in the 1970s was very different from the response in the 1980s. Between 1973 and 1979 Yugoslavia covered the extra cost of oil and the fall in the relative importance of remittances by letting the current account go into deficit. As a result, in 1979 only 75 per cent of payments for imports and net interest was covered by exports and other net receipts. In the new climate of the 1980s, Yugoslavia was obliged to follow a different pattern of adjustment and to concentrate on changing the volumes of its commodity exports and imports. Unfortunately, most of these efforts were directed towards reducing non-oil imports, which had damaging effects on domestic production. There was, however, some increase in exports, especially, as we have seen above, in the two-year period 1983–5. The turnaround in the current balance was heroic, from −25 per cent of total payments to +6.0 per cent. But the cost to the economy of the method of achieving this result was enormous

The distribution of Yugoslav commodity trade by major groups of countries is shown in Table 9.3. Although Yugoslavia does a substantial amount of trade with OECD countries, it also has large trade connections with the Soviet Union and the socialist countries of Eastern Europe. Its trade with developing countries, especially those in the Middle East and North Africa, is also considerable. The pattern of trade in recent years has been

TABLE 9.3. *Commodity Trade by Area, 1979, 1984, and 1987*
(percentages of total export and import values)

	Exports			Imports		
	1979	1984	1987	1979	1984	1987
Developed countries	46.0	36.5	50.1	66.3	47.5	57.4
of which:						
West Germany	11.4	8.7	11.6	22.5	14.0	18.3
Italy	11.0	8.2	13.0	8.9	8.5	10.3
United States	5.7	4.2	6.4	8.2	5.5	5.7
Socialist countries	42.3	47.0	35.4	27.7	34.7	30.2
of which:						
USSR	21.6	27.3	19.4	13.9	17.4	15.3
Developing countries	16.3	16.4	14.5	15.0	24.0	12.4
Addendum:						
Petroleum and products	3.0	3.5	1.9	16.0	29.3	17.4

Sources: 1979 and 1984 area trade: OECD (1987, Table L); 1987 area trade and petroleum data: *Indeks*.

much affected by the price of oil. The rise in the oil price after 1979 was mainly responsible not only for the growth in the share of this group of products in total imports from 1979 to 1984, but also for its decline during the following three years. This factor also accounts for the changes in the shares of imports taken from the Soviet Union and the developing countries in these years. Almost all petroleum imports by Yugoslavia come from the Soviet Union, Iraq, Libya, and Algeria.

The commodity composition of Yugoslavia's foreign trade, averaged over the five years 1980–4, is shown in Table 9.4. Here again, the importance of petroleum imports is apparent. The other major import group was machinery and transport equipment, the largest sources of which were West Germany, Italy, the United States, the Soviet Union, Britain, and Czechoslovakia. Important suppliers of raw materials other than petroleum were the United States (oil seeds, coal), Australia (wool), the Soviet Union (cotton, coal, iron ore), and Egypt (cotton). Major markets for Yugoslav products were Italy (hardwood), the Soviet

TABLE 9.4.   *Commodity Composition of Foreign Trade, Average of 1980–1984*
Values
(percentages of total exports and imports)

	Exports	Imports
Food, drink, and tobacco	10.8	5.2
Raw materials other than petroleum	5.3	11.7
Petroleum	2.5	26.5
Chemicals	10.9	13.0
Semi-processed products[a]	22.4	15.4
Machinery and transport equipment	30.1	25.4
Other finished goods	17.6	2.7
Unclassified	0.4	0.1
Total	100.0	100.0

[a] Including edible oils and fats.

Source: YB85 (121–12).

Union (machinery, transport equipment and parts, ships, furniture, clothing, and footwear), France and Poland (transport equipment and parts), Liberia (ships), the United States (furniture), and West Germany (clothing and footwear).

It is often said that Yugoslavia exports lower-quality products to the Soviet Union and Eastern Europe than to the West. For example, an article in *Danas* (6 January 1987) stated: 'Up to now we have produced one quality of product for the home market, another for Western markets, and a third quality for the East.' But Comecon markets may be becoming more competitive. In 1986 the Soviet Union returned goods worth $7.2 million to Yugoslavia on the grounds of inferior quality, and a smaller quantity of such goods was returned also by East Germany (*EP*, 21 March 1988). In that year inferior goods were returned by forty-nine countries in all, including all Yugoslavia's major Western markets. Another reason for Yugoslavia's large exports to the Soviet Union is said to be that in this way the Soviet Union can obtain Western products which would not otherwise be so easily available to it. In addition, since trade with the Soviet Union is intended to be bilaterally balanced, it has been necessary to find some Yugoslav products to supply to the Soviet

Union in return for its petroleum and other raw materials. For this reason, the Soviet Union is still a 'soft' market for Yugoslavia, especially for Serbia, while higher-quality products are shipped to the West, especially from Slovenia and Croatia. These regional differences in trade patterns are important in determining regional attitudes to alternative arrangements for allocating scarce foreign exchange.

2. The Allocation of Foreign Exchange

Throughout the postwar period, Yugoslavia has been short of foreign exchange, and never more so than in the 1980s. Like many other developing countries, Yugoslavia followed a development strategy that was biased towards import replacement rather than exports. This bias was strengthened by the nature of a socialist regime, which always has a preference for an autarkic system, which can be controlled and 'planned', over free trade, which is subject to the 'unbridled forces of the market'. Despite the fact that Yugoslavia was more market-conscious than some other socialist countries, the development of exports was never given priority in its industrial strategy. The consequence was that very few Yugoslav enterprises were established mainly to satisfy export demand. The need for exports is too often regarded by Yugoslav enterprises as a 'necessary evil' imposed on them by the government.

When a country has a persistent shortage of foreign exchange, two kinds of policy question arise. The first concerns the best method of allocating the scarce foreign exchange currently available. The second is how to move the economy towards a position in which the balance of payments will be closer to equilibrium. The standard economic answer to both these questions is that the price of foreign exchange should be raised in terms of the domestic currency. Then both the earners and the users of foreign exchange will know its real opportunity cost, and they will adjust their behaviour so as to economize on foreign exchange in the short term and to earn more of it in the long term. But in a country such as Yugoslavia, which has a 'structural' disequilibrium in its balance of payments because of past mistakes and accumulated debts, the price of foreign exchange which would bring current demand and supply into equilibrium might be so high as to be very painful to some well-entrenched interests. This is one reason why the Yugoslav government has tried to avoid raising the price of foreign exchange. But the other reason is that the price of foreign exchange can be raised only if the supply of domestic currency is reduced in relation to the available supply of foreign exchange. This means imposing a tight domestic monetary policy, which, as already pointed out, is very distasteful to most governments, and especially to socialist governments.

If a government cannot bring itself to introduce a completely free market for foreign exchange (at least for current transactions), there are many possible alternative policies. Usually, these involve the establishment of multiple markets and multiple prices for foreign exchange. By this means a government can ensure that part of the supply of foreign exchange is surrendered to it at a low price to be used to satisfy the demands of privileged groups, including itself, while the remainder is left for more or less free disposal by the recipient enterprises, either on an official market at a more favourable rate, or on a free or 'black' market. In an extreme case, the government may insist on the surrender to it (or to the central bank) of all foreign exchange. In that case, it has to take responsibility for allocating all foreign exchange to the users by administrative methods.

For many years the Yugoslav system of allocation was to allow exporters to retain a certain proportion of their foreign exchange earnings and to surrender the remainder to the National Bank. Since the purpose of allowing enterprises to retain part of their foreign exchange earnings was to enable them to finance their essential import needs, the retention ratios varied between industries. But there was always much debate about the level at which each ratio should be set, and much bitterness when an industry considered itself badly treated. The problem is, of course, that, with only a few exceptions, there is no unique relation between an industry's inputs of imported materials or components and its exports. Imported materials are pooled with home-produced materials, and output consists of both exports and sales on the domestic market. There was, therefore, usually some scope for an enterprise to substitute domestically produced materials for imported materials, and there was never any guarantee that foreign exchange retained by enterprises would be used solely for producing exports.

Moreover, when one group of enterprises is given the privilege of retaining foreign exchange while others are obliged to apply for administrative allocations, which they know that they will frequently not receive, or to buy foreign exchange on the black market at a high price, the latter enterprises begin to think of all sorts of reasons why they too should receive part of the foreign exchange proceeds of exports. After all, the exporters are not living in a vacuum: they rely on domestic producers for many of their materials, power, transport, and other services. Logically, these latter producers can claim that they contribute to the value of exports, and are therefore entitled to part of the proceeds. And the enterprises that supply *them* with goods and services can make a similar claim; and so on. An input–output analysis would show approximately how much of every $100 of exports is ultimately produced by each domestic industry, and how much by imports. But the argument would not even stop at that point. For the producers of material X, for example, although not currently selling X to exporting firms, can argue that, if they were not supplying firms that sell only on the home market, those firms would have to buy imported supplies of X, and that, if the firms that now supply X to exporting firms were unable to do so, they would be able to take their place. In the end, it must be accepted that exports are produced through the co-operation, to a greater or lesser extent, of every enterprise in the economy.

This was the kind of discussion that developed in Yugoslavia under the system of retention ratios. And it led to all sorts of 'self-management agreements' between enterprises on the reallocation of foreign exchange. But the agreements were not enforceable, or at any rate were not enforced. For example, in 1985 the steel industry, which relies on imports of both coking coal and iron ore, and which does not export enough to cover these require-ments, made an agreement with the metal-working industry, which is a net exporter, to sell it $67 million of foreign exchange during the year. But up to the end of May 1985, the steel industry had received from the metal-working industry only $360.000. Nor was it able to buy sufficient foreign exchange from other sources. As a result, it decided to increase its exports of steel. But it could do this only by making a substantial cut in its prices, in fact to prices below the cost of steel imports (*EP*, 12 August 1985). There is also a regional dimension to this problem. For much of Yugoslavia's receipts of convertible currency are earned by Slovenia and Croatia, either from commodity exports to OECD countries or from tourism. The retention ratio system ensured that a large proportion of these receipts remained in these two republics, either to be used directly by the exporting enterprises or to be sold to other enterprises in the same republic. It was almost certainly the growth of dissatisfaction with this arrangement in the other republics and provinces that led to the abandonment of the retention ratio system at the end of 1985. This feeling can be discerned in the comments of the Federal Executive Council (the federal government) on the draft of its new law on foreign exchange (*EP*, 15 July 1985). It declared that the linking of the right to pay for imports to the receipt of foreign exchange was 'an unacceptable principle', because the system led to 'the obstruction of foreign exchange flows between regions and banks, the reduction of the role of the dinar as a single currency and means of payment in a unified Yugoslav market . . . and the strengthening of autarkic tendencies'.

Against the strong objections of Slovenia and Croatia (but ultimately without their veto), the retention ratio system was replaced at the beginning of 1986 by a system which claimed to be directed towards the establishment of a free market in foreign exchange. From that date, all foreign exchange receipts were to be surrendered to authorized banks at the official rates of exchange. Enterprises that needed foreign exchange to pay for imports or for other purposes were then to make application to the banks, which were to determine the amount of each enterprise's 'socially verified needs', based on its use of foreign exchange in the previous year and its export performance in that year. But this elaborate system of administrative allocation was not applied in practice, because there was not enough foreign exchange to meet all the 'socially verified needs'. In the event, the government had to resort to Article 110 of the law, which comes into operation when there is a shortage of foreign exchange at the rates determined by the National Bank.

Under this article, foreign exchange is allocated on a system of priorities (OECD 1987, 70–1). The first priority is the servicing of foreign debts and other foreign contracts. Then come the

foreign exchange needs of net exporters, followed by the needs of
enterprises that could be net exporters if they were not obliged to
give priority to the home market. Next are the priority needs of
federal agencies and organizations, then imports of energy, and
finally imports of consumer goods. The application of such a
system must inevitably be arbitrary. According to *NIN* (9
November 1986), since available supplies of foreign exchange
have to be given to priority industries, non-priority enterprises
have received nothing. Yet there is no guarantee that the
'priority' industries contribute more to social product or to the
balance of payments than 'non-priority' industries.

In order to compensate firms for the loss of their retention
rights, the federal government set up a scheme of export
subsidies. But it had great difficulty in finding the necessary
funds for this purpose, and, partly for this reason and partly
because of sheer bureaucratic inefficiency, the payment of the
subsidies was always much delayed. The incentive to export
seems to have been considerably reduced, and in 1987 Yugoslavia
found itself in an increasingly difficult balance of payments
position. In August the Slovene delegation to the Skupština
launched a strong criticism of the new system, which, it
maintained (*EP*, 24 August 1987), had 'irrefutably shown for a
year and a half that it is inefficient, and that the centralization of
foreign exchange, the administrative allocation of import entitle-
ments, and priority for the servicing of debts have brought
disastrous results for exports and for the inflow of foreign
exchange'. Among the reasons given for this conclusion were that
the system imposes long delays in obtaining foreign exchange for
essential imports, thus putting a brake on exports; that the rate of
exchange was not adjusted sufficiently; and that in the absence of
retention rights the exporters had lost their motivation for
exporting. The Slovenes, therefore, proposed that the existing
foreign exchange allocation system should be abandoned, and
that there should be a return to the previous system of retention
ratios. The Slovenes were given some support from Croatia, but
the majority of the republics and provinces were unwilling to
return to the old system. A temporary compromise was found,
without satisfying the Slovenes and Croats, and a new arrangement was promised for later in 1988.

In the meantime, some exporters had found a typically

'Yugoslav' solution to the problem of paying for their essential imports. They made agreements with their foreign customers to be paid in goods instead of money. Apparently, such agreements are not contrary to the law, or else are winked at. According to *Eknomska politika* (20 July 1987), these agreements covered at that time about half of the value of exports to the convertible currency area, so that only about half of these exports were generating an inflow of foreign exchange. Such arrangements, although of advantage to the enterprises concerned, are clearly damaging to the rest of the economy. It is not surprising, therefore, that in the latter part of 1987 the Yugoslav government failed, for the first time, to pay interest on its foreign debt. Moreover, barter agreements are a very inefficient method of trading, and their continuation would have depressed Yugoslavia's economic performance even further.

An example, although perhaps a rather extreme one, of the disadvantages of barter concerns the case of some construction work done in Iraq and Libya (*EP*, 17 August 1987). The original contracts were for payment in dollars. But after a while the Yugoslav government took them over, and converted them into agreements to supply oil. The result was long delays in settlement. The foreign oil producers were slow in supplying oil, and there were delays in loading and off-loading it (and in waiting for a full ship-load). Finally, the Yugoslav government held up payment to the construction enterprises for several more months, and then paid them in dinars at the current rate of exchange, which was considerably worse than the rate applicable at the time when payment was originally due. As a result, one of the enterprises decided to sue the government for compensation.

While a system of retention ratios is certainly a 'second-best', it is clearly preferable to a system of administrative allocation according to 'priorities'. For the latter system greatly reduces the incentive to export and leads to a progressive worsening of the balance of payments. A system of retention ratios at least gives exporters part of the benefits due to them, since they are assured of most of their import needs, and can sell any surplus foreign exchange on the black market to other enterprises, who also benefit by being able to obtain foreign exchange at a price instead of being at the mercy of administrative decisions by bureaucrats. In late 1987, a return to the retention ratio system was favoured by the Economic Chamber of Yugoslavia, as well as by the governments of Slovenia and Croatia. For many months the federal government seemed to be wavering. Eventually, however, in May 1988 it signed a new agreement with the IMF, under which, in return for a supply of new foreign loans, it agreed to relax foreign exchange controls and open an effective foreign exchange market. Since these measures were to be accompanied by a tight control over the supply of bank credits, there seemed to be a reasonable chance that the new policy would succeed in bringing the foreign balance closer to a state of equilibrium.

Regional Problems

When Yugoslavia came into existence in 1918 it was called the Kingdom of the Serbs, Croats, and Slovenes. Serbia, which had been semi-independent from 1817 and fully independent from 1878, and which had played a considerable part in the First World War (and suffered enormous losses), was the nucleus of the new state. Serbia already included present-day Macedonia and Kosovo; and, by the addition at the end of the war of Vojvodina and Bosnia and Herzegovina, the new state acquired a considerable addition of people of Serbian language and religion. Montenegro, which had partially maintained its independence for many centuries, was another added area of people of mainly Serbian characteristics.

Serbia (including Macedonia and Kosovo) and Bosnia and Herzegovina had been under Turkish rule for four or five centuries. They were predominantly small peasant economies, with scarcely any industry. But the other two main additions to the new kingdom—Slovenia and Croatia—had been under the rule of Austria or Hungary for approximately the same period of time. They were also mainly peasant economies, but they had a significant number of industrial enterprises (many of which were the ancestors of today's 'organizations of associated labour'). Both Slovenia and Croatia were Catholic and 'western'. They used the Latin script, and they had been part of the western world from the time of the Roman Empire. Although economically underdeveloped by modern standards, they were more advanced than the rest of the new kingdom (except Vojvodina), and especially in comparison with mountainous Montenegro and Bosnia and Herzegovina, and with southern Serbia, including Kosovo and Macedonia.

In the interwar period there was a small expansion of industry, but in 1941, when Yugoslavia was occupied by the Axis powers, the country was still predominantly a nation of poor peasants. When the communists took over in 1945, they were determined to industrialize and, at first, to eliminate the private peasants. They believed that Yugoslavia's backwardness was the fault of capitalism and that a period of socialism would put it right. This doctrine, of course, implied that the large inherited differences in the level of economic development in the different regions of Yugoslavia would also disappear under socialism. But, as they say in Yugoslavia, 'it didn't work like that'. In fact, although over the past forty years there has been a major transformation of the Yugoslav economy, inter-regional differences are at least as great as they were before, and in some cases even greater.

In the first section of this chapter we shall study some indicators of present inter-regional economic differences in Yugoslavia. At the top of the league is Slovenia, and at the bottom Kosovo (although Macedonia is not in a much better condition). The economic problems of Kosovo merge with—and accentuate—its political problems, which arise from the conflict between the majority Albanians and the shrinking minority of Serbs and Montenegrins. The 'Kosovo problem' has had strong repercussions in Serbia and has stimulated a revival of Serbian nationalism, which now threatens the stability of Yugoslavia. Because of the seriousness of this issue, the second section of this chapter is devoted to an analysis of the background to the Kosovo problem and an assessment of current policies towards it.

1. Inter-regional Economic Differences

Table 10.1 presents some estimates of differences in average levels of labour productivity and income in the six republics and two autonomous provinces of Yugoslavia in 1986. It may first be noted, from column (1), that there is a fairly wide dispersion in population size between these eight federal components. Their resident population ranges from more than 5.5 million in Serbia in the narrow sense (without its two autonomous provinces of Vojvodina and Kosovo) to about 600,000 in Montenegro. Croatia and Bosnia and Herzegovina both have more than 4 million inhabitants, and the other four regions (Slovenia,

TABLE 10.1.   *Regional Differences in Productivity and Income, 1986*
(indexes: Yugoslavia = 100)

Region[a]	(1) Resident population (000)	(2) Real social product per head	(3) Output per worker in social sector	(4) Net personal income per worker in social sector Nominal	(5) Real
Slovenia	1,871	179	145	145	124
Croatia	4,437	117	106	108	102
Vojvodina	1,977	133	103	92	101
B and H[b]	4,155	80	85	87	96
Serbia (N)[b]	5,574	94	93	93	93
Montenegro	604	80	90	81	84
Kosovo	1,760	36	69	73	89
Macedonia	1,954	75	75	70	80
Yugoslavia	22,334	100	100	100	100

[a] Listed geographically from west to east and from north to south.

[b] 'B and H': Bosnia and Herzegovina; 'Serbia (N)': Serbia in the narrow sense, without the autonomous provinces of Vojvodina and Kosovo.

Sources: col. (1): total population from *Indeks* −1.5 times the no. of workers abroad in 1981, from *Jugoslavija 1945–85*, p. 202; col. (2): social product from *Indeks*; resident population from col. (1); relative cost of living from estimated income needs of a family of four in each region in *EP* · (24.8.87); col. (3): social product and no. of workers in the productive social sector from *Indeks*; col. (4): *EP* (28.3.88); col. (5): col. (4) adjusted for relative cost of living as in col. (2).

Vojvodina, Kosovo, and Macedonia) are all slightly below 2 million. Serbia in the 'wide' sense, including Vojvodina and Kosovo, has a resident population of more than 9 million, although less than 7 million of these are Serbs. There are, however, more than a million Serbs living in other republics, mainly in Croatia and Bosnia and Herzegovina.

Because of its federal structure and the close interest taken by Yugoslavs in differences between conditions in the different republics and provinces, there are abundant official statistics about each region. (Indeed, there is even a large amount of

statistical information about each of the more than 500 communes.)
It is easy, therefore, to discover the average level of per capita
social product in each region. In 1986 these varied from 209 per
cent of the Yugoslav average in Slovenia to 30 per cent of the
average in Kosovo—an enormous range of difference for a
single country. These figures, of course, are measured in dinars.
But in a country with such wide differences in standards of living,
the real value of the currency is not equal in every region.
According to an official survey, the income needs in terms of
dinars of a family of four in early 1987 varied from 17 per cent
above the Yugoslav average in Slovenia to 18 per cent below the
average in Kosovo. The nominal differences in real social
product per head, therefore, have been corrected by this set of
estimates to yield the figures in column (2) of the table.

Even with this correction, the range of variation in real social
product per head between the republics and provinces is very
wide. At the extremes, there is still a 5:1 ratio between Slovenia
and Kosovo; and Bosnia and Herzegovina, Montenegro, and
Macedonia are also much below the levels of the northern
regions of Slovenia, Croatia, and Vojvodina. There is, in other
words, a marked difference in Yugoslavia between the 'North'
and the 'South'.

These differences reflect many influences. In Kosovo there is a
high dependency ratio, because the Albanians have large families
with many children. Moreover, among persons of working age in
Kosovo, less than a quarter have jobs in the social sector,
because there are many small peasant households (with very low
incomes) and a high level of unemployment. The proportion of
persons of working age who have jobs in the social sector is low
also in Bosnia and Herzegovina, and slightly below the Yugoslav
average of 43 per cent in Montenegro, Macedonia, and parts of
Serbia. In Croatia, however, this proportion is 51 per cent, and
in Slovenia 67 per cent.

Even when a worker has a job in the productive social sector,
his or her output varies considerably between the different
republics and provinces. As shown in column (3), output per
worker is twice as great in Slovenia as in Kosovo, and, in general,
there is a difference between the levels of productivity in the
North and the South. These differences are reflected in the levels
of net personal income per worker (or net money earnings) in the

different republics and provinces (column (4)), although the real differences, after correction for the variation in the cost of living, are somewhat smaller (column (5)).

Some additional indicators of regional economic differences are given in Table 10.2. The first column shows that the poorest regions tend to have the highest ratios of foreign debt to social product. This is partly because, at least in the cases of Montenegro and Kosovo, large foreign loans were raised for investments in infrastructure and heavy industry (much of which turned out to be unprofitable). The second column also shows that there is a wide variation between regions in the proportion of exports to foreign debt. Once more, it is Slovenia that excels,

TABLE 10.2. *Other Indicators of Regional Differences*

Region[a]	(1) Foreign debt as % of social product	(2) Exports as % of foreign debt	(3) Job-seekers as % of workers in social sector	(4) Workers abroad as % of those in social sector	(5) Natural rate of growth of population 1986
Slovenia	15	180	1.7	5	3.4
Croatia	22	75	7.7	10	2.0
Vojvodina	16	86	15.2	8	0.3
B and H[a]	28	76	23.9	13	9.5
Serbia (N)[a]	23	90	17.7	9	2.7
Montenegro	72	25	24.5	6	9.8
Kosovo	60	20	55.9	13	24.5
Macedonia	34	53	27.0	11	11.8
Yugoslavia	24[c]	83[c]	16.2	10	6.4

[a] See notes to Table 10.1. per thousand persons.
[c] Excluding foreign debt of $5.5 billion owed by the federal government.

Sources: col. (1): foreign debt at the end of 1983 from *EP* (22.2.88) × 380 dinars per dollar to convert to 1986 dinar values, ÷ the dinar values of the social product in 1986 from *Indeks*; col. (2): exports in 1987 from *Indeks* as % of social product in 1986 as in col. (1); col. (3): job-seekers and no. of workers in the social sector in 1986 from *Indeks*; col. (4): workers abroad in March 1981 from *Jugoslavija 1945–85*, p. 202; no. of workers in the social sector in 1986 from *Indeks*; col. (5): *Indeks*.

and Kosovo that brings up the tail. Exports, of course, are not the only source of foreign exchange. Croatia, Slovenia, and Montenegro (especially the first of these) have large earnings from tourism, and all regions receive substantial amounts from remittances. But it is clear that both Montenegro and Kosovo have a critical foreign debt problem.

There are no reliable figures of unemployment, because no effort is made to distinguish between job-seekers who are available for work and those who are still at school or college, or working on the family farm. Nor are there reliable figures on the total work-force (which is always a problem in a country with a large peasant population). The figures in column (3) show the number of registered job-seekers as a percentage of the number of workers in the social sector (both productive and non-productive). These, again, show a remarkable variation between Slovenia, where there is clearly 'full employment', and Kosovo, where there is more than one job-seeker for every two workers at present employed in the social sector. As usual, there is a general difference between the North and the South. Apart from actual job-seekers, there are hundreds of thousands of Yugoslavs working 'temporarily' abroad, mainly in Western Europe. These represent another 10 per cent in relation to the total number of workers already with jobs in the social sector. If they were added to the registered job-seekers, the employment problem would appear to be even worse. (And if the 1.5–2 million surplus workers now in jobs were added, it would be seen to be catastrophic.)

The final column of Table 10.2 gives the natural rate of growth of population in each region in 1986. The rates of growth are lowest in the North, including Serbia, and highest in the South, especially in Kosovo. This is probably a reflection partly of larger peasant populations in the South, but also of religious and cultural differences. It is well known that the Albanians, who predominate in Kosovo and in parts of western Macedonia, tend to have very large families, Such rapid rates of growth of population in areas of poverty and high unemployment are naturally a matter of great concern to the authorities. But attempts to encourage family planning encounter obstacles not only of an economic nature but also of a religious, cultural, and possibly also political nature.

Estimates of the net saving of enterprises given in Chapter 7 showed that the amount of net saving had become more and more negative in the 1980s. Table 10.3 throws some light on regional differences in enterprise saving in 1987. In that year, even the official figures show that total net saving of all enterprises was negative, at a rate of approximately $250 per worker. But there were also wide regional variations. In Slovenia net saving was positive, and in Croatia nearly so; but in Bosnia and Herzegovina, Montenegro, and Kosovo net saving was approximately −$800 per worker. When these figures are compared with the amounts of net personal income paid in the same period, it can be seen (column (4)) that about 40 per cent of net personal income in these three regions was financed out of net dissaving (or losses).

The Yugoslav government has always been very concerned

TABLE 10.3. *Net Enterprise Saving per Worker and Net Personal Income per Worker, 1987*

Region[a]	(1) Net enterprise saving per worker	(2)	(3) Net personal income per worker	(4) Net saving as % of net personal income
	(thousand dinars)	($ US)	(thousand dinars)	
Slovenia	+466	+605	3140	+14.8
Croatia	−31	−40	2208	−1.4
Vojvodina	−139	−181	1885	−7.4
B and H[a]	−651	−845	1736	−37.5
Serbia (N)[a]	−273	−355	1846	−14.8
Montenegro	−606	−787	1522	−39.8
Kosovo	−668	−868	1418	−47.1
Macedonia	−318	−413	1399	−22.7
Yugoslavia	−193	−251	2045	−9.4

[a] See footnotes to Table 10.1.

Sources: col. (1): net enterprise saving from *EP* (28.3.88); no. of workers in the productive social sector in 1986 (from *Indeks*) inflated by 2% for growth in 1987; col. (2): col. (1) ÷ 770; col. (3): *Indeks*; col. (4): col. (1) as % of col. (3).

about the wide regional differences in economic achievement.
Since the early 1970s it has attempted to raise the level of the less
developed republics and provinces (Bosnia and Herzegovina,
Montenegro, Kosovo, and Macedonia) by heavily subsidized
loans from a special fund financed by the other republics and
provinces, in 1987 at the rate of 1.56 per cent of their social
product. In addition, the federal government makes grants for
current purposes to the less developed regions. In the 1970s the
total volume of transfers through these two channels was nearly 3
per cent of the social product of the more advanced republics and
provinces, and even in the more difficult 1980s this ratio has
amounted to almost 2½ per cent. When the size of this transfer is
compared with the volume of similar international transfers
between rich and poor countries, it can be seen as being a very
considerable effort; and it imposes a heavy burden on the more
advanced regions, especially on Serbia, which has an average
social product per head below the Yugoslav average.

Despite this large volume of inter-regional aid, there is
no evidence that the *relative* position of the less developed regions
has improved. A comparison of social product per head in the
1950s with that in 1986 (in current dinars, unadjusted for
regional differences in the cost of living) shows a significant
improvement for Montenegro (from less than 60 per cent of the
average to 77 per cent) and, at the other end of the scale, for
Vojvodina (from less than the Yugoslav average to 21 per cent
above it). The main losers in this period were Bosnia and
Herzegovina and Kosovo, while the relative positions of the other
regions (Slovenia, Croatia, Serbia, and Macedonia) did not
change significantly. But most of the changes that did occur took
place over 1950–70; since the latter year there appears to have
been little change in the relative positions of the different
republics and provinces in social product per head.

Why is it that, despite such large financial contributions to
the less developed regions, there has been no appreciable
improvement in their relative economic performance? Difference
in birth rates is clearly one reason. But the more important
reasons are 'economic', and arise from the nature of the economic
system. The bulk of the transfers have been. made to the
governments of the less developed regions to be used at their own
discretion. According to *NIN* (23 November 1986), the developed

regions have no influence on how the Federal Fund for the development of the less developed regions is spent. 'Any suggestion of this kind is rejected as an infringement of sovereignty. The local bureaucracies of the less developed regions have unfettered freedom in spending these funds, and they have made many disastrous mistakes.' An article in *Politika* at the end of 1986 (10 December), when the rate of inflation was moving up towards 100 per cent, reported that loans from the Federal Fund were given at 10 per cent (9 per cent in Kosovo) with a repayment period of twelve years. In some cases this money had been spent on 'magnificent sports centres, public buildings, and libraries', as well as on useless projects such as FENI.

Such hard experience has taught the Yugoslavs that there is no guarantee that 'foreign aid' solves the problem to which it is directed. Since 1976 they have tried to encourage the donor regions to use part of their contributions to the Federal Fund for direct investment in enterprises in the less developed regions. From 1976 to 1980 they were allowed to use 20 per cent of their contributions in this way, from 1981 to 1985 they were allowed to use 50 per cent, and since then the permitted ratio has been 60 per cent. It is reported (*EP*, 28 December 1987) that in the past five years Slovenia has taken full advantage of this arrangement. However, in another report (*EP*, 26 January 1987) it is said that the average proportion of all contributions to the Federal Fund used for direct investment has not exceeded 2.5 per cent. There is, in fact, very little incentive for enterprises in the more developed regions to engage in such investments. Because of the sanctity of the self-management system, any enterprise that makes a direct investment in another enterprise (through so-called 'pooling labour and resources') has no control over the activities of the recipient organization and can expect no return other than interest on its investment (at a sharply negative rate).

In a few cases, investing enterprises may have hoped to ensure supplies of scarce raw materials or energy supplies. At one time, some enterprises in the more developed regions invested in hotels on the Dalmatian coast in order to obtain scarce foreign exchange through the retention ratio system then in operation. But this is no longer feasible. In any case, as *NIN* (26 January 1986) pointed out, many enterprises that built factories in other areas in order to supply materials or for other reasons have had these factories taken away from them, often through their conversion into independent basic 'organizations of associated labour'. The incomes of these basic organizations thereafter belonged to the area in which they were located and were lost to the parent organization. 'Not long ago a campaign was launched in some republics and provinces to convert the branches of "foreign" organizations into separate basic organizations. The campaign was successful, but it put a stop to any interest in investing in "foreign" territory. The outcome has been that, over the past fifteen years, there has been 'a huge expropriation of accumulated labour, several times greater than the expropriation which immediately followed the war'. In spite of this, new efforts are still being made to encourage enterprises in the more advanced regions to make direct investments in the less developed regions. Under a social compact which runs until the end of 1990, the investing organizations will pay lower income taxes. But, since this will be at the expense of their own republican or provincial governments, it is doubtful whether it will be regarded as a significant incentive.

The Yugoslav government has clearly been right to try to switch inter-regional aid from a grant (or 'loan') basis to a direct investment basis. In principle, direct investment brings with it better management, improved technology, and marketing expertise. Yugoslavia itself has benefited considerably from a few such direct investments from foreign countries, especially in the automobile industry. But under the rules of self-management direct investment is heavily discouraged, since the investing firms can obtain no long-term control over the management of their 'subsidiaries', and have no prospect of receiving reasonable profits (or even other alternative advantages). Thus, the self-management system creates insuperable obstacles to the mobility of capital, management, skilled labour, and technology; and this virtually guarantees that the less developed regions will continue to lag behind. The great advantage of capitalism, recognized by Marx, is that it spreads capital and new technology wherever it is allowed to do so. Marxist ideology, of course, adds that this brings 'exploitation'. State socialism has not been very successful in transferring technology between countries, and has brought its own kind of exploitation (as the Yugoslavs discovered in the first few years after the war). But Yugoslav experience has shown that self-management, and especially socialist self-management, is incapable of solving this problem, even within the confines of a single country.

2. The Special Problem of Kosovo

The area of Kosovo (which covers what was previously known as Kosovo and Metohija) is an approximate square with a side of about 70 miles, equivalent to half the size of Wales. It is situated to the south-west of Serbia, bordering Montenegro, Albania, and Macedonia. It is high country, with some moderately good agricultural land and substantial deposits of lignite and non-ferrous metals. Apart from products based on these natural resources, including electric power, Kosovo has little industry except some textiles and leather products. It was occupied by Slav tribes in the ninth and tenth centuries, and it was near the heart of the Serbian Empire of Stevan Dušan in the fourteenth century. Indeed, a large part of Serbian history and culture was centred on Kosovo until the Serbian feudal state suffered a decisive defeat at the hands of the Turks in 1379. The battle of Kosovo Polje, in which the flower of the Serbian nobility was destroyed, is one of the legends of the Serbian national epic.

During the Turkish occupation, many Serbs migrated north-wards across the Danube into the area now known as Vojvodina. The lands that they abandoned were gradually occupied by Albanians, most of whom had been coverted to Islam. By at least the eighteenth century, the Albanians were in a majority. In 1953 they constituted 65 per cent of the population, and in 1981 they were 77 per cent. More recent figures suggest that by 1987 Albanians amounted to as much as 85 per cent of the population of Kosovo.

From the time of the re-establishment of Serbian rule over Kosovo in 1878, the Albanian population of the province was persecuted, and throughout the interwar period their hostility to Serbian rule continued to mount. In 1941 Kosovo was occupied by the Italians and annexed to Italian-controlled Albania. After the German invasion of the Soviet Union, the Albanian Communist Party organized resistance to the Italians, and many

Albanians in Kosovo participated in this activity. At that time, there were good relations between the Yugoslav partisans, led by Tito, and the Albanian resistance. But the Yugoslavs were worried by the links between the Albanians of Kosovo and the Albanians of Albania. The Albanian Communist Party was in favour of the adherence of Kosovo to Albania after the liberation, and the Yugoslav Party was adamantly opposed to any loss of prewar Yugoslav territory (although insisting on the Italian surrender of Istria).

During most of the war, the partisan movement in Kosovo was weak, but at the end of 1943, after the surrender of the Italians, the Yugoslav Party organized a conference at Bujan, in Albanian territory, with the aim of establishing a national liberation committee for Kosovo. This conference, all but three or four of the forty-nine delegates being members of the Yugoslav Communist Party, adopted a resolution which included the following passage (*Danas*, 2 June 1987):

Kosovo and Metohija is a region inhabited mainly by Šiptars [Albanians], and today, as always in the past, it wants to be united with Šipnija [Albania]. Consequently, we consider it our duty to indicate the correct path which the Šiptar people must follow if it is to realize its aspiration. The only way that the Šiptars of Kosovo and Metohija can be united with Šipnija is through a common struggle with the other nations of Yugoslavia against the occupiers and their lackeys. For that is the only way to achieve freedom, after which all the nations, including the Šiptars, will be able to decide their future, with the right of self-determination, including secession. This is guaranteed by the National Liberation Council of Yugoslavia, as well as by the National Liberation Council of Šipnija with which it is closely linked.

With the help of this resolution, Albanian support for the partisan movement in Kosovo began to increase, although most of the partisans in that area continued to be Serbs and Montenegrins.

This resolution was not repudiated by the Yugoslav Party during the war. Indeed, it was not repudiated until 1987, when, under pressure from the Serbian Party, the Presidency of the Provincial Committee of the League of Communists of Kosovo issued a statement 'invalidating' the Bujan Conference (*Politika*, 20 June 1987). This statement referred to a letter sent by the Yugoslav Party Central Committee to the Kosovo Party in

March 1944 expressing some reservations about the decisions of the Bujan conference. But the letter did not explicitly repudiate the promise of self-determination for the Albanian people after the war. Subsequently, the regional committee of the Communist Party of Kosovo and Metohija passed a resolution in June 1944 which referred to 'some mistakes, errors, and failures', but without explicit reference to the Bujan conference. It was on the basis of these two documents that the 1987 statement declared that 'From that moment the position taken by the Bujan conference is considered to be invalidated.'

At the end of the war, when the Yugoslav Party had established its complete control over Kosovo, the Assembly of Kosovo and Metohija decided *unanimously* that Kosovo and Metohija should form part of Serbia. No opportunity was ever given for the 'Šiptars' to exercise their promised right of self-determination. But some concessions were made to the Albanians. Albanian become one of the official languages of Kosovo, and Albanian schools were established. Under the 1946 Constitution, Kosovo and Metohija became an autonomous region of Serbia, like Vojvodina. Finally, in 1974 both Kosovo and Vojvodina were given the status of autonomous provinces, nominally within the republic of Serbia, but in practice with semi-republican rights of direct access to the Yugoslav federal Skupština, the federal government, and even to the leading bodies of the Party.

But Albanian 'nationalist' feeling was not pacified. More and more Albanians were recruited into the Kosovo Party, until eventually they became a majority. The Albanian birth rate was much higher than the birth rate of Serbs ánd Montenegrins, and the composition of the population steadily shifted in their favour. There was also some emigration of Serbs and Montenegrins, which accelerated after 1981. Major demonstrations by Albanian 'nationalists' took place in 1968 and 1981, and smaller demonstrations in the mid-1970s and in 1983. Their principal demand was that Kosovo should become a full republic, like the other republics inhabited mainly by one 'nation', of which Slovenia and Macedonia have only slightly larger populations, and Montenegro a much smaller one (see Table 10.1.). Many Serbs believe that such a concession would soon lead to a demand for secession. But the 1974 Constitution does not, in fact, give a republic the right to secede without the approval of all the other republics and provinces (Article 5). In any case, it is very doubtful that the majority of Albanians in Kosovo would want to become part of Albania. The Albanians of Kosovo have a legitimate grievance. They have never been given equality of status with the other 'nations' of Yugoslavia, and even under the benign 1974 Constitution they are conscious that they are regarded as inferiors, barely tolerated by the Slav peoples of Yugoslavia, and especially by the Serbs. Many of the latter, of course, regard Kosovo as a sacred part of historic Serbia which can never be 'surrendered'.

The demonstrations of 1981 were more serious than on any previous occasion. They were described at the time as an attempt at 'counter-revolution', and in subsequent years many thousands of Albanians have been arrested and punished. There was also a party purge. But the principal party leaders in Kosovo are still Albanians. Many Serbs believe that they are secret 'nationalists' who, in the words of Svetomir Lalović, Serbian Secretary for Internal Affairs (i.e. the man in charge of the Serbian police), 'work in the morning for us, and in the afternoon illegally' (*Danas*, 4 November 1986). There is an undercurrent of anti-Albanian prejudice in Serbia which emerges whenever there is a new 'incident'. The Serbian press is full of anti-Albanian reports, and from time to time Albanian shops in Serbia are wrecked. Very few Serbian leaders are willing to extend the concept of 'brotherhood and unity' to the Albanians in their midst.

The rise of Serbian nationalism

Although the general heading of this section is 'the special problem of Kosovo', it would be more accurate to describe it as 'the special problem of Serbia'. The problems of Kosovo, as we saw in the previous section, are mainly economic. They are problems of poverty, inefficiency, and unemployment, which are reflected in other symptoms of backwardness, such as corruption and law-breaking. But the 'national' problem of Kosovo is a consequence of a long history of Serbian oppression and chauvinism, which has provoked the natural response of Albanian nationalism. Short of mass expulsion or the annihilation of the Albanians of Kosovo, the problems of Kosovo will never be solved until the Serbs accept the Albanians as an equal national component of Yugoslavia, entitled to the same treatment as all the other Yugoslav nations.

But in the past few years the trend has been in the opposite direction. There has been an ominous growth of Serbian nationalism, which is independent of Kosovo, but uses the situation in Kosovo as a means of arousing popular sentiment. The roots of Serbian nationalism go back at least to the Empire of Stevan Dušan in the fourteenth century. Both the nineteenth-century kingdom of Serbia and the twentieth-century kingdom of Yugoslavia were triumphant demonstrations of Serbian revival. But then came the collapse of 1941, the emergence of the communists as the leading force in the resistance, and the ultimate discrediting of Mihailović and the Četniks. At the end of the war, under communist control, Yugoslavia became a federation, and Serbia lost not only its dominant position but also large areas that had previously been regarded as part of its territory. Macedonia became a separate republic, and Vojvodina and Kosovo became autonomous regions, and eventually autonomous provinces. Nevertheless, the Serbs continued to dominate the army and (until 1966 through Ranković) the secret police and the 'nomenklatura'. The fall of Ranković, after the Brioni plenum of the Central Committee of the Party, deprived the Serbs of their Yugoslavia-wide control of crucial appointments in the Party and the security apparatus. From that time onwards each republic, and even each autonomous province, could select its own top officials, judges, prosecutors, and policemen. Yugoslavia was finally 'federalized'.

Since the death of Tito in 1980, and with the growing economic crisis, which is felt by Serbians to have particularly affected them (although there is, in fact, little evidence that Serbia's relative position has fallen in comparison with Yugoslavia as a whole), a growing number of Serb intellectuals have been looking back over the past and asking themselves whether Serbia was discriminated against under 'Titoist' rule. In 1986 the Serbian Academy of Sciences and Arts appointed a commission of Serbian intellectuals to consider some of these problems, and by the autumn of that year a working group of that commission had prepared a draft 'Memorandum' which, although supposed to be confidential, was published in the Serbian press. According to a report in *NIN* (9 November 1986), the memorandum claimed that the prewar Comintern was hostile to Serbia, that the Serbian delegates to the second session of the Anti-fascist Council of National Liberation of Yugoslavia in 1943 (at which major decisions were taken about the postwar composition of Yugoslavia) were elected not by organizations within Serbia but by Serbian personnel who were in the partisan armies in Bosnia and Herzegovina at that time, and that postwar Yugoslavia was largely under the control of Tito, a Croat, and Kardelj, a Slovene.

Although this memorandum was immediately denounced and repudiated, there is no doubt that it touched some sensitive nerves. Moreover, subsequent events suggest that Serbian nationalism is deeply entrenched in the Serbian Party. As will be described below, the leader of the Serbian communists, Slobodan Milošević, has played a major part in whipping up anti-Albanian feeling in Kosovo. In 1987 he and his supporters finally decided to have a 'show-down' with other leading Serbian communists who were urging a more liberal policy. In October 1987 the Presidency of the Central Committee of the Serbian Party summoned a special meeting of the Central Committee to consider the case of Dragiša Pavlović, who was at that time president of the Presidency of the Belgrade City Committee of the Party. Pavlović was accused of having spoken to a group of journalists and others about the dangers of Serbian nationalist attitudes towards Kosovo, and the importance of avoiding 'direct action' and using only correct legal methods to deal with Albanian nationalism. It was suggested that he had implied a criticism of Milošević when he used the phrase 'easy promises of quick success'.

The meeting of the Central Committee lasted two long days, during which eighty-eight delegates spoke, some of them at great length. Commentators have described it as a 'Stalinist trial', not only of Pavlović but also of others who hold similar views. By a large majority, the Central Committee decided that Pavlović should be expelled from its Presidency, and immediately thereafter Pavlović also offered his resignation from his post in the Belgrade City Presidency. The Central Committee then circulated to the Serbian Party a document which was to form the basis of compulsory discussions in all party organizations, with the accompanying demand that there should be a 'differentiation'. 'Differentiation' means inquisition, witch-hunting, denunciations, and punishment (including in some cases expulsion) of any member who fails to agree completely with the current party line. (This resurrection of medieval church practice was Lenin's special contribution to the modern working-class movement and the one-party state.) Some of the early victims of 'differentiation' were the director of the firm that publishes *Politika*, the chief editor of the weekly journal *NIN*, and—the supreme prize—the Prime Minister of Serbia, Ivan Stambolić. Stambolić was a long-time friend and 'patron' of Pavlović. He held the same views about the dangers of Serbian nationalism, and he tried to defend Pavlović from his accusers. The witch-hunt then moved on to try to unseat the editor of *Borba*, and it is clearly the intention of the Serbian nationalists, who have seized control of the Serbian Party, that they should control all newspapers and journals published in Belgrade, even if they are federal organs such as *Borba*. The Serbian Party is also beginning to put pressure on the press in other republics, especially in Slovenia and Croatia.

In December the City Committee of the Belgrade Party (which is the largest city organization of communists in Yugoslavia, with nearly a quarter of a million of members, many of whom are highly influential federal and Serbian bureaucrats) elected as its new president Professor Radoš Smiljković, professor of political science at Belgrade University. In an interview with *NIN* (27 December 1987), Professor Smiljković announced his full support for the new political trend in Serbia, and in particular for 'differentiation', the rooting out of 'opportunism', and the replacement of old cadres by new ones. He claimed that there is a new surge of enthusiasm in the Serbian Party for crushing the 'counter-revolution' in Kosovo (which he also described as 'genocide'), and for solving the economic crisis. He expressed himself in favour of ideological purity, strictly in accordance with Marx, Engels, and Lenin, and for purging members who deviate. He insisted on a greater commitment to Marxist education, and he expressed the belief that the Serbian revival was spreading to other parts of Yugoslavia. This kind of combination of Serbian nationalism with dogmatic Marxism will create serious dangers for the future of Yugoslavia.

Serbian agitation in Kosovo

Parallel with these events in Belgrade, and in mutual interaction, there has been growing anti-Albanian agitation among the Serbs and Montenegrins in Kosovo. A major complaint of the Serbs is that their proportion of the Kosovo population is steadily shrinking. In the census of 1981, Albanians were 77.4 per cent of the population of Kosovo, Serbs 13.2 per cent, Montenegrins 1.7 per cent, Muslims 3.7 per cent, Turks 0.8 per cent, and Gypsies 2.2 per cent (*Politika*, 1/2 May 1987). *NIN* (29 November 1987) claims that the proportion of Albanians in Kosovo has now reached 85 per cent, which would imply that the proportion of Serbs and Montenegrins has fallen to about 11 per cent.

There are two main reasons for the changes in these proportions. The first, and most important, is that the natural rate of increase of the Albanian population is about 2.5 per cent per annum, while the corresponding rate among Serbs and Montenegrins is probably below 0.5 per cent. (The average rate in Serbia without the provinces is less than 0.3 per cent.) From 1981 to 1986 the total population of Kosovo rose by about 220,000, and of this increase about 200,000 may have been Albanians. The second reason, which has attracted much more publicity, is the steady, but slow, net emigration of Serbs and Montenegrins from Kosovo. In the same five years from 1981 to 1986 this amounted to nearly 20,000. After allowing for a few thousand of natural increase, the Serb and Montenegrin population of Kosovo would have fallen from 237,000 in 1981 to about 220,000 in 1986. This, in itself, is scarcely the disaster that Serbian nationalist propaganda makes it out to be. But the degree of sensitivity on this issue is now such that the emigration of a single Serbian individual or family is blown up to a national crisis.

In view of the depressed state of the Kosovan economy and the high rates of unemployment, it is scarcely surprising that there is continual emigration of Serbs and Montenegrins from the province (and presumably also of Albanians, although no one bothers to record that aspect). It is also claimed that there has been a great deal of harassment of Serbs and Montenegrins by Albanian nationalists, who hope to drive them out and establish an 'ethnically pure' Kosovo. This harassment, according to *Borba*

(7 November 1986), takes the form of writing slogans on walls (the principal slogan is 'Kosovo republic'), shouting abuse, distributing pamphlets, stoning cars and buses, destroying tombstones, damaging crops, arson, and rape. The emotive subject of rapes has been given a great deal of publicity, and every case of an alleged rape of a Serbian woman by an Albanian is used as a pretext for fierce agitation among the Serbian population. Official figures for the period from the beginning of 1982 to October 1986 (*Danas*, 11 November 1986) report 118 rapes in Kosovo, of which 16 were by 'Albanian irredentists' on Serbian or Montenegrin women, 5 were by Serbs or Montenegrins on women of their own community, and 97 were by Albanians on Albanians. It was further reported (*Danas*, 10 November 1987) that in the first nine months of 1987 there were 17 rapes in Kosovo, every one of which was between two members of the same ethnic group, and that in this period the incidence of rape in Kosovo was lower than in other parts of Yugoslavia.

The Albanians of Yugoslavia (not only those in Kosovo but also elsewhere, especially in Macedonia) consider themselves to be an oppressed people, who have always been discriminated against by the Serbs, whether under the monarchy or under communist rule. They have never been accepted as an equal 'nation' within Yugoslavia; they have difficulty in obtaining recognition for their language (except in Kosovo, where however there is now a threat that in future the official language will be Serbocroatian, and that all Albanian children will be forced to learn it at school); and they consider that Serbs, in particular, regard them as inferiors and potential enemies. They have also suffered much officially approved harassment. For example, in the five years from 1981 to 1986, 176 Albanian teachers, 11 Albanian professors, and 511 Albanian students were expelled from schools or universities in Kosovo, and 1,600 Albanians were expelled from the Party (*Danas*, 11 February 1986). No student can be enrolled at the university without a certificate from his local authority that he is 'morally and politically suitable' (*Politika*, 8 September 1987). From 1981 to 1986, more than 1,000 Albanians were prosecuted for political crimes, and more than 6,000 for offences with a political element (*Danas*, 1 July 1986). In the middle of 1986, more than 150 Albanian members of an organization called 'Marxist–Leninists of Kosovo' were on trial in Priština (*NIN*, 18 May 1986). Moreover, under Kosovo law it is illegal for Serbs or Montenegrins to sell land or buildings to Albanians (*Politika*, 13 June 1987). When a Serbian family in the village of Zakuti sold some of their land to Albanians, the local committee of the Party decided that this was an act of 'treachery', and demanded that in future the law banning sales to other nationalities should be strictly enforced. They also decided that two Albanians who had recently bought land in Zakuti should be boycotted, and that they should not be accepted as residents of the village (*Borba*, 18 June 1986).

In 1985 the Serbs in Kosovo Polje, a suburb of Priština, collected 2,011 signatures to a petition, in which they complained of constant pressure from the Albanians, amounting to 'fascist genocide', and of the failure of the Kosovo government to protect them. They presented fifteen demands designed to protect the rights of Serbs and Montenegrins in Kosovo. These included a change in the constitutional status of the province so as to make it subordinate to Serbia, the imposition of Serbocroatian as the official language, the dismissal from the Kosovo government of 'Albanian chauvinists' and of Serbian 'opportunists and careerists', and the return to Kosovo of Serbian emigrants (*NIN*, 9 November 1986). The Priština committee of the Party issued a statement which described the organizers of this petition as 'nationalists, chauvinists, and fascists', and alleged that they were in contact with 'hostile elements' in Belgrade. The Presidency of the Serbian party also issued a statement which, while attacking the organizers of the petition, admitted that there were some serious problems in Kosovo which demanded urgent attention (*Danas*, 31 December 1985).

On Wednesday, 9 April 1986, the Kosovo police (who are, of course, controlled by the Kosovo Party) arrested Kosta Bulatović, an agricultural engineer living in Kosovo Polje, on suspicion of 'carrying out a criminal act of hostile propaganda' (punishable under Article 133 of the Criminal Code of Kosovo). They also removed from his house a large amount of material, including copies of petitions signed by Belgrade intellectuals, copies of the 'Petition of the 2,011', and various letters. The latter probably included correspondence with Colonel Filipović in Belgrade, who has been active for many years in agitating for firmer action against Albanians in Kosovo (*NIN*, 13 April 1986). Soon a large crowd gathered outside Bulatović's house, protesting against his arrest. This crowd, and many cars, continued to grow over the next two days. A delegation was elected to go to Belgrade and Priština, and the crowd was promised that high functionaries would soon come from both capitals to meet them. The demonstrations, however, continued, and it was then decided that as many people as possible should go to Belgrade on the following Monday in order to demonstrate in front of the Skupština. Late on Saturday night Bulatović was released without charge, and on the next day Ivan Stambolić, who was at that time the president of the Serbian Party, spoke to a mass meeting of many thousands in Kosovo Polje. On the Monday morning 550 people arrived in Belgrade and marched through the streets to the Sava Centre (a luxurious conference centre) in New Belgrade, at which they had a six-hour meeting (and lunch) with top party officials, including Stambolić.

These events were quite unprecedented in a communist country, where no one is allowed freely to demonstrate or march without the approval of the Party. In Yugoslavia it was especially sinister that the Party should have connived at demonstrations by a single ethnic group, thus undermining their central doctrine of 'brotherhood and unity'. It was the beginning of a process that can only lead to the final alienation of the Albanians from the present regime.

In June 1986 the Serbian inhabitants of a village in Kosovo, Batusi, threatened to organize a mass migration to Serbia if the authorities failed to protect them from Albanian harassment (*NIN*, 27 June 1986). They were rewarded by the promise of a factory, and we shall discuss the implications of this decision later. In November a new delegation of about 200 Serbs and Montenegrins visited Belgrade to protest about two alleged rapes of Serbs (one a woman of twenty and the other a girl of eleven) by Albanians. They met some high officials and were promised that their demands for protection would be considered by the Skupština (*Politika*, 4 November 1986).

In the same month the Serbian Secretary for Internal Affairs, Svetomir Lalović, made a statement to the Serbian parliament (*NIN*, 9 November 1986). He said that the problems of Kosovo could not be solved by the police. Kosovo was 'up to its ears' in debt, and was suffering from corruption, high unemployment, low productivity, an irrational educational system, and a neglected agriculture. This situation had arisen because of the existence of 'an uncontrolled regional oligarchy, blinded by a model of Marxism–Leninism which is irresistible for only one reason: that it permits the exercise of unlimited political power'. Kosovo, he said, approximates to the 'Hobbesian state of nature'. There was a high degree of voluntarism in the payment of taxes, contributions, import duties, and rents. The Slavs in Kosovo were losing hope and were continuing to emigrate. But by repeated sending of delegations to Belgrade, they were weakening their influence inside the province.

It was also in November 1986 that an Albanian member of the Presidency of the Kosovo Provincial Committee of the Party made a speech attacking not only Albanian chauvinists but also Serb and Montenegrin nationalists (*Politika*, 6 November 1986). The latter, he said, 'help to create the idea that it is impossible to live in a community with Albanians, and that the Albanians in Kosovo have been given too many rights'. They attack Tito, local Serb and Montenegrin officials, and the Kosovan leadership, and they encourage emigration.

But the most decisive event occurred in May 1987. A meeting had been called in Kosovo Polje of 300 party delegates, of which the majority would, as a matter of course, have been Albanians. But the local Serbs and Montenegrins converted it into a mass demonstration of about 15,000 of their own people, including a number of Serbs who had come specially from Belgrade. The star speaker of the meeting was Slobodan Milošević, who was now president of the Serbian Party, and a strong supporter of Serbian nationalism. Riding on the crest of the wave of nationalist emotion of the meeting, Milošević committed the Serbian Party to full solidarity with the Serbs and Montenegrins in Kosovo. During the thirteen-hour meeting there were a number of fierce attacks on Albanians in general, and on Albanian leaders of the Kosovo Party and government in particular. No one repudiated these attacks or rebuked the people who expressed such nationalistic views. Two Albanians who tried to address the meeting were booed (*Danas*, 19 May 1987). This was the beginning of the final stage of the nationalist takeover of the Serbian Party, which has already been described above.

The Serbian Party's policy for Kosovo

Since 1985, the Serbian Party has launched a series of new policies intended to solve 'the problem of Kosovo'. In the first place a group of measures has been designed to halt, and possibly even reverse, the trend of emigration of Serbs and Montenegrins. The Kosovo law prohibiting the sale of land and buildings by Serbs or Montenegrins to Albanians has already been mentioned. At Priština University the children of Serb or Montenegrin families returning to Kosovo are accepted regardless of their academic attainment (*Politika*, 8 December 1986), and in 1987 Serbs or Montenegrins with special qualifications were promised that, if they returned to Kosovo, they would be guaranteed jobs, flats, jobs for their wives, and schooling for their children. Any such people who wished to visit Kosovo in order to study conditions at first hand were to be given free hotel accommodation for this purpose (*Politika*, 27 May 1987).

Such measures of positive discrimination are remarkable enough in a communist country, especially one that emphasizes 'brotherhood and unity'. But an even more extraordinary policy along similar lines was the one adoped in order to pacify the Serbian villagers of Batusi. When they threatened to organize a mass emigration, they were offered the construction of a factory in their village to employ about 100 workers in the assembly of electronic components. At first, the inhabitants of the village were worried that it would not be possible to fill all these jobs without importing Albanians. But it soon turned out that the authorities were determined to ensure that there would be no such outcome. The factory was built in the record time of three months by a Belgrade firm, and it was opened on Republic Day 1986 in the presence of a number of high officials from Belgrade, but in the absence of any representative of the Kosovo government (*Politika*, 2 December 1986). When the latter were criticized for failing to attend the ceremony, they issued a statement explaining that they stayed away because they disagreed with the establishment of an 'ethnically pure' factory (*NIN*, 21 December 1986). An Albanian member of the Presidency of the Provincial Committee of the Kosovo Party said (*Danas*, 13 January 1987): 'We are opposed both in principle and in practice to ethnically pure areas and ethnically pure economic activities.' He pointed out that the Kosovo authorities had built many factories in which workers of all nationalities were employed. But of the 140 Albanians who had applied for a job at the Batusi factory, not one had even been called for interview. Subsequently, in response to a question by an Albanian delegate in the Serbian assembly, the Serbian minister stated that the Batusi factory employed 58 Serbs, 6 Montenegrins, and 3 Croats, and that it was therefore not 'ethnically pure' (*Danas*, 17 February 1987).

Despite every measure of positive discrimination, it is unlikely that the flow of Serbian emigration from Kosovo can be completely stopped, let alone reversed. Even Serbian and Montenegrin officials who have been given leading management and political positions in Kosovo frequently have homes outside the province, and send their children away for schooling. The paper *Jedinstvo* alleged that many of these people had used housing credits given to them in Kosovo to build houses or buy flats outside (*NIN*, 3 August 1986). Increasingly, the Serbian Party is becoming preoccupied with the rapid rate of population increase of the Albanians in Kosovo. A much-publicized meeting of the Central Committee of the Yugoslav Party was entirely devoted to the problem of Kosovo (*Politika*, 27 June 1987). But, despite many rhetorical speeches, the only practical recommendation was that a family planning programme should be established in Kosovo to restrain the excessive rate of growth of the population (implicity, of the Albanian population).

Attempts are also being made to undermine Albanian confidence in the rightness of their demands and in their (official communist) leaders. The 'repudiation' of the decisions of the Bujan conference has already been described. Another measure aimed in the same direction has been the discrediting of Fadilj Hodža, an Albanian party leader since the time of the partisan struggle, and a 'national hero'. For more than forty years, Hodža occupied leading positions in Kosovo and also in the government and Party of Yugoslavia. He was closely associated with Tito, but many Serbs believe that he was always secretly an Albanian 'irredentist'. In retirement, in the autumn of 1986, he spoke at a gathering of veterans in Kosovo and referred to the problem of rapes. By way of a coarse and foolish joke, he suggested that the way to reduce this problem was to import prostitutes, since

Albanian women would not be willing to perform such services. This remark was kept secret for about a year, and released to the press in 1987 to coincide with the surge of anti-Albanianism in the Party, led by Milošević. In response, there were large demonstrations by Serbian women in Kosovo, with slogans such as 'We are not prostitutes', and 'Bring in the army'. Soon after, Hodža was deprived of his remaining political privileges and expelled from the Party. *NIN* (8 November 1987), under new management, proceeded to publish a 'Sketch of a Political Portrait of Fadilj Hodža', which was full of smears and innuendoes about his early work in the Party and the resistance movement.

But the fundamental aim of the Serbian Party is to take over direct control of Kosovo; and on 9 July 1987 the Presidency of the Serbian Party adopted a set of proposals to this end. They called on the Party in Kosovo to carry out a 'differentiation', in order to eliminate not only 'counter-revolutionaries' but also members who had been weak or tolerant in their attitude towards Albanian nationalism. Party members working as judges and lawyers in Serbia were to be seconded to work in Kosovo, so as to speed up the settlement of cases against Albanian nationalists. By the end of August all public signs in Kosovo, including street names, were to be written in Serbocroatian as well as Albanian. Land and finance was to be provided to assist Serbs and Montenegrins to settle in Kosovo. Factories were to be built in Kosovo to employ Serbs and Montenegrins, and firms in Serbia and elsewhere were to be asked to send management personnel to Kosovo to help to make its enterprises more efficient. Albanians were to be encouraged to leave Kosovo in order to be trained and obtain jobs elsewhere. All schoolchildren in Kosovo were to be taught not only their mother tongue but also their 'non-mother' tongue. Priština University was to accept more Serb and Montenegrin students, and universities in other parts of Serbia were to take more Albanian students (*Politika*, 7 July 1987). Whether the Serbian Party has either the authority or the resources to carry out such a programme is doubtful. Despite the strict deadlines, the last of which was to be the end of 1987, there does not seem to have been any report on how much of the programme has actually been implemented.

The final instrument on which the Serbian Party pins its hopes is a revision of the Yugoslav Constitution, so as to reduce the status of Kosovo and give Serbia the right to control its affairs. It will be necessary also to amend the Serbian Constitution, but this can be done only if amendments are first made at the federal level. The procedure for amending the Yugoslav Constitution is complex and takes between one and two years, even if no special difficulties are encountered. At the end of the process, no amendment can be made unless it receives the unanimous agreement of the assemblies of all the republics and provinces. But the Serbian demands can be met only by reducing the status of both the autonomous provinces, Kosovo and Vojvodina; and the majority of the people, and of the Party, of both these provinces are opposed to such changes. Kosovo politicians, who are mainly Albanians, have to be careful what they say in public about these matters. They live under constant threat of 'differentiation' and removal from power. But the leaders of Vojvodina are not so constrained and have made quite clear that they will not agree to any proposals that would reduce the province's autonomy.

The process of changing the Yugoslav Constitution was started at the beginning of 1987. In March 1988 details of proposed amendments were finally published. They cover a much wider range of issues than the changes in the status of Serbia's autonomous provinces, which was the original impulse that set the process going; and further discussion of these issues will be postponed until the next chapter. Although the Serbian Party is determined that its desired changes shall be implemented, it seems doubtful that they can be forced through within the framework of the existing Constitution. The Serbian Party may try to use the rule of 'democratic centralism' to force the party leaders of the provinces to accept the Serbian proposals. But, since the Party itself is now very largely 'federalized', there is no guarantee that the Serbs can get what they want by this method. The President of the autonomous province of Vojvodina has declared bluntly (*Danas* 17 November 1987): 'democratic centralism cannot be above the Constitution'.

The tragedy of Serbia is that Serbian nationalists have now taken over the Serbian Party, the government, and the press, and that, instead of trying to find political solutions to their relations with the Albanians of Kosovo, they are driving relentlessly towards a confrontation. If they continue along this line, they will undermine the authority of the present pro-Yugoslav Albanian leadership of Kosovo, and will push all self-respecting Albanians into the camp of the Albanian nationalists. The outcome will be another 'West Bank', with incalculable consequences for the future of Yugoslavia as a whole.

II

Politics

1. The Problem of Political Change under Communism

Elementary Marxism, and even ordinary common sense, suggests that, when a country has been in a state of growing economic crisis for seven or eight years, there is likely to be pressure for political changes. There are some signs of such pressure in Yugoslavia, although not yet as great as might have been expected. But so far there have been no significant changes. Why is this so? There are, in the first place, some fundamental reasons why it is difficult to make changes in any communist country; and in this section we shall consider those reasons. Subsequent sections will be concerned with (1) the growing sense of disillusion in Yugoslavia, (2) the question of whether the Yugoslav Party is capable of changing course, and (3) the prospects for the establishment of a genuinely democratic system in Yugoslavia.

There are three main causes of political immobility in any communist country. The first is the obvious one that the system is a dictatorship, which severely restricts freedom of speech and the press, and completely prohibits freedom of organization and free elections. It is very difficult, therefore, in such a society for alternative views about economic policy or political institutions to be publicly discussed, and impossible for them to be voted on. But this is not all. When there is no freedom of information and organization, with government having control over all organs of opinion, the people are kept ignorant, divided, and intimidated. In such a society it is very difficult for anyone to formulate an alternative political programme, and virtually impossible, except in a severe crisis, to win popular support for it.

The second great obstacle to change is the 'new class'. This phrase, first used by Djilas in a book of that name, refers to the class of party officials, bureaucrats, and officers in the army and police, as well as many thousands of petty party officials, organizers, delegates, and the like, all of whom have a vested interest in the maintenance of the status quo. The main perquisite of the 'new class' is power; but its members also enjoy economic privileges, the importance of which varies with their position in the hierarchy. Djilas described in another book (1985, 15–17) the first steps in the establishment of this class in Yugoslavia. As soon as the partisans entered Belgrade, Tito selected for himself a fine royal palace in Dedinje (a wealthy suburb of Belgrade), a villa, hunting preserves, and various estates. He also took over the royal train. All the other leaders, from the federal level down to the lowest district level, followed his example. A new ruling class materialized, 'spontaneously and systematically'. Together with it came the inevitable envy and greed. The top leaders did nothing to halt the process but merely corrected some of the worst excesses.

In all communist countries, after the first flush of the revolution, and the mass killing of opponents (and anyone found guilty by association), there is systematic recruitment to the 'new class', and the new recruits are trained in Marxism–Leninism and promoted to positions of power. Along with power goes privilege, to ensure loyalty and fear of disapproval by those above. Soon the whole vast apparatus becomes firmly rooted and self-perpetuating. In the words of Velizar Škerović, a member of the Federal Presidency of the Socialist Alliance (*NIN*, 22 December 1985),

The political and other bureaucracies are more and more cut off from the masses, and they have, it seems to me, become completely self-satisfied. They are afraid of public discussion, and their greatest enemy is anyone who points out their monopoly and privileged position . . . Obviously, the bureaucracy develops into a class enemy of the working class and of the self-management system. Every bureaucracy, by strengthening its position, achieves a monopoly of control . . . especially when it achieves a monopoly over cadres' policy . . . It does not regard people as agents who create policy but rather as servants or subjects.

In Yugoslavia, as in all communist countries, party officials enjoy many privileges. They are well paid, they are given the best housing (at heavily subsidized rents), and they can look forward to good pensions. As pointed out by a member of the Central

Committee of the Yugoslav Party in a discussion at its 21st Session (*EP*, 4 November 1985), while most young people leaving school have to wait for years for a job, supported by their parents (who are often pensioners), the children of officials 'have no material problems, nor difficulty in being registered in a preferred university; nor do they have to wait for a job'. Not surprisingly, the percentages of various social groups who are members of the Party are estimated to be as follows (*EP*, 10 March 1986): managers, 76; experts, 42; teachers, 40; industrial workers, 8; and private peasants, 2–3.

In addition to the above two obstacles to change in a communist country, there is a third, which is probably the most difficult to overcome. The ideology of Marxism–Leninism asserts that Marxism is a *scientific* theory, which provides *certain* answers to all economic, social, political, historical, and philosophical problems. Moreover, this superior knowledge is the monopoly of the communist party, the 'vanguard' which can be safely trusted to lead the workers and all working people to the ultimate goal of a perfect society. The members of the Party are both the warriors and the philosophers (the 'scientists') of communist society. They alone are endowed with a knowledge of truth.

How is it possible that such a 'vanguard' can lead society into a state of permanent crisis? This is a riddle to which communist parties have never been able to find an answer. Inconsistently with Marxism, they attribute the disasters of communism to the personal defects of the leaders—to 'the cult of personality', or to the influence of 'the Gang of Four'. Nevertheless, the strict hierarchical structure of communist parties ensures that the 'leader' is usually all-powerful in his lifetime, and that major changes in policy and personnel can be made only after his death, when it is safe to criticize him. In general, one leader can only be replaced by another, who must also be declared to be all-knowing and above criticism. It is ideologically awkward if the new leader pursues a policy different from that of the old one; even worse if he denounces the old one. But at least it is possible by this method to have some change in the system without opening the door to free discussion and free elections. In Yugoslavia, however, this method of transition is excluded.

For nearly forty years Yugoslavia was ruled by the towering personality of Tito. Although Tito was not a great original thinker or theoretician of Marxism, he was a tough and able leader, who combined dedication to communism with a determination to defend the independence and unity of Yugoslavia. Despite his personal vanity and luxurious life-style, he was genuinely popular. But his most indispensible quality was that, although he was a Croat by birth and upbringing, he was not identified with any one nation or nationality. He was the incarnation of Yugoslavia. Before his death, realizing that there was no one who could succeed him in that sense, he proposed the system of rotation of political posts which has been in operation ever since. This ensures that no one person, identified with one 'nation' or republic, can hold power for more than a few years, and in some cases (e.g. the President of Yugoslavia, or president of the federal Party) for more than a single year. The system is well designed to quell fears of domination by one nation or republic. But it also ensures that no single leader can emerge to guide the Party, and hence the country. It is strictly in contradiction with the concept of an all-knowing 'scientific' party, above such 'bourgeois' idiocies as nationalism. In reality, Tito's pragmatic compromise on the leadership question undermined a fundamental concept of Marxism–Leninsm. It was an acknowledgement that the vanguard is not guided solely by Marxist truth, but is capable of nationalist error. But, if the vanguard is capable of error, the concept of 'scientific' socialism collapses.

Given the impossibility of finding a new leader with the 'supranational' qualities of Tito, the Yugoslav Party tries to maintain that its leaders are 'the best', and recommends that in the elections of delegates and governments the criterion of 'the best' should prevail. Nevertheless, since all leading party and government bodies at federal level are carefully balanced in national composition (and in several other respects also), it is obvious that the principle of choosing only 'the best' is not applied in practice. Even if it were applied, it would not provide any solution to the political problem. The disillusion of one Yugoslav with the whole concept was shown in a letter that he wrote to *NIN* (19 January 1986) at the time of the 1986 'elections':

We are in the midst of elections for the party and government bodies.

There is a general determination that the people nominated and elected to the various posts should be the best, the most able, the most creative, the most highly qualified, and the most highly principled; and all after the most careful comparison. The same principles were applied in the last elections. But now we know to what extent and in what manner they were realized in practice.

2. The Growth of Political Disillusionment in Yugoslavia

The Yugoslav system is remarkably robust. Despite seven or eight years of increasing economic crisis, there are no immediate signs of complete loss of confidence in the system. But there is a growing sense of disillusionment. While this disillusionment is not yet so great as to lead to organized (illegal) opposition, there can be no doubt that, if free elections were allowed, the present government would be replaced by a new one.

Disillusion affects different groups in different ways. Many intellectuals, journalists, and directors of enterprises are deeply dissatisfied with the economic policies of the government, and would welcome a shift towards a more freely competitive self-management system. There is much criticism of the present system by young people, especially students, and especially in Slovenia. There is also a great deal of apathy. For example, at a party conference in Bosnia and Herzegovina, it was said (*Politika*, 30 January 1987) that there is an increasing tendency for young people to exhibit passivity, indifference, and neutrality, reflecting their dissatisfaction with current conditions. Dissatisfaction among manual workers has been expressed mainly in the form of strikes, of which there were a large number in 1987. As described in Chapter 6, some of the demands put forward in those strikes were of a political character; and in some cases there were signs of deep dissatisfaction with the official trade unions. As real personal incomes in the social sector continue to decline, there will be more strikes, and more of them are likely to generate political demands.

Probably the most deeply disillusioned group are the directors of enterprises, especially the more capable and more enterprising directors. They are completely frustrated by government intervention, both in its direct form and through government manipulation of the foreign exchange and banking systems. On all sides they are subject to rules and social compacts, which limit their scope for independent decision-making. It is becoming almost impossible for a director to make a success of his business. Even a few years ago, the director of a firm in Ohrid said (*NIN*, 29 December 1985):

Politics are so dominant over the economy that the simplest economic logic is denied. We business people have a common language, irrespective of which republic we work and live in. We find that we are overburdened, that economic laws are not respected, and that it is an illusion to expect results from complicated political agreements. We want to be linked with economics, not politics . . . In work organizations there is now a dangerous defeatism; all motivation has been lost, and there is an increase in shirking . . . In [my firm] there has been an increase in passive resistance, absence from sickness is twice as great as last year, and absenteeism has also increased. We are also confronted by large-scale thefts by a growing number of workers. It seems that the workers have lost hope, which is not surprising when they earn less than 30,000 dinars a month [about $100 at the current rate of exchange]. We have gone beyond the limits of endurance. We are losing control.

One year later, in a New Year survey of the opinions of directors, the Zagreb journal *Privredni vjesnik* invited seventy directors from all parts of Yugoslavia to discuss prospects for 1987. The answers indicated a deep sense of disillusionment with government policies. Examples of points of criticism quoted in the summary report in *NIN* (28 December 1986) included: consistent failure by the government to implement agreed policies, despite repeated promises; constant resort to administrative methods; inflation, unemployment, and technical stagnation; the giving of rights without corresponding duties; failure to distinguish workers from idlers; the levelling of incomes; and the domination of dogmas. All agreed that Yugoslavia could not expect to compete on the world market unless there was free competition on the internal market.

A journalist writing in *Danas* (30 December 1986) pointed out that, in the elections in the previous spring, all sorts of promises were made. Although after the elections there were some changes in the composition of the government, with the inclusion of a larger number of young people, there was not much evidence of a change of policy. At the recent meeting of the Central Committee of the Party it was recognized that six months had been wasted. Inflation was accelerating, and two republics and one province were bankrupt. The creation of ethnically pure villages, and even factories, in Kosovo was driving the wedge of nationalism deeper. The Party itself was becoming the prisoner of nationalism. Some people believed that Yugoslavia was moving towards a new 'balkanization'.

Dr Zoran Popov, Director of the Institute of Economic Science in Belgrade, also wrote in *Danas* (3 June 1986):

In essence, the Yugoslav crisis is a crisis of the political and economic system, which is obvious from the fact that it has already lasted more than six years . . . Since all the evidence suggests that there is no prospect of more fundamental changes in the political and economic system in the near future, there is little real prospect that the Yugoslav economy will emerge from its crisis in the next few years . . . So it is more realistic to expect that we shall have approximately the same economic trends as in the previous six years. This is, apparently, the highest economic level of performance of which the present socio-economic system is capable.

Yugoslavia, he added, has 'a feudal organization of economic life'; and 'The basic characteriistic of a feudal economy is a slow or nearly stagnant rate of development.'

In an interview with *NIN* (2 February 1986), Professor Josip Županov, a distinguished professor of sociology at Zagreb University, said that in the previous five years conditions had greatly deteriorated. Parents were having to support their unemployed children, and two or three generations were living in the same dwelling. Although conditions had been more difficult in the early postwar years, people were now losing perspective, 'and that loss of perspective can be a depressing psychological factor'. People had also been losing their self-respect. They now thought nothing of dumping rubbish in the street and failing to keep their blocks of flats clean. The system established in 1974 was 'made for angels, not men', and this utopian system opened the door to government intervention.

In all sections of the population, there is a sense of growing impoverishment. According to *Borba* (5 September 1986), a large section of the working class is living below a socially acceptable level of existence, and among these there is a lack of faith in the future of the revolution. At the other end of the social scale,

Professor Dragoje Žarković, of the University of Novi Sad, wrote (*Danas*, 27 October 1987) that his monthly income from teaching, including a supplement for holding a chair, was at the level of the income of a cleaning woman in a good enterprise or public institution. As a result, university staff are forced to look for outside work, at the expense of their teaching.

A major source of disillusionment for most economists has been the failure of the Government to implement the Long-term Programme of Economic Stabilization. This programme consisted of a series of reports and recommendations prepared by a commission of eminent persons, several of whom had served in previous governments, as well as in other top party posts. The first report on 'Basic Principles' (literally, 'starting bases') was published in April 1982, and the remaining fifteen reports were published over the following twelve months.

The main thrust of the Programme was the need to reduce detailed government intervention in the economy and to establish a market economy in which independent self-managed enterprises would compete. This, the commission maintained, would not only be in accordance with the logic of the self-management system, but would also be consistent with the Constitution, the Law on Associated Labour, and previous decisions of party congresses. It must be remembered, however, that these previously adopted official statements also included the concepts of social ownership, social compacts, and social planning, by virtue of which Yugoslav governments at all levels acquire the right to intervene in the affairs of enterprises. The commission went out of its way to affirm its support for these concepts, and even recommended the strengthening of pressure on enterprises to abide by their social compacts.

Although the 'Basic Principles' of the Long-term Programme of Economic Stabilization were accepted unanimously by the 12th Congress of the Party in June 1982, and the remainder of the Programme by the Central Committee during the following year, the Programme has never been implemented. Indeed, it is often pointed out that the Mikulić government, which was appointed in May 1986, has moved consistently in the opposite direction, towards more intensive intervention in the economy. The government constantly reiterates that it is firmly committed to the Programme, and blames its inability to implement it on disagreements between the republics and provinces, which impose a 'blockade' on introducing the necessary measures. However, what scarcely anyone points out is that the Long-term Programme of Economic Stabilization is internally inconsistent, since it asks for a free market system within a 'social compact' economy. It is probably also true, as Kiro Gligorov, a leading member of the commission, has said (*Danas*, 14 July 1987), that 'The huge state apparatus in the widest sense, including the apparatus of the League of Communists, the Trade Unions, and the Socialist Alliance, is by its methods of operation an obstacle to the implementation of the Long-term Programme of Economic Stabilization.'

With the passage of time, the Long-term Programme of Economic Stabilization has lost some of its earlier appeal. Economists and others are beginning to realize that issues that were avoided by the commission, such as social ownership, social compacts, and social planning, are of fundamental importance. Moreover, as inflation has accelerated, and the control of inflation has become a dominant preoccupation, it has been increasingly realized that the commission's treatment of this problem was unsatisfactory. The commission's Anti-inflationary Programme, which was one of its special reports, proposed to reduce inflation by improving efficiency, reducing demand (especially for investment), reducing costs of production, and introducing price controls (Bajt 1985, 115). There was to be a gradual slowing down of the rate of growth of the money supply, but it was to be adjusted to 'the possibilities of the economy'. This 'programme' proposed, therefore, two tasks that are outside government control—improving efficiency and reducing costs—and three that are in its sphere of influence—reducing demand, imposing price controls, and providing an 'accommodating' supply of money. The Yugoslav government has, broadly speaking, followed this advice. It has restricted demand (except in 1986), it has frequently resorted to price controls, and it has provided an accommodating supply of money. But this combination of policies has resulted in an increasing rate of inflation, a decline in enterprise efficiency, and a rise in costs of production. The 'anti-inflation programme' has proved to be a disaster.

When the Mikulić government took over in May 1985, it gave

a firm promise that the rate of inflation would be reduced to 20 per cent by the end of the year (*Politika*, 2 November 1986). Instead, inflation continued to rise, and in 1987 reached an unprecedented level. It is the failure of the government to solve this problem, and all its unpleasant consequences, that is mainly responsible for the growing disillusion with it, and also with the present methods by which governments are 'elected'. Increasing public discussion of these questions coincided with the decision to revise the Federal Constitution, although the original motive for starting this procedure was to satisfy the demands of the Serbs for greater control over Kosovo. But the Presidency of Yugoslavia, in its outline of recommended changes to the Constitution (*Politika*, 12 February 1987), made only the feeblest gestures towards improving democratic accountability. It is proposed that the rights and duties created by social compacts and self-management agreements should be more clearly formulated, that the system of election and recall of delegates to assemblies should be 'simplified', and that the *possibility* of organizing direct elections to the chambers of local communities in the communes should be 'discussed'. The process of revising the Constitution continues, but there is widespread dissatisfaction with the absence from the final proposals submitted for public discussion of any significant moves to improve democratic accountability.

This is the background to what Professor Dušan Bilandžić, of Zagreb University, has called (*Danas*, 22 September 1987) a 'sudden and rapid decline in the legitimacy of the political leadership'. This judgement is consistent with the results of a periodic small-scale telephone public opinion survey organized by *NIN* (21 June 1987) with a sample of 100 persons drawn at random from telephone directories covering the whole of Yugoslavia. Some of its results are shown in Table 11.1. Despite the smallness of these samples, and their selection from a special group of the population, the downward trend in public confidence is quite evident.

3. Can the Party Change Course?

In 1987 the League of Communists of Yugoslavia had a membership of 2.1 million, a large number for a country with a

TABLE 11.1.   *Trends in Public Opinion, 1983–1987*

	April 1983 (%)	June 1984 (%)	April 1986 (%)	June 1987 (%)
To what extent has the Federal Executive Council [the government] justified your expectations?				
Completely	36	20	19	10
Not at all	10	11	23	35
When will the country's economic problems be resolved?				
In a few year's time	46	46	26	13
Impossible to say	40	50	72	79

population of about 15 million adult persons. Of the total membership, however, less than 30 per cent were 'workers'. During the previous four years the number of members fell by 775,000, and the proportion of members aged less than 27 fell from 33 to 21 per cent (*Danas*, 5 January 1988). From a survey made by the Marxist Centre of the Central Committee of the Serbian Party, it appears (*EP*, 1 April 1985) that 28 per cent of members (presumably in Serbia) were 'inactive' and 27 per cent 'moderately active'. *Ekonomska politika* commented that 'one can reasonably assume that, in fact, more than half the members do nothing except pay their dues'. From a national survey made at the end of 1985 on a sample of 4,500 people employed in the social sector, it emerged that there were about 1.3 million former party members, and that there was a good deal of dissatisfaction and uncertainty among those currently in the Party. Of the latter, 28 per cent were of the opinion that the reputation of the Party was low, and 18 per cent had considered leaving the Party (*NIN*, 19 October 1986).

These facts reinforce a conclusion that may be drawn on wider grounds, namely, that, if the rule of the League of Communists is to survive in Yugoslavia, there will need to be a major shift in its policies and methods of work. The crisis of Yugoslavia is rapidly becoming a crisis of the Party. But the crucial question is whether the Yugoslav Party is capable of making the necessary changes. Apart from the difficulties that any communist party has in reforming its policies, which were discussed in the first section of this chapter, the Yugoslav League of Communists is faced by three special problems.

The first is the *de facto* federal structure of the Party. Each republican and provincial party is, in effect, an independent organization, with its own congresses, its own central committee and presidency, and its own cadres policy. At the republican and provincial congresses, which are held in advance of the all-Yugoslav congresses, the regional parties adopt their own policies and nominate their own candidates for the all-Yugoslav Central Committee and Party Presidency. Consequently, the federal leadership is strictly a 'federalized' leadership, in which no individual has an all-Yugoslav constituency. A small, but significant, symptom of the degree of federalization of the Party is the fact, reported in *NIN* (15 November, 1987), that articles in the official party journal *Komunist* are sometimes suppressed by republican editors in charge of their own editions. For example, an article about Kosovo was rejected from the Serbian edition, because it commented unfavourably on the behaviour of some Serbs and Montenegrins in Kosovo.

According to Dr Žarko Pukovski (*Danas*, 15 March 1988), the Yugoslav Party has now disintegrated into eight national parties. Professor Dušan Bilandžić (*Danas*, 22 September 1987) has pointed out that, 'In the circle of leading personalities, both at the Yugoslav and at the republican level, there is a permanent state of conflict'. Professor Josip Županov argues (*Danas*, 6 May 1986) that it is these 'intellectual and ideological divisions among the political élite' that are responsible for the 'unclear and inarticulate language used in our conclusions and resolutions':

Our political culture does not permit the public articulation and expression of differences between various interests and points of view. That would be called factionalism and nationalism. So we cram the interests of all sections of the political élite into our resolutions . . . In this way we maintain the illusion of the unity of the élite, and also make it possible for each regional and local élite to interpret general decisions in whichever way suits them . . . So there emerge compromise, omnibus, resolutions which are, in general, not operational, i.e. which it is impossible to implement.

A similar point was made by Mitja Ribičić, a veteran party

leader from Slovenia, when he said (*Danas*, 7 April 1987) that the most common attitude in Slovenia towards the federation was: 'Agree to everything in Belgrade, but look after your own interests when you get back home.' There can be little doubt that this attitude prevails also in the other republics and provinces.

The second difficulty, which is related to the first, is the apparent lack of individual party leaders of sufficient stature to command the support of a majority of the Party for a set of major reforms. This weakness of leadership is considerably increased by the system of rotation of offices inside the Party, at both regional and federal levels. The weakness of leadership imposed by this system was strikingly revealed in a public opinion survey in Slovenia (*EP*, 13 May 1985), in which it was found that 90 per cent of respondents did not know the name of the president of the Presidency of the League of Communists of Yugoslavia. A member of the Presidency of the Central Committee of the Croatian Party, Ivica Račan, has also pointed out (*Danas*, 29 December 1987) that the rotation system undermines responsibility. People appointed to important positions just hope to survive their period of 'mandate' without disaster.

But while federalization and rotation of offices are serious impediments to fundamental changes in party policy, these difficulties could be overcome if it were not for the third and greatest difficulty, which is that the Yugoslav Party is confronted by a fateful ideological and practical dilemma. Any change from the status quo compels the Party to make a choice between two very unpleasant alternatives. The first is to return to a system of central control and central planning—to the old Stalinist system, foreshadowed by Lenin when he wrote (in *State and Revolution*) that under the communists 'The whole of society will have become a single office and a single factory.' But this alternative is now almost excluded: central planning has failed; both the Soviet Union and China are moving away from it; and—the decisive point—it is totally incompatible with Yugoslav federalism, which is the only basis on which Yugoslavia can survive in the long term.

The other alternative, which is even more unpleasant to most communists, would be to move to a freely competitive system of mixed self-managed and privately owned enterprises under a predominantly *laissez-faire* state. This would mean repealing the

Law on Associated Labour, scrapping existing social compacts, abandoning 'social planning', and depriving governments at all levels of the right of detailed intervention in the activities of enterprises and banks. It would also mean abandoning the attempt to enforce detailed accounting rules and income distribution policies on enterprises. Foreign exchange and price controls would be removed, but the federal government, in conjunction with the National Bank, would gradually tighten the money supply until everyone, both in Yugoslavia and abroad, began to regard the dinar as a currency with a reasonably stable value.

Such a policy, combining microeconomic freedom with macroeconomic restraint, would cause severe temporary adjustment problems. Unemployment would rise, and some enterprises would go bankrupt. There would, therefore, be a need for more generous provision of unemployment benefits, and assistance with retraining. But there would also be an enormous release of pent-up energy and enterprise, which would soon turn Yugoslavia from the 'sick man of Europe' into a booming Mediterranean economy. Within a few years, if the economic reform were followed by the establishment of parliamentary democracy, Yugoslavia could join the European Community, and participate in the surge of economic development which is likely to come from that direction.

But the ideologues and dogmatists would regard such a programme as 'counter-revolution', the revival of capitalism, and the abandonment of Marxism–Leninism. And they would be supported by the entrenched ranks of bureaucrats and party officials, whose power and privilege would be threatened by the proposal. In the words of Dr Božidar Jakšić (in *Danas*, 5 April 1988), there is a 'professional political apparatus' inside the Party of several tens of thousands, who are mainly executants of decisions taken at higher levels. In each republic and province there is also a small oligarchic group which, although not having a formal right to do so, in fact determine the policies carried out by the wider stratum of the political apparatus. The role of the broader party membership is merely to approve these policies by acclamation. According to Radiša Gačić, who holds the influential post of secretary of the Presidency of the Central Committee of the Yugoslav Party, 'We have reached the point where, in many cases, the Party is dominated by a middle stratum of officials. This stratum supports the status quo; in fact, it neither wishes nor is able to carry out the desired social changes' (*Politika*, 16 February 1987).

In the final analysis, the greatest difficulty is one of ideology. Stalin used to attribute all the defects of socialism to the 'remnants of capitalism' in men's minds. The problems of the communist states today, including Yugoslavia, are due most of all to the 'remnants of Marxism–Leninism' in men's minds. As Professor Županov has pointed out (*Danas*, 15 March 1988), no reform has ever been successful in a socialist country, because 'socialism is fundamentally hostile to the market'. But, as Lenin used to say, 'facts are stubborn things'. The fact of Yugoslavia's decline and persistent stagnation is undeniable, and will become ever more disturbing to the Yugoslav people. Sooner or later, the Party will have to make major changes in its ideas and its behaviour; or it will be pushed aside.

4. The Prospects for Wider Democracy

Ultimately, as almost all communist reformers realize, it is not enough for the Party itself to change its line. It is necessary for the people as a whole to have a say, and a choice; there is a need for real, not bogus, democracy. The reason is that reform of the Party and reform of the political system are interdependent. No political party, in the long run can be an 'island'. But this, of course, is where the real problems start. Communist reformers want *glasnost* and wider popular participation in economic and political affairs; but they also want to retain the monopoly position of the Party. The two aims are inconsistent. In the final analysis, the question whether democracy can be established depends on the people, not on the Party, although it helps if there are genuine reformers inside the Party.

Although Yugoslavia is not a fully totalitarian country, of the pre-Gorbachev Soviet or Czechoslovakian type (not to mention Maoist China, Cambodia, Cuba, Ethiopia, and the like), it is a country in which basic freedoms of speech, the press, organization, and political choice are heavily circumscribed, or even totally absent. It may be useful, therefore, to remind the reader of the

differences between even a relatively 'liberal' communist country
like Yugoslavia and the countries of parliamentary democracy.

In Yugoslavia there has been for many years much greater
freedom of information than in any other communist country.
There is an abundance of official statistics which, although not
always entirely reliable, do not seem to be deliberately falsified.
In this respect, Yugoslavia has had *glasnost* for more than a
generation. Reporting of social and political events is not so
accurate or uninhibited, but it has been improving in recent
years. The great limitation is that the entire press is in the hands
of people appointed by the Party, or by it satellite organizations.
While individual journalists or papers do from time to time show
some independence, they are ultimately at the mercy of the
Party. In Serbia, as mentioned in the previous chapter, there has
recently been a purge of the press, and no Serbian journalist now
dares to express an opinion deviating from the official line on
Kosovo, and to a large extent on all other questions. The Serbs
are trying to impose similar restraints on journalists in other
republics, especially in Slovenia and Croatia. So far, they have
been resisted by the political establishments in these two
republics; but the future is uncertain.

The Slovene youth paper *Mladina* is constantly in trouble with
the authorities for articles to which they object, and complete
issues have been banned. The editors of this and other papers
have been threatened with prosecution, and, if the Slovene Party
leadership so decided, they could be removed from their posts.
Another means of pressure on journalists is through the League
of Journalists. In 1986 Dušan Bogavac, the editor of the Party's
official journal *Komunist*, was removed from his post on the
grounds that for the previous five years he had held 'anarcho-
liberal and nationalist' views. A group of 91 Serbian journalists
signed a protest against this decision and set up a fund to give
Bogavac financial support. Contributions were received from 200
journalists and others, including the well-known economist
Branko Horvat (*Borba*, 6/7 September 1986). In the spring of
1987 Bogavac himself and two journalists in Vojvodina were
expelled from the League of Journalists for being associated with
this fund, whose supporters, according to a 'Council of Honour'
of the association of Serbian journalists, had 'openly expressed
their determination to oppose the basic directives of a socialist

self-management society' (*Politika*, 10 April and 5 May 1987). Bogavac was also expelled from the Party, and his journalistic career is clearly in ruins. Meanwhie, the Slovene Society of Journalists has proposed that the rules of the League of Journalists of Yugoslavia should be amended to remove the rule that journalists must be 'conscientiously loyal to the ideas of Marxism–Leninism' (*Danas*, 21 October 1986). But this proposal was attacked by a paper in Bosnia and Herzegovina, and it seems unlikely that it will be accepted.

Authors other than professional journalists also suffer from censorship and persecution. In 1985 Professor Dragoljub Petrović, of the Philosophy Faculty of the University of Novi Sad, published an article in *Kniževna novina* which aroused violent criticism. Demands were made at all sort of meetings and bodies for him to be excluded from the university. The journal published a statement defending Petrović's right to publish articles with which other people disagreed, since this was a 'constitutional right'. But the Belgrade police brought Petrović before the local court in Novi Sad, and he was sentenced to sixty days' imprisonment (*NIN*, 8 December 1985). As usual, no information was given about the nature of the statements that were alleged to have constituted his offence.

Professor Ferid Muhić, who is professor of philosophy at Skopje University in Macedonia, gave an interview to *Danas*, in the course of which he commented on the fears expressed in Macedonia about the growth of the Albanian population in that republic. He asked, 'Are these people Yugoslav citizens or not?' If they are, he said, there should be no objection to their increase on the grounds that they were Albanians. These remarks prompted some sharply hostile letters to the paper *Nova Makedonija*. One group of correspondents alleged that Muhić's statements were contrary to the Programme of the League of Communists of Yugoslavia, and to all subsequent party resolutions. 'Is it not time', they asked, 'that Muhić should be the subject of investigation by his basic organization, the university committee, and the city committee of the League of Communists of Skopje?' (*Danas*, 1 March 1988).

The system of censorship of books is illustrated by the treatment of a book by a Serb, Veselin Djuretić, entitled *The Allies and the Yugoslav Drama*. Publication of this book was banned by the Belgrade district court on the grounds that Djuretić stated in it that the Četniks were anti-fascist. This, said the court, is contrary to 'established fact'. So the book was banned (*Politika*, 27 March 1987).

As many quotations cited earlier in this book show, there is a good deal of freedom of discussion in Yugoslavia. But there are strict limits to the opinions that can be expressed. No one is allowed with impunity to challenge the official story of the national liberation struggle, to criticize the behaviour of Tito, or to dispute the right of the Party to be the sole interpreter of the national interest. A leading Slovenian politician, Jože Smole, said at a meeting in Ljubljana (*Politika*, 21 January 1987): 'Today we can discuss everything; there are no longer any taboos.' But he immediately went on to denounce any talk about a multi-party system, which, he said, 'is quite contrary to our socialist self-management interests'. Democracy should not allow the spread of 'reactionary ideas', although in his opinion it was acceptable to discuss 'rational' proposals, such as those of the environmentalists or the peace movement. Despite these discouraging remarks, there is some movement towards freer expression of opinion in Slovenia. Indeed, at Christmas 1986 a Slovenian party leader came on television and wished his fellow citizens a happy Christmas (*NIN*, 4 January 1987). Such a thing had not happened for forty years. The public was astonished, and journalists in Belgrade were asking for official confirmation of this extraordinary development.

While there is a limited, but precarious, right to freedom of discussion, such tolerance does not extend to any attempt to organize a group of citizens for a political purpose, either inside or outside the Party, with which the party leadership does not agree. In this respect, Yugoslavia is still completely Stalinist. An example of the official attitude to independent organizations was the response to the creation of the 'Solidarity Fund' on behalf of Dušan Bogavac. When a group of journalists, including persons working for such prominent papers as *Borba*, *Politika*, and *NIN*, sent out an invitation to people in all parts of Yugoslavia to support the organization, an article was published in *Komunist* (the journal of which Bogavac had previously been the editor) denouncing the Fund and declaring it to be, in effect, an attempt to set up a new political party.

If sanctions such as dismissal, expulsion from the League of Journalists, and expulsion from the Party are not thought to be sufficient to enforce compliance with official policies, resort can be had to the police and the law. While the normal rule is that people who are arrested must be brought before a court within seventy-two hours, a Belgrade lawyer has pointed out (*EP*, 29 June 1987) that the Law on Internal Affairs in Serbia (and similar laws in the other repubics and provinces) gives the police the right to hold a person indefinitely without bringing him to court, if they suspect that his activities are 'a danger to public order'. According to another report (*Politika*, 22 January 1987), the police receive each year about 210,000 reports of violation of order and peace, as well as more than 260,000 reports of criminal offences. There are many complaints, the paper states, that people are arrested without justification and held in prison for twenty-four hours, during which time they are beaten and tortured. When accused persons are brought before the courts, they are entitled to be represented by lawyers of their own choice, but they can be sure that the judges have been carefully vetted by the Party's cadres department. In 'political' cases there is no impartiality. The courts are an essential instrument of the Party's dictatorship.

But the fundamental cause of all these infringements of human rights is the total absence of free elections. The Yugoslav communists, like those in other countries, have erected a great façade of 'socialist democracy', the key characteristic of which is that, while people have the right (and even the duty) to *vote*, they have no right to *choose*. The Yugoslav system of 'elections' provides a guarantee that no candidate for an assembly or government post will ever be nominated without the approval of the Party, and that, except in rare cases, there will never be more than one candidate from which to choose. Under the Yugoslav system of indirect elections, the first level of 'delegates' is 'elected' in the manner described in Chapter 2. The lists of approved candidates for these 'delegations', exactly equal to the number of vacancies, is drawn up by the trade unions (for delegates from the 'organizations of associated labour') and by the Socialist Alliance (for delegates from the local communities). Both of these organizations are party satellites, and it is quite likely that all delegates are ultimately approved by the Party's cadres department. Even if some people of independent views were somehow to slip through this net, the next stage of elections, to the commune assemblies, ensures that there will be no such mistakes. And so it goes on up the pyramid, to the assemblies of the republics and provinces and to the federal Skupština. According to *Danas* (22 December 1987), in the four years 1983–7, all but 9 out of 1,260 delegates to the Skupština were members of the Party. *Politika* (30 January 1987) has also reported that, of 308 delegates to the Skupština, 134 were professional 'functionaries', i.e. full-time officials of the Party or of one of its satellite organizations.

This system of 'democracy' not only stultifies any serious discussion of political and economic issues, both in the assemblies and among the public at large, but it cuts the assembly members off from the people they are supposed to represent. Both aspects are illustrated by the reflections of Vjekoslav Vidjak, a Croatian delegate to the Federal Chamber of the Skupština during the period 1982–6 (*NIN*, 16 March 1986):

When he first arrived in Belgrade, he said, he was full of enthusiasm for his task. He 'hoped to change the world'. But he was rapidly disillusioned. 'The majority of delegates to the highest organ of government relapse into pessimism.' They decide just to fill in their time until the end of their 'mandate'. Vidjak himself, being a conscientious person elected to represent associated labour, thought that he should try to find out the views of his constituents. As a consequence of the system of indirect elections, Vidjak had been elected by delegates from all the 113 communes of Croatia. Since it was clearly impossible to keep in touch with all of these, Vidjak decided to concentrate on five communes in his own part of Dalmatia. He began to visit them regularly; but, although they were hospitable, he found that they were not really interested in his work. Nor did he find that members of the republican government of Croatia had any time for him, because they relied on the Croatian delegates to the Chamber of Republics and Provinces to take care of their interests. 'So I can say', he concluded, 'with a full sense of responsibility, that no one, neither the electors, nor the communes, nor "my" republic, showed any kind of interest in me as a delegate.' He recommended, therefore, that in future each delegate should be elected directly by between one and three communes.

While the replacement of indirect elections by direct elections would be a small step foward, it would not make any great difference so long as there is a ban on multiple candidates. The Slovenes carried out an experiment in this direction in the spring of 1988 by allowing multiple candidates for the post of president of their republic (*Danas*, 22 March 1988). With the approval of the party president, Milan Kučan, a number of candidates were nominated, all members of the Party. When they were invited to be interviewed about their 'programmes' on Slovene television, several withdrew; and only one of those finally interviewed, a woman journalist, expressed any radical opinions. She favoured a mixed economy, absence of administrative interference in enterprise decisions, and political democracy, with independent courts and direct elections. Although she had the support of the youth paper *Mladina*, she was unlikely to win the election (nor, in fact, did she), more especially because the 'electors' were a stratum of 'delegates' at a lower level of the electoral pyramid. But that she was allowed to give her opinions on television was an important step towards democratic practice in Slovenia.

Although Slovenia is in the forefront in allowing democratic experiments, there is also widespread support for more democracy in other republics and provinces. In a national survey at the end of 1985 of workers employed in the social sector, out of a sample of 4,500, 71 per cent said that workers and citizens have little or no influence on the choice of delegates, and 79 per cent said they were in favour of multiple candidates (*NIN*, 25 May 1986).

While direct elections and multiple candidates are indispensable conditions for greater democracy, they are not sufficient conditions. Questions that will still need to be resolved include: Must all candidates be members of the Party? Are alternative candidates, whether members of the Party or not, to be allowed to offer alternative programmes? Will they be allowed to present their programmes in the media before the election? Will they be allowed to gather their supporters and to organize and electoral campaign? Will there be a genuinely free and secret ballot? The standard communist answer to all these questions (except the first and the last) is 'absolutely forbidden'. Above all, there must never be an alternative organization, any 'opposition party'.

Yugoslav defenders of the one-party system often rely on the argument that, if multiple parties were allowed in Yugoslavia, some or all of them would be 'national' parties, and the unity of the country would be destroyed. This, of course, is an argument that is inconsistent with Marxist theory, which maintains that 'class' interests override 'national' interests. But that is a debating point. More relevant is the observation that Yugoslavia already has eight 'national' parties, although they are all officially parts of the League of Communists of Yugoslavia. The country is already 'confederalized', fragmented, and disunited. Democracy has its risks; but it is more likely to produce coherent policies and effective governments than the present system.

But the movement towards democracy will not proceed very far unless it has the support of the workers. Manual workers are not so interested in *glasnost* and freedom of discussion as intellectuals and professional and managerial employees. They worry more about the security of their jobs and the size of their real incomes. It is only when they are convinced that things cannot go on as they are, and that the country is steadily sinking without hope of recovery, that they will be ready to accept radical new ideas about the organization of the economy. But the most important of these 'radical new' ideas is the long-established Yugoslav idea that the workers should have genuine rights of self-management. Since 1974 these self-management rights have been progressively undermined, and have now almost completely disappeared. The economy has been wrapped in a cocoon of social compacts and detailed legislation which has squeezed the life out of self-management. The best hope for the reformers, therefore, is to reach out to the workers with the message that the solution to the country's problems lies in the establishment of genuine self-management; and that democracy in the work-place requires also democracy in the political sphere.

12

General Conclusions

By an accident of history, in the agony of war, a small group of dedicated and well-organized communists was able to win control over the Yugoslav resistance movement and, at the end of the war, to seize control of the state. Having established the usual one-party dictatorship, they proceeded with a Stalinist programme of nationalization of industry, most services, and part of agriculture, and planned to collectivize the remainder of agriculture as soon as they conveniently could. But, suddenly, a great storm came out of a blue sky. Stalin denounced the Yugoslavs as traitors to the revolution and arranged for them to be excommunicated—unanimously—from the international communist movement.

After recoiling from this shock, and gradually coming to terms with the new situation, the Yugoslav communists started in 1950 on a new course. They rejected 'Stalinist' state socialism and launched the slogan of 'The factories to the workers!' Step by step, they moved towards a new system of 'socialist self-management'. They abandoned central planning, gave the workers in enterprises significant nominal rights of control, and directed them to operate in future in the market. But 'society' (which meant in practice the party-state) retained the ownership of enterprise assets, and retained effective control over managerial appointments and credit allocations by the banks. The new system was finally codified in the Federal Constitution of 1974 and the Law on Associated Labour of 1976.

Under these laws, every aspect of political and economic activity was regulated in extraordinary detail. The Yugoslav political system was thoroughly federalized (as had been promised during the wartime resistance); and socialized enterprises were, on the one hand, fragmented into basic 'organizations of associated labour' and, on the other, subjected to an entangling net of social control through 'social compacts' and 'social planning'. The liberating doctrine of 'self-management' was transformed into its opposite—a new system of all-embracing state administrative intervention and control—the dominant purpose of which was to ensure the maintenance of (federalized) party power.

The 1974 system can be defined as *federalized socialist self-management*. Political power now rests in the hands of the political élite—the 'new class'—of each of the eight republics and provinces. The Party itself—the League of Communists of Yugoslavia—is effectively federalized on the same principle. Economic power within each of these regions is in the hands of the same regional élite, operating through the regional state apparatus of the republics, provinces, and local communes. This is the 'socialist' component of the system. As for 'self-management', this is now not much more than a phrase, or a slogan, endlessly repeated but increasingly empty of practical significance.

Self-management has real advantages over a command economy of the usual Marxist–Leninist–Stalinist type. It releases the energy and initiative of workers and managers, especially of the latter; and, because it requires a system of market relations, at least in respect to transactions in goods and services, it brings a certain measure of economic rationality into enterprise decision-making. The introduction of self-management was one reason for the rapid economic progress of Yugoslavia in the 1950s and 1960s. (And it might have a similar beneficial effect, for a time, in the Soviet Union and other communist countries.)

But self-management has certain inherent weaknesses. Even under *laissez-faire* conditions, and even if the workers in each enterprise were also its owners, a system of universal, compulsory self-management would lack the competitive spur of potential, and actual, new entry of enterprising privately owned firms. Moreover, even under optimal rules, self-management would, for reasons explained in Chapter 5, encourage excessively capital-intensive investment decisions, the immobility of labour and capital, both between enterprises and between regions, and internal organizational inefficiency arising from lack of managerial authority and declining labour discipline. All these defects are exacerbated under conditions of *socialist* self-management, where the workers have no ownership rights, and where their rights to

influence the most important enterprise decisions—on investment, technology, and managerial appointments—are heavily
circumscribed, or even completely eliminated. In Yugoslavia the
process of expropriation of the workers' self-management rights
has been concealed under the soothing formulae of 'social
ownership', 'social compacts', and 'social planning'.

But Yugoslav federalism, although in itself a worthy aim, has,
when combined with socialist self-management, created a
monstrous amalgam. For the 'dictatorship of the proletariat' is
now in the hands of each republican and provincial party-state,
and, even worse, is in the hands of the political élite of each of
more than 500 communes. As a result, the Yugoslav market has
been fragmented, economic and financial decisions have been
biased towards autarky, industrial capacity has been duplicated,
there is little domestic competition, and the inter-regional
immobility of labour, capital, and technology has been greatly
intensified. While federalism, socialism, and self-management
may each, separately, have some positive features (at least within
carefully specified limits), their combination seems to be a
formula for an enormous waste of human and material resources.

In the balmy days of the 1950s and 1960s, when the liberating
effects of self-management were still dominant, and with the help
of substantial amounts of Western aid and the remittances of
Yugoslav workers employed in Western Europe, Yugoslavia
made good progress. But the 1970s were increasingly characterized
by a waste of resources, and especially by a waste of the huge
inflow of foreign loans which followed the first oil shock. By the
irony of history, the first oil shock coincided with the introduction of
the 1974 Constitution, which weakened the competitive freedom
of self-managed enterprises precisely at the moment when they
needed to draw on all their entrepreneurial resources in order to
cope with a more difficult world economic environment. After the
second oil shock, and the rapid decline in the inflow of foreign
loans, the Yugoslav economy entered a period of stagnation and
decline which has already (in 1988) lasted for nine years. Unless
there is a radical change in the system, this decline seems likely
to continue.

The policies followed by successive Yugoslav governments in
the 1980s have been directed at the symptoms of the crisis rather
than at its underlying causes. Imports and investment have been

savagely cut, prices and workers' incomes have been temporarily frozen, and the system of allocation of foreign exchange has been changed from time to time. But the government has never voluntarily relinquished its right to print money in sufficient quantity to cover its own priority needs, and to rescue loss-making enterprises and banks. As a result, inflation has risen in eight years from an annual rate of 30 per cent to an annual rate of over 150 per cent. The distorting effects of rapid inflation, when added to the distortions created by persistent government intervention in enterprise decisions, has seriously weakened the strongest feature of the Yugoslav system—its reliance on the market. The Yugoslav economy is now in a tragic mess, in which its inherent powers of recuperation and advance are frustrated by an arbitrary, and to a large extent inefficient, party–state bureaucracy.

Yugoslavia was an artificial creation of the Versailles settlement. Although the great majority of its inhabitants are Slavs, they belong to different national groups moulded by differences in history, language, culture, and levels of economic development. The acceptance of these national differences by the communist partisans, under the slogan of 'brotherhood and unity', was their strongest weapon in the national liberation struggle. This led, naturally, to the wartime promise of postwar federalism, although this was clearly inconsistent with the simultaneous intention to follow the Soviet path of Stalinist central planning. Under the stimulus of the 1948 excommunication, it was central planning that was abandoned, and the door was opened to genuine federalism. 'Self-management' at first threw the political responsibility for overseeing enterprise decisions to the communes; later, a considerable part, but not all, of these powers was assumed by the governments of the republics and provinces. With the adoption of the 1974 Constitution, the process of establishing 'federalized socialist self-management' was complete.

The purpose of the 1974 Constitution was to 'kill nationalism by kindness'. To a large extent, this aim was achieved. But one major 'national' problem was left unresolved: the problem of Kosovo. The Albanian people of that province, who now constitute over 80 per cent of its population, were given a wartime promise of 'self-determination', which was never fulfilled. Never accepted as an equal 'nation' in Yugoslavia, and with a long memory of Serbian oppression, the Albanians of Kosovo believe that their region is entitled to the status of a republic, like Montenegro with less than a third of its population, or Macedonia and Slovenia, with approximately the same population size. This claim is strongly resisted by a large proportion of the Serbs, who regard Kosovo as part of their ancient homeland. Until the mid-1980s, this dangerous 'inter-national' conflict was kept under control by. a combination of a restrained Serbian Party leadership and a collaborative Kosovan leadership. But continued Serbian emigration from Kosovo, the rapid growth of the Albanian population, and the stagnation and decline of the Serbian economy provoked a Serbian nationalist movement, which has now taken over the Serbian Party, government, and press. The Serbs are pressing for a revision of the 1974 Constitution which will deprive Kosovo of a considerable measure of its autonomy and allow the Republic of Serbia to obtain direct control over its government, personnel, and the management of its economy. This pot continues to boil; and, as the temperature rises, it threatens to bring disaster not only to Serbia and Kosovo, but to Yugoslavia as a whole.

Other potential national conflicts are caused by the wide economic differences between the various republics and provinces, and especially between Slovenia and (to a lesser extent) Croatia on the one hand, and Montenegro, Kosovo, and Macedonia (together with parts of southern Serbia) on the other. These differences have existed throughout the forty years of communist rule, and probably for hundreds of years before that. But in a period of general economic stagnation and decline, they become even harder to bear. They come to the surface when there are arguments about economic policy, for example over the method of allocating foreign exchange, or monetary and fiscal policies. The Mikulić government seems to be trying to widen the gulf between Slovenia and Croatia and the other republics and provinces, arguing that the former two republics favour the existing decentralized system while the others support a stronger federal government. This is Mikulić's response to the demands that have come from Slovenia and Croatia for his resignation. But it is a dangerous game.

These national conflicts merge with, and to a large extent are caused by, the general sense of discontent with the state of the economy. There is an increasing sense of impoverishment in almost all sections of society, and a growing sense of despair that conditions will ever improve. In the spring of 1988 the Mikulić government, which had started its 'mandate' two years previously with a proud termination of the 'stand-by' arrangement with the International Monetary Fund, once more agreed to submit to IMF conditions. The money supply is to be kept under tighter control, interest rates are to be raised, incomes are to be held back, and prices are to be progressively freed. Unless the Yugoslav government takes full responsibility for this programme, and fights for its implementation, the social discontents which it will cause will be blamed on the IMF, and the programme will fail. Previous experience of the Mikulić government gives no great cause for confidence that these conditions will be met.

Among many intellectuals and managers of enterprises, and a few politicians, there is a growing demand for changes in the present system. Some keep insisting on the need to implement the Long-term Programme of Economic Stabilization; but others are beginning to realize that that programme does not go far enough. The latter group are calling for a reconsideration of the 1974 Constitution and the Law on Associated Labour, which riveted on the Yugoslav economy the system of social compacts and social planning, and which has squeezed out the freedom of the market and the independence and effectiveness of enterprise self-management. Another, partly overlapping, group is calling for more democracy, with direct elections and multiple candidates. So far, there is little public demand for freedom of political organization; but that demand will emerge, especially if the Party itself fails to rise to the needs of the situation.

The Party is, of course, faced with a great dilemma. Unlike the Soviet Union and its satellites, Yugoslavia long ago abandoned central planning and introduced market incentives. These other countries are now considering whether to follow the Yugoslav path. But the Yugoslavs have already found that their system has lost its dynamism. Their choice is either to go back to central planning, or to go forward to a more truly free market economy, while perhaps retaining a bias towards self-management. If the Gorbachev trend continues in the Soviet Union, it is difficult to conceive of a Yugoslav reversion to 'Stalinism', although the irrational thrust of Serbian nationalism raises the threat of military rule. But the other alternative is difficult for a dogmatic Marxist–Leninist party to swallow; and it arouses the hostility of the entrenched bureaucracy of the 'new class', who would to a large extent become redundant.

The Yugoslav Party is in desperate need of a courageous leader, who is prepared to tell the people the truth and give them much greater rights of participation in decision-making, both within enterprises and in the political sphere. Such a leader would raise again the banner of self-management, and ensure that self-managed enterprises were allowed, and obliged, to operate in a freely competitive market. Private enterprise, including foreign subsidiaries, would be allowed to compete with self-managed enterprises on equal terms. Politicians, at all levels, would be deprived of their rights to intervene in enterprise decisions, and to influence bank credit allocations. The appointment of managers in self-management enterprises would be left entirely to workers in those enterprises, without supervision and control by the Party, the commune authorities, and the trade unions. Governments would limit themselves to the provision of those services which lie in their direct field of responsibility, and to macroeconomic controls through fiscal and monetary policies. The supply of money would be regulated so as to squeeze inflation out of the system and strengthen the dinar, thus opening the way for the abandonment of foreign exchange controls over current transactions.

The implementation of such a programme would necessitate the provision of more substantial unemployment benefits, and possibly other measures to assist workers on low incomes. But Yugoslavia, under present conditions, simply does not have the resources to protect all of its people from poverty. The present system of forcing social sector enterprises to employ more and more unwanted workers provides 'guaranteed' employment for some, but at the expense of persistently driving down the productivity and real earnings of all social sector workers. More and more social sector workers spend their time doing little or no work, or doing private work in company hours. After taking things easy in official hours, they go off to earn extra money 'moonlighting'. As productivity in the social sector sinks, it becomes increasingly difficult for it to pay · even minimum incomes, let alone to support the huge overheads of taxes and contributions to cover government expenditure, social services, and pensions. A social sector that was no longer obliged to carry such a burden of overmanning (not only in industry, but also in government and semi-government administration, together with the swarming mass of 'functionaries') would respond to market opportunities with rapidly rising productivity, out of which it could afford to contribute to necessary welfare programmes.

A programme of reform along the above lines would open the way to genuine democracy. The separation of detailed economic and business decisions from politics would ensure that the progress of the economy would develop its own independent momentum, and so validate the decision to dismantle the party–state monitoring apparatus. Once politics was put in its proper place, as a minor adjunct to the life of the community (at least in peacetime), it would be easier to relax the grip of authoritarian rule and trust the people to choose their own governments. It is no accident that a market system has always been the precondition for political democracy.

What lessons does Yugoslav experience provide for communist parties in other communist countries? It demonstrates that the introduction of market relations, even within a one-party state and subject to the condition that all industrial enterprises are obliged to be self-managed and 'socially owned', can release some of the potential energy and initiative of the people. As a result, for a significant period of time the economy makes good progress, the standard of living rises, and political freedom is slightly increased. But the Yugoslav experience also shows that the above-defined system contains inherent contradictions, which eventually bring its progress to a halt. If progress is to be resumed, on both the economic and the political fronts, the frontiers of freedom must be pushed much further. In the economic sphere, self-managed enterprises must be allowed to compete under *laissez-faire* conditions; private enterprises must be allowed to operate freely in a mixed economy; workers in self-managed enterprises must be allowed to acquire ownership of the equity capital of their businesses; government administration must be severely reduced; strict fiscal and monetary policies must be used to curb inflation; and the exchange rate must be allowed to adjust to a level at which the balance of payments is in equilibrium. Such economic reforms would open new opportunities in the political sphere, by both requiring and permitting a relaxation of obstacles to freedom of expression, freedom of nomination for political office, free elections, and, ultimately, freedom of political organization. After nearly one-and-a-half centuries, the glowing words of Marx and Engels should be directed towards their followers. In the communist countries, above all, 'the workers have nothing to lose but their chains'.

APPENDIX

Adjusted Estimates of Social Product

In business accounts, the credit side of current operations includes both the value of sales and the value of changes in stocks. On strict accounting principles, the value of changes in stocks should be estimated by comparing physical quantities of stocks at the beginning and end of the period (usually a year), and expressing those changes in the average prices ruling during the year. However, in order to avoid the difficult and costly process of making estimates in this way, a standard accounting procedure is to subtract the value of stocks held at the beginning of the year from the value of stocks held at the end of the year, and to assume that this difference represents the value of the change in stocks during the year. But when prices are changing this procedure is inaccurate; and when prices are changing rapidly it is very inaccurate.

The source of this error may be illustrated by an example. Suppose that physical stocks are constant, but that their value at the beginning of the year is 100 and at the end of the year 120. According to the standard accounting rule, the change in the value of stocks would be recorded as 20. But, by assumption, there has been no change in physical stocks and, even with a 20 per cent rise in stock prices, the value of the change in stocks should still be zero. The difference between these two figures ($20 - 0 = 20$) is called 'stock appreciation', or the 'inventory valuation adjustment'. In a period of significant changes in prices, it is important to adjust estimates of business and national accounts for stock appreciation.

In Yugoslav national accounts, there seems to have been no adjustment for stock appreciation, and as a result, in recent years of rapid inflation, estimates of investment in stocks have been excessive. The same error has also inflated the values of social product and enterprise saving, both in current and in constant prices. It is important to realize that deflation of unadjusted figures, which include stock appreciation, does not correct for this error in the estimates of constant price series. In the above example, the unadjusted estimate of stock change in current prices was 20. If this figure is deflated by the index of stock prices (1.2), the constant price estimate of stock change appears to be 16.7. But, by assumption, it should be zero. Hence, in order to obtain correct estimates of stock changes at constant prices, it is necessary to deflate the values of the stocks themselves, not the *changes* in their values.

Estimates of the required stock appreciation adjustments, and of the adjusted values of social product, for Yugoslavia in the years 1975–85 are given in Table A1. The estimates have been made by the following methods. End-of-year values of stocks for the years 1974–84 were taken from Madžar (1985, Table 1), supplemented by the value of stock change in 1985, given in the national accounts tables in *Indeks*. (Madžar's figure for 1978 of 459.34, which yields implausible results, was assumed to be a misprint for 405.93.) It was assumed that the average prices at

TABLE A1.   *Estimates of Stock Appreciation Adjustment and Adjusted Social Product, 1975–1985*
(billions of dinars)

	Current price series		Series at 1972 prices		
	Stock appreciation adjustment	Adjusted social product	Stock appreciation adjustment	Adjusted social product	
				Total	Social sector
1975	22.5	480.5	13.0	276.9	230.2
1976	19.8	572.8	10.1	291.2	242.3
1977	61.6	672.6	27.3	298.0	246.8
1978	49.3	852.6	19.0	328.8	279.9
1979	90.5	1074.8	28.9	343.4	291.7
1980	173.8	1379.4	42.6	338.1	286.1
1981	244.6	1963.3	42.8	343.6	290.3
1982	347.3	2577.2	46.2	342.8	286.1
1983	503.5	3561.3	47.6	336.7	281.3
1984	1002.5	5322.7	62.1	329.7	274.5
1985	1980.3	9286.2	69.2	324.5	272.5

which stocks are valued is the September price in each year; and consequently the social product annual deflator, derived from OECD (1983 and 1987, Table A), was adjusted to its September value by reference to monthly changes in the index of prices of industrial products, derived from *Indeks*.

The values of stocks were deflated by the above-estimated September values of the social product deflator to bring them to average 1972 prices, and the successive differences between these constant-price stock values were assumed to be the appropriate estimates of constant-price changes in stocks. Comparison of this series of stock changes at 1972 prices with the official estimates of stock investment in 1972 prices, given in OECD (1983 and 1987, Table A) yielded the series of stock appreciation adjustments at 1972 prices. In order to obtain estimates of stock appreciation adjustments at current prices, this series was inflated by the annual social product price deflator (which appears to be the same as the deflator for stock changes used in the official accounts). Adjusted estimates of social product, in both current and constant prices, and of the social product of the social sector at constant prices, were obtained by subtracting the appropriate stock appreciation adjustment figures from the official figures for these series, taken from YB85, 102–7, and *Indeks*.

In some of the text tables, use is made of adjusted social product estimates for years before or after 1975–85. Approximate estimates of adjusted social product at 1972 prices for the years 1960, 1970, and 1974 were made with the help of estimates given in World Bank (1975, Appendix Tables 2.3 and 2.4). Approximate estimates of stock appreciation adjustments and adjusted social product at current prices for the years 1986 and 1987 were made with the help of recent data published in *Indeks* and *Ekonomska politika*.

References

Daily Yugoslav newspapers:
Borba, published in Belgrade.
Politika, published in Belgrade.
Vjesnik, published in Zagreb.

Weekly Yugoslav papers:
Danas, published in Zagreb.
Ekonomska politika, published in Belgrade (abbreviated to *EP* in actual references).
NIN, published in Belgrade.

Regular statistical publications:
Statistički godišnjak Jugoslavije (Statistical Yearbook of Yugoslavia). References to particular editions and tables are in the following form: YB85, 102–13 means the 1985 edition, Table 102–13.
Indeks, a monthly bulletin of statistics.
Both of the above are published by the Federal Statistical Office in Belgrade.

Other sources:
Babić, M. (1987), 'Yugoslav external debt: causes and consequences', in *Economic Development and the World Debt Problem* (below).
Bajt, A. (1985), 'Trends and cycles in the Yugoslav stabilization', *Est-Ovest*, no. 4.
Bajt, A. (1987), 'Stvarni i potencijalni društveni proizvod 1980' (Actual and potential social product in 1980), *Privredna kretanja Jugoslavije*, no. 171.
Djilas, M. (1985), *Rise and Fall*, Macmillan, London.
Economic Development and the World Debt Problem, Faculty of Economics, Zagreb, 1987.
Goldstein, S. (1985). *Prijedlog 85: glas iz privrede* (1985 proposal: a voice from the economy), Scientia Yugoslavica, Zagreb.
Grgić, M. (1987), 'External disequilibrium and Yugoslav indebtedness', in *Economic Development and the World Debt Problem* (above).

Horvat, B. (1985), *Jugoslovensko društvo u krizi* (Yugoslav society in crisis), Globus, Zagreb.

Jugoslavija 1945–1985, Savezni zavod za statistiku (Federal Statistical Office), Belgrade, 1986.

Kos, M. (1986), 'Kriza inovacija: kriza tehničke inteligencije' (Crisis of innovation and of the technical intelligentsia), in *Kriza, blokade i perspektive*, Globus, Zagreb.

Lydall, H. (1979), *A Theory of Income Distribution*, Oxford University Press.

Lydall, H. (1984), *Yugoslav Socialism: Theory and Practice*, Oxford University Press.

Madžar, Lj. (1985), 'Revalorizacija zaliha, fiktivna komponenta i iluzija rasta ' (Revaluation of stocks, the fictitious component, and the illusion of growth), *Ekonomist*, vol. 38.

Mates, N. (1986), 'Problem nagolimanih gubitaka u finansijskom sistemu SFRJ' (The problem of accumulated losses in the financial system of Yugoslavia), *Naše teme*, vol. 30.

Meade, J. E. (1974), 'Labour-managed firms in conditions of imperfect competition', *Economic Journal*, vol. 84.

Mencinger, J. (1987), 'Inflation in Yugloslavia in the 1980's (mimeo), Working Paper 215, Department of Economics, University of Pittsburgh; subsequently published, after revision, as 'Acceleration of inflation into hyperinflation: the Yugoslav experience in the 1980s', *Economic Analysis and Workers' Management*, vol. 21.

OECD (1982, 1983, 1984, 1987, 1988), *Economic Survey of Yugoslavia*, OECD, Paris.

Parker, R. H., and Harcourt, G. C. (eds.) (1969), *Readings in the Concept and Measurement of Income*, Cambridge University Press.

Petrin, T. (1986), 'Kriza male privrede' (The crisis of small industry), in *Kriza, blokade i perspektive*, Globus, Zagreb.

Tyson, L., Robinson, S., and Woods, L. (1984), 'Conditionality and adjustment in socialist economies: Hungary and Yugoslavia' (mimeo), Berkeley Roundtable on the International Economy, Working Paper no. 20, University of California, Berkeley.

Ward, B. (1958), 'The firm in Illyria: market syndicalism', *American Economic Review*, vol. 48.

World Bank (1975), *Yugoslavia: Development with Decentralization*, Johns Hopkins University Press, Baltimore.

Index

Abdić, Fikret 168–9, 171
accounting rules, new
  described 70, 134–6
  effects of 5–6, 136–8
accumulation, meaning of 11
administration, cost of 146–8, 153
Agrokomerc 154, 156, 168–71
Albanians 7, 37–8, 187, 189, 191, 229,
  238–9
  discrimination against 204–5, 208–9,
  210–11
  prohibited to buy land in Kosovo 205
  see also Kosovo, special problems of
Anti-inflation Programme 95, 221
Arzenšek, Vladimir, on strikes and trade
  unions 34–5
assemblies, political 18–19
associated labour
  basic organizations of 13
  complex organizations of 13
  work organizations of 13
Associated Labour, Law on 8, 11, 13, 60,
  100, 105, 109–11, 112, 115, 119,
  122, 152, 220, 226, 235, 240
  recommendations for repeal of 124

Babić, Mate 48, 55, 56, 161
Bajt, Aleksander 83, 158, 221
balance of payments 25, 49–51
  policies towards 53–7
bank credits 6
  allocation of 156, 157
banks
  control of 14, 155
  effects of exchange depreciation on
  164–8
  system of 154–8
Batusi factory 206, 208–9
Belgrade, Party in 201, 202
Bilandžić, Dušan 222, 224

Bogavac, Dušan 228–9, 230
Bosnia and Herzegovina 37, 85–6, 186–
  93, 217
  and Agrokomerc 168–71
  strike in textile factory in 25
Brioni plenum 81, 200
'brotherhood and unity' 38, 80, 206, 208,
  238
Bujan conference 197–8
Bulatović, Kosta 205–6

capital-intensive bias 74–5
cadres department of Party 22, 155, 231,
  232
cadres policy 224
Četniks 200, 230
Church, attacks on 3
Churchill, Winston 1
collective consumption
  changes in 46
  defined 15
collectivization 2, 3, 22
Cominform 1, 80
Comintern, attitude to Serbia 38, 201
Committees for National Defence and
  Social Self-protection 34
communes
  incomes of 148, 151
  number of 18
Constitution, Federal (of 1974) 4, 8, 11,
  13, 39, 50, 59–60, 64, 65, 81, 93,
  100, 111, 112, 122, 148, 198–9, 220,
  235, 237, 238
  proposals to change 7, 36–7, 151–2,
  211, 221–2, 239, 240
consumption, changes in 25, 43, 46
consumption per capita see consumption
corruption 27, 31–2
Critical Analysis of the Political System of
  Socialist Self-management 36
Croatia 39, 84–5, 86, 89, 137, 169, 179,

Croatia (*cont.*)
182–3, 185, 186–93, 232
directors in 114

decision-making in enterprises 104–8
defence, cost of 146–8
delegates, election of 14, 18
democracy
industrial 102–8
political, prospects for 227–34
depreciation 5, 128–33, 134–5
dictatorship of the proletariat 1, 22
'differentiation' 202, 210, 211
directors
appointment of 14, 105–6
disillusionment of 217–18
functions of 14, 105–8, 111–14
powers of 75–6, 118–19
discipline *see* incentives and discipline
Djilas, Milovan 213–14
Djuretić, Veselin 229–30
Dodik, Petar 170
Dolanc, Stane 117
Dragičević, Adolf 99
Dušan, Stevan 196, 200

economic chambers 17
economic crime 7, 31–2
Economic Reform 2, 81, 88, 111
economy, the Yugoslav definition of
12–13
education 4
expenditure on 27–8, 145–7
finance of 14–15
elections
absence of freedom of 232–4
method of 18–19, 216–17
proposal for direct 7, 222, 233
electricity, production of 86–7
employment in social sector 87–9
changes in 43
Engels, F. 202, 243
enterprise, private, hostility towards 3
exchange depreciation 54–7
exports
changes in 5, 46
failure to stimulate 52–3, 179
quality of 178–9
see also foreign trade
'extra' income 152

'The factories to the workers' 2, 235
federal budget 147–8

Federal Executive Council 21, 95, 159,
182
federal fund for the development of the
less developed regions 193–4
federalism 94–5
effects of 79–82
FENI iron ore processing plant 83–4,
194
Ferronikl alumina plant 85
'feudal socialism' 81, 219
Filipović, Colonel 205
fiscal policy 62–5, 144–53
foreign debt 4, 5, 25, 44–5
regional differences in 190–2
waste of 53, 67, 82
foreign exchange
allocation of 179–85
deposits of 6, 156, 166
'differences' 134–6
foreign trade 172–9
barter in 184
undervaluation of 172–4
see also imports and exports
fragmentation of enterprises 110–11
freedom, restriction on 3, 228–34
free riders 75

Gačić, Radiša 226
Gams, Andrija 98
Gligorov, Kiro 221
Goldstein, Slavko 100, 106, 111, 112,
115, 122–5
Gorbachev, Mikhail 227, 240
Greece 8
Grgić, Mato 49

health 4
expenditure on 26–7, 145
finance of 14–15
Hodža, Fadilj 209–10
Horvat, Branko 81, 228
hours worked 118
housing 4, 28–30
imports
changes in 5, 25, 46–8
of petroleum 175–8
see also foreign trade
INA–Petrokemija fertilizer plant 84–5
incentives and discipline 114–19
see also work-shirking
incomes policy 59–62, 62–3
inequality in housing 29
inflation 5, 6, 25, 62–3, 65–7, 238

effects on enterprise accounting 128–34
'programming' of 158–9, 162, 175
intellectuals
    attitudes of 7
    and Marxism 23
interest payments
    in foreign balance 176
    on foreign exchange debts 51, 149–50
interest rates 6, 29–30, 156, 161–2
International Monetary Fund 6, 45–6, 51 n., 52, 131, 161, 162, 185, 240
inventions, rewards for 116
inventory gains 5
inventory valuation adjustment see stock appreciation
investment
    changes in 5, 25, 43, 46–7
    duplication of 81, 86
    mistakes in 82–7
    'invisible hand', lack of 142

Jakšić, Božidar 226
Jerovšek, Janez 112
job-seekers see unemployment

Kardelj, Edvard 39, 201
Kaštelić, Vinko 110
Korošec, Štefan 91
Korošić, Marijan 28, 100, 124
Kos, Marko 116
Kosovo 6, 7, 18, 30, 32, 37, 38–9, 68, 85, 86, 150, 186–94
    ethnic composition of 203
    and revision of Federal Constitution 222
    Serbian agitation in 203–12
    Serbian Party's policy towards 208–12
    special problem of 187, 196–212, 238–9
Kosovo Polje
    agitation among Serbs in 205–6, 207
    battle of 196
Kučan, Milan 98, 233
Kuzmanović, B. 32

Labin, coal strike in 121
labour productivity
    changes in 4, 24, 25, 43
    regional differences in 188–9
Lalović, Svetomir 199, 206
League of Socialist Youth 21

Lenin, V. I. 103, 202, 225, 227
Letica, Slaven 116
liquidity
    of banks 157
    of enterprises 135, 157, 162
Long-term Programme of Economic Stabilization 52, 69, 91, 138, 150, 220–1, 240
losses
    defined 16
    size of 25, 68, 87, 136
Macedonia 6, 7, 30, 68, 83, 120, 155, 186–93, 229
Madžar, Ljubomir 42, 246
Maksimović, Ivan 98, 100
managers see directors
market economy 3
Marx, K. 202, 243
    on advantages of capitalism 195
    and definition of production 12
Marxism 3, 22–3, 79, 93, 195, 202, 207, 213, 214, 215, 216, 226, 227, 234, 241
Marxism–Leninism see Marxism
Mastnak, Tomaž 37
Mates, Neven 166, 167
Meade, J. E. 89
Medjugorje 8
Mencinger, Jože 58–9, 68, 99
Metohija see Kosovo
Mihailović, Draža 39, 200
Mikulić, Branko 35–6, 37, 91–2, 141, 220, 221–2, 239, 240
    and inflation 158–9
    on wasted foreign credits 53, 82
Milošević, Slobodan 201, 207, 210
monetary policy see banks and money supply
money supply
    control of 6, 54–5, 63–7, 158–64
    definition of 66
Montenegro 6, 86, 94, 186–93
moonlighting 6, 31, 117, 241
    amount of 25
Muhić, Ferid 229

National Bank of Yugoslavia 65, 100, 150, 156–7, 158–61, 166, 169, 170, 180, 182, 226
net income of enterprises, defined 15
net worth of enterprises 132–4
    effects of new accounting system on 136

'new class' 213–14, 236, 240
new entry 74–5, 78, 89–93
nomenklatura 200
    see also cadres department

Obrovac aluminium refinery 84
oil shock
    of 1973–4: 50, 67, 84, 176, 237
    of 1979: 4, 50, 67, 176, 239
overmanning 25, 88–9, 118–19, 242

partisans 1
    in Kosovo 197
Party
    crisis of 223–7
    dilemma of 225–7
    federalizationof 224–5
    membership of 19, 215, 222–3
    privileges of 214–15
Party–state intervention 78–9
Pavlović, Dragiša 201, 202
peasants, Party attitude towards 22, 187
pensions
    cost of 146
    for disability 30–1
    finance of 14–15, 30–1
personal incomes
    changes in 25–6, 44
    control of 4, 5, 60–2
    proposed new system of determining
        70–1, 138–41
    regional differences in 188–90
Petrin, Tea 91
Petrović, Dragoljub 229
police, powers of 231
political effects of the crisis 35–9
'political factories' 87
political immobility under communism
    213–17
political organization 17–23
'pooling labour and resources' 194–5
Popov, Zoran 219
Popović, Stašimir 82
population
    regional growth in 190–1
    by regions 187–8
poverty 6, 25, 219
Pozderac, Hamdija 169
Presidency, federal 21
press, control of 228–9
prices
    changes in 60, 163, 164

control of 5, 57–9, 62–3
    see also inflation
private enterprise, attitude towards 22,
    91–3
productive activities, definition of 12–13
'programmed' inflation see inflation
public opinion, trends in 222–3
Pukovski, Žarko 224

Račan, Ivica 225
railways, organization of 110
Ranković, Aleksandar 81, 200
rapes, in Kosovo 204, 206, 209–10
regional differences 6, 187–96, 239
remittances from workers abroad 50–1,
    175–6
republics and provinces
    attitude to federal budget 149
    disputes over foreign exchange
        between 182
    and income tax 150–1
    revenues of 148
    veto power of 19
    see also regional differences
reserve funds of enterprises, defined 15
retention ratios; see foreign exchange,
    allocation of
Ribičić, Mitja 224–5
rotation of offices 21–2, 216, 225

Savin, Davor 171
saving of enterprises 5, 25, 127–32
    regional differences in 192
self-financing of enterprises 133–4
self-management 3, 4, 9
    advantages and disadvantages of 236–7
    aims of 102–3
    competitive 73–6
    and democracy 103–8
    and efficiency 108–19
    and federalism 80–2, 238
    meetings 106–7, 118
    need to revive 234
    proposal for reform of 122–5
    socialist 76–9
    theory of 72, 82
self-management agreements 13, 17
    on foreign exchange 181
self-management communities of
    interest 14, 15
    number of 153
    revenues and expenditures of 144–5
Serbia 6, 7, 18, 37, 84, 86, 94, 169, 179,

186–94, 228, 231, 239
directors in 112
nationalism in 38–9, 187, 199–212
party members in 223
Serbian Academy of Sciences and Arts,
memorandum of 38–9, 200
Serbs
emigration from Kosovo 203
harassment in Kosovo 203–4
ship-building 52
Singer, Aleksandar 171
Šiptars see Albanians
Škerović, Velizar 214
Smederevo steel works 53, 84
Smiljković, Radoš 202
Skupština, composition, election, and
powers of 18–19, 232
Slovenia 7, 28, 29, 37, 39, 86, 91, 93, 98,
116, 119, 120, 150, 169, 179, 182–3,
185, 186–94, 217, 225, 228, 230, 233
directors in 112
small enterprises 90–3
Smith, Adam, definition of productive
activity 12
Smole, Jože 170, 230
Social Accounting Services 170
social compacts 4, 17, 20, 60
Socialist Alliance, role of 18, 19–20, 231
socialism, meaning of 9, 94
social ownership 76, 94–5, 96
social planning 16–17
social product
changes in 4, 24–6, 43
definition of 12–13, 41–2
social property, waste of 32
social sector, definition of 12–13
socio-political communities 18
socio-political organizations
definition of 12
description of 19–21
Soviet Union, trade with 160, 176–9
Stalin, J. V. 1, 103, 227, 235
Stalinism 1, 3, 23, 80, 87, 94, 201, 225,
230, 235, 238, 240
Stambolić, Ivan 202, 206
statism 2, 23, 94–5
'statistical' dollars 172–4
stock appreciation
correction for 24, 42–3, 128–30, 245–7

and new accounting rules 134–7
strikes 20, 32–5, 119–22, 217

taxation 16, 144–53
number of authorities 153
progressive 152–3
structure of 150–2
see also fiscal policy
Tito, J. B. 1, 2, 4, 200, 207, 209, 214,
215–16, 230
and attitude to Serbia 39, 201
on 'political factories' 87
on rotation 21
tourism 3, 18, 20
trade unions 3, 18, 20
attitude to strikes 34–5
travel, freedom of 3
Trepča lead and zinc plant 85
Trifunović, Miljko 98
Turkey 8
Tyson, Laura 51 n.

unemployment 2, 5, 25, 44
regional differences in 191

verbal crimes 93
Veterans' Federation 20–1
Vidjak, Vjekoslav 232–3
Vojvodina 18, 39, 86, 158, 186–93, 198
directors in 113
and opposition to changes in the
Federal Constitution 211

Ward, Benjamin 73
work community, defined 13
workers abroad
numbers of 2, 44, 50
regional differences in 190–1
workers' councils 14, 106
work-shirking 4, 5, 218
see also incentives and discipline

young people, attitudes of 7

Žarković, Dragoje 82, 98, 100, 220
Žarković, Vidoje 96
Županov, Josip 36, 219, 224, 227
Zvornik alumina plant 85–6